# The Smiler
## A DJ'S LIFE

### BY ROB TISSERA & ANDREW WOODS

Published 2023 by Music Mondays Publishing, 125 Knella Road, Welwyn
Garden City, Herts, AL7 3NA

Copyright © **Music Mondays**

First Published in Hardback in 2023

**Cover design:** NeMedia Creative Soliutions
**Proofing:** Dan Brightmore and Wendy Matthews
**Photographer credits:** Warren Simmens, Louise Savage Photography,
Rob Farrell, Elle, Leo Dyson (RIP), Liberation, John Stables Photography,
Brian O'Mahony, Paul Dry (Ravin Pix), Storm, Eventography UK, James
Abott Donnelly, Francis William Johnson, Craig Dewse and Boocas.com

**Contributors:** Graeme Park (Haçienda), Amadeus Mozart (Tidy Boys),
Evil Eddie Richards, Nick Halkes (formerly XL Recordings and Positiva),
Ian Bland (Dream Frequency and Dancing Divaz)
and Tommy Smith (Blackburn rave promoter).

A catalogue record for this book is available from the British Library
**ISBN:** 978-0-9934732-8-9
Printed by Dolman Scott Ltd.
www.dolmanscott.co.uk

FOR MY MUM AND DAD
AND MY BEAUTIFUL FAMILY

# INTRO>>

*The music stopped. We could now hear the barking police dogs and the helicopter circling outside. I plugged the headphones into the back of the mixer and used it as a makeshift microphone. I could see thousands of ravers packed into this warehouse. I raised the headphones up and tapped them to make sure they were working. "Oi! Oi! Listen!" Heads started turning towards me. I now had their full attention. "Look, if you guys want the party to continue, we're gonna have to fight the bastards!" A roar of approval went up and the atmosphere started to get very dark. Very quickly.*

*The party was now a full-scale riot. Ravers started breaking up wooden pallets bordering the industrial unit. KERRRRRRRUUNCH! The planks of wood were now being launched through the windows; the smashed glass shattering onto the police in the street below, like crystal rain. Anything close to hand was being lobbed through the windows to keep the police from entering the building.*

*I left the makeshift DJ booth and climbed up onto a container that some of the ravers were using as a vantage point from where they could peer through the broken glass. You could hear the shouting first and then once I'd popped my head up over the ledge I could see a blurry fug of torches and police car headlights lighting up the early morning. Another strafe of light was coming from the helicopter circling above.*

*There must have been 300 Old Bill in riot gear, with batons, shields, the lot, and even more ravers making a run for it. The party had a thousand ravers inside, but possibly up to another 4,000 outside and we heavily outnumbered the police. But any thoughts that our greater numbers would force the police to retreat were soon extinguished.*

*Because when I looked out that window and surveyed the devastation below, I could see there was no way these guys were going to give up. Not in a million years. What the fuck had I done?!*

**July 21st, 1990**

# Contents

rob
Tissera

# Elvis, Technics And Auntie Queenie

CLUNK! Dad whacked the 8-track cartridge of Elvis Presley hits into the stereo of our bright green Ford Capri. These family car trips with the music blasting and Dad's rather passionate driving, would hold me in a trance. Indeed, a love for loud music and even louder cars, was borne from those family drives as the 60s gave way to the 70s. We would tear around the Buckinghamshire countryside shouting along to The King.

Although I was born in South Kensington Hospital, West London (March 1966), I can't really lay claim to being a proper Londoner as we moved around the south coast for a bit while I was a toddler. And most of my early memories are rooted in Bletchley, Milton Keynes. And you couldn't get much more 70s than the modernist new town of Milton Keynes, which was only three years old when the decade kicked off.

We lived in the much more historical Anglo-Saxon town of Bletchley, which was a little over three miles from the roundabouts of Milton Keynes. Bletchley Park was of course famous during the Second World War as the headquarters of Alan Turing and the Enigma codebreakers.

Some of my happiest childhood memories are of sitting in the back of the green Capri with the sweet black bonnet, driven at pace by Dad, or Mum, while listening to Elvis Presley, The Rolling Stones and Little Richard as the Bucks countryside flashed past the open windows. My dad liked to drive fast, which had a massive influence on me. My mum didn't mess around in a car, either.

My parents moved to Bletchley in 1967, having left their London home in Westbourne Terrace, Queensway, following a brief residency in Westcliffe, Essex. My mother, Patricia, or Pat as she was fondly known, was living in Kilburn, London when she met my dad, Alfred Tissera or Alfie. Mum was originally from Dublin and my dad wasn't a native to the UK either, having moved from Sri Lanka at the age of 20, hence the surname Tissera (which translates from the original Portuguese as 'elm tree').

Mum, Dad, my older sister Diane and I made the switch to Bletchley when Dad got a job working as a camera technician for a repair firm in Luton, which was only a 20-mile commute. Dad was an expert at repairing professional cameras like Pentax, Rolleiflex and Leica at a time when people didn't throw things away as soon as they stopped working. Dad could repair anything from a Kodak Box Brownie all the way up to the large frame, top quality cameras the professionals used. Some of Dad's clients would have included the paparazzi, studio photographers and photojournalists. He would also fix cameras for the customers of high-street retailers too, who subcontracted the work to my dad's firm.

My sister Diane and I definitely had a healthy bout of sibling rivalry back then, but nothing over the top. Diane was incredibly bright, but was a real firebrand back then; bloody hard work! But let's make no bones about it, I should imagine that having such a hyperactive, annoying brother like myself was probably hard work for her.

The Tisseras lived in a council house on Shenley Rd, Bletchley and although it was a modest upbringing, we never went short for anything. We didn't live in a particularly fancy house, but we were lucky enough to have a car, a decent one at that, as well as the latest in audio technology both in the motor and at home. My parents were such an inspiration to me and they loved music. Dad was obsessed with the audio stack systems that were popular at the time and our pride and joy growing up was a Technics belt-driven turntable that sat atop the amp, tuner and cassette decks.

My parents could play too. Dad could get a decent noise out of his guitar and Mum was a pianist. My sis played the violin and the sax. Music was a big thing at home and I was a sponge, soaking it all up. Weekends were usually when the stereo was cranked up. You might hear The Carpenters, followed by a bit of country all the way through to hard rock, funk and disco. We had a big collection of records. An album, well, double album, that had a big effect on me, was the movie soundtrack to *Shaft* which would later become a sampler's playground [e.g., the 1989 Young MC track *Know How*, which sampled Isaac Hayes' *Theme from Shaft*]. I played that album to death.

The first record I ever bought was *not* Suzi Quatro's 1974 hit *Devil Gate Drive*, which is what I've told people for many, many years. Why the deceit? Well, because my first ever 7" single, purchased in 1973, was *I'm The Leader Of The Gang (I Am)* by Gary fucking Glitter! Of course, Gary fucking Glitter's work is not the kind of material you shout about these days, and for good reason, and so for many years Suzi held that coveted spot as my first 7" single. And so, it's with great disappointment that I have had to make this confession. Sorry, Suzi!

Britain was in the grip of glam rock during the early 70s. T. Rex, Slade, David Bowie, The Sweet, Alice Cooper and Gary Glitter were everywhere. That stomping drumbeat and fuzzy guitar soundtracked my youth, although a lot of what we were listening to at home was American rock, country, funk and disco. Britain was in the grip of long hair, tank tops and high-waisted, flared trousers known as 'Oxford Bags'. Bags were popular back in the 20s at the top universities, but by the early 70s they'd become associated with the Northern Soul scene, before entering the high street. Football fans would often be seen marching down to the ground in these wide, flapping trousers; silk scarves tied around their wrists. Baggies, which were usually black or brown – there was a lot of brown in the 70s – had the highest waistband ever complete with a ton of buttons, plus, there were buttons on the side pockets and even more buttons on the back. So many buttons! The waist was tight and the trousers instantly widened at the thigh and just flared out. The only shoes that could make any kind of impact with the Oxford Bag were platform boots or Doc Martens.

I wasn't a very well-behaved kid by the time I got to middle school. I was a little shit, to be fair. I was far too influenced by a lot of other little shits as well. There were always one or two kids taking a wrong turn, and I was often a willing participant in whatever antics they'd planned. One of the most embarrassing situations involved being summoned to the headmistress' office one afternoon, aged 8, after David Cook and I were spotted smoking behind some bins. Cooky and I considered a complete denial of any involvement in the crime, a tactic that was quickly abandoned when the headmistress opened the top drawer of her desk. "We have collected your cigarette butts," she announced, before plopping a see-through bag of stinky Benson & Hedges butts onto the table. It was a proper piece of theatre and any courage we'd built up in the corridor quickly evaporated when we saw that bag. Of course, there was no CCTV back then, but we weren't savvy enough to simply refute her claims. In our eyes, we were absolutely banged to rights.

Even worse than seeing the headteacher was knowing that my parents would be informed as well. That really sucked. Although oddly my parents were never told of our maleficence. But that was my first brush with authority, at the tender age of eight.

I was lucky enough to be brought up, not dragged up and I knew right from wrong. My parents were not bohemians, but they were not the strictest either and they afforded me a lot of freedom. As a result of that, I like to think I've got pretty impeccable manners for which I am eternally grateful. I don't always do the right thing, but at least I *know* it's wrong. And a winning smile, coupled with the occasional use of the phrase 'soz' would always help me avoid recrimination.

*** 

I didn't get to meet my grandparents when I was young because my mum's family had already passed away when I was very young, and my dad's parents were still in Sri Lanka. So, Auntie Queenie and Uncle Sid, who lived virtually opposite our house, were like my grandma and grandpa. I would spend most of my time after school with them. They would sometimes take me to school and back so Mum and Dad could go out and earn money. They were absolutely awesome and I spent a lot of time with them; they were in their late 30s I guess. They were so kind and incredibly generous to all our family. I can't thank them enough for being our second mum and dad. That was a super solid relationship. My Uncle Sid always used to smell of brown sauce. Even now, the smell of HP reminds me of him.

**rob tissera**

# Dirty Leeds, The Angry Yorkshireman And The Love Of Synths

Our council house on Shenley Road had an outside wall down one side of the garden. We lived on the end of a row of houses and I used to play 'pass and move' against that wall, before smashing the ball home in between these two trees that acted as goalposts. The grass in the garden was like a winter football pitch, churned to mud by my sessions with the ball. I used to severely piss off the guy next door. It got to a point where the ball went over the garden wall so many times our neighbour, this Yorkshireman called Vince, started getting quite tetchy. Vince would often pop my footballs before launching them back over. We had a bit of a tempestuous relationship with the neighbours, to be fair. Well, Vince was a grumpy old bastard, which was a bit of a shame really. It was like a scene from the *Beano* comic, with the angry neighbour getting into a red-faced fury as Dennis The Menace sends another football straight through the greenhouse.

My love of football was sparked by the Leeds/Chelsea FA Cup Final in 1970. It was a brutal match, which would have seen at least six red cards in the modern era in a game that featured headbutts, kung-fu kicks and some awful scything fouls. I remember watching that game at Wembley on my parents' TV and just getting caught up in all the high drama. The game finished 2-2 before going onto a replay at Old Trafford the following week. As soon as that Wembley final ended, I ran out into the garden with my football to re-enact the most dramatic moments, some of which involved actual football, rather than outright thuggery.

As live televised football was so rare back then, the FA Cup Final was probably the biggest day in the footballing calendar, especially as league games were usually only ever shown as highlights. The game was live on two of the three available channels back then: BBC1 and ITV. It was BBC2 for those who didn't want to watch it. But many did, and a then record 28 million watched the replay at Old Trafford, which Chelsea won 2-1.

Rickley Park was another huge place for me growing up. I spent so much of my time there while at junior school, playing football with some older lads, which really toughened me up. Football was becoming a big thing for me and I spent years and years playing 'headers and volleys' at Rickley Park.

Around the age of 8, I would accompany my dad into work on a Saturday morning. The camera repairs company was situated in Luton, right across the road from Kenilworth Road, home to the mighty Hatters. The workshop was 200 metres from the entrance of Kenilworth Road and once he'd finished work we'd eat our sandwiches before going over to watch Luton Town. My very first game was on my eighth birthday in 1974 and we were right behind the goal. I remember the goalkeeper Keith Barber came over at one point and signed my programme and from that moment on, that was me. I was a Luton Town fan through and through. Luton beat Leyton Orient 3-1 that day and went on to get promoted under the managership of 'Happy' Harry Haslam. Following that, Dad and I would go to most home games together. It was a great first season seeing Luton return to the top-flight.

A lot of my youth was spent kicking a ball and I signed up to play for Bletchley Colts aged nine. I was a slight, short kid back then, but I was really nippy and loved playing on the right wing. My first football coach was Colts manager Mick O'Leary; a builder of Irish descent with a strong London accent. Mick taught us everything we needed to know regarding discipline and the importance of a strong work ethic. Mick had a massive influence on my life in terms of knowing that you weren't going to get anything easy, and you had to work your balls off in training if you wanted to be in his team. Mick was a Brian Clough type from that school of tough love and as a result I honestly don't think there's anything wrong with telling somebody to sharpen their shit up depending on the circumstances. Mick was hard, but he was also awesome. He taught me a lot.

I definitely had to work at the football, although I would eventually display a natural, instinctive style of play. I spent a lot of time practising skills and training. Football carried me all the way through my youth really.

The first friend I made at Rickley Park School was Danny James. Danny had just moved to the school from Hemel Hempstead and oddly enough, he was a Watford fan – Luton's biggest rivals! We must have been well suited though, as even that footballing rivalry couldn't prevent us from becoming firm friends. I guess we both supported teams that were considered pretty average and so we had a lot in common.

Danny lived about a mile from my house, and I used to spend all my time walking backwards and forwards from his to mine when I wasn't with Auntie Queenie and Uncle Sid. Danny lived in a slightly posher area of town than us and was the first person at school to get an Atari console. Everyone used to go to Danny's house to play *Space Invaders*. Meeting Danny was an important moment in my life and he was a truly solid geezer, well, boy, back then. And he's still my best mate to this day.

My parents bought me a bass guitar for my 12th birthday in 1978. I *wanted* a Yamaha CS-5 synth because I was into Ultravox, Human League and Tubeway Army and all that early UK electronica, which would be everywhere by 1979. We had a decent quality organ in the house and so I'd always been messing around with little bits of music. You could press a button and it would accompany you with a bossa nova or whatever. That keyboard led me to plink, plink, plinking away.

We went to the local music shop Chappell Of Bond Street in Milton Keynes, which had this little synthesiser section with all the latest Yamaha models. I started this CS-5 up, imagining that you would just nudge a few buttons and out would come all this Ultravox and Tubeway Army. However, that wasn't what happened. Instead, we treated the other customers to a discordant chorus of random bleeps and noises – this was nothing like Human League. In fact, it didn't even sound as good as the organ at home. I didn't realise you had to actually programme that shit, and *know* how to make it work. My spirit was a little crushed by the CS-5, or was it my ignorance?

However, my dad had a really nice semi acoustic guitar he'd been playing since I was a kid and so he thought I might prefer to get a bass guitar. It made a lot of sense to be honest and so my parents bought me a Rickenbacker copy. Now, my best mate in school, Danny, was a drummer and so having the bass meant we could accompany each other while we learnt to play.

My mum and dad were certainly not rich, but their ability to pay for birthday presents like my bass guitar was because they both went out to work to make sure we were looked after. And so, a massive thank you to Uncle Sid and Auntie Queenie, who were my second parents, really, while my folks were out grafting.

And so Mum and Dad got me this bass guitar and an amp. I would just sit in my room and play the same riff all the time, which must have driven them crazy. I would always be trying to play the pop music of the time. I was taught the violin for a bit when I was eight, but when it came to bass, I was pretty much self-taught. My dad showed me a few things, but I was a stubborn little bugger and wanted to do it my way. I really wanted to learn the riffs of the music I was listening to. From about the age of 12 I would have been listening to Blondie, The Clash and Sex Pistols. I discovered John Peel on Radio 1 around then too and would tape his late-night shows.

I discovered The Clash through John Peel. I was a bit too young for punk really, and didn't truly understand what it was all about, but I *loved* the rebellious nature of it. And some of the older kids I knocked around with at school were into punk and so we got into the tail end of the Sex Pistols thing. But because it was such a profound movement, punk stuck around for quite a few years, even after Sid Vicious had died and the group had split. My mate Danny and all our mates were influenced by the Pistols who were proper legends. And then off the back of the Pistols came Crass, Public Image Ltd, Killing Joke and A Flux Of Pink Indians, and the whole post-punk scene. Those bands got me into the tribal movement of music where people were united by a common passion. The tribes included greasers, teds, mods, rude boys, soul boys, skinheads, punks and an emerging new scene known as new romantic. It was just like that back then. Tribes. David Bowie was a big inspiration to the new romantics. I loved the way Bowie shifted from one persona to the next. I have always loved artists who just keep morphing. I knocked around with a lot of people who aped Bowie's sense of style that influenced Vicious Pink, Psychedelic Furs and Toyah. Toyah was *definitely* a teenage crush.

# CH. 3

## rob tissera

# Bloodied Nose, Racist Yobs And A Judo Master

The National Front was a very prominent force back in the 70s. The NF achieved 1.3% of the vote in the 1979 general election, a poor performance for them in some respects due to promises of tighter immigration controls by the new Prime Minister Margaret Thatcher. Many high streets across the UK would witness the Union Jack-waving extremists demanding that immigrants be packed off 'home'. Just bear in mind, that this was before the internet and mobile phones, so to get a few hundred or more racists to turn up to a rally, was quite the undertaking. They were not covering their faces either. Even at school, you would see 'NF' scratched into the desks. It was an awful time, particularly as my dad was one of only a handful of people of a different ethnicity in our neighbourhood.

My dad came over to the UK by boat from Sri Lanka aged 20, with one of his best mates. In those days you spent three weeks or so on the boat doing a crossing like that. And so he had to fight for everything he had. Britain was a pretty rough ride for Asians back then because you were living in a time of signs outside boarding houses shouting, 'No Blacks! No Asians! No Irish! No dogs!' which made it pretty difficult for Dad *and* Mum because of her Irish ancestry. They would have always been last in line, and so it's amazing how they made good for themselves.

My name Tissera marked me out at school as someone who didn't quite fit into the racists' ideas of 'normality' and subsequently there were a few incidents. It was definitely a character-building period. There was us and a family from the West Indies in our predominantly white area. Then another kid came through the school who was a Ugandan refugee and when she arrived the heat eased up on me a little bit.

1978, aged 12, I was at high school when the whole racism thing seemed to be peaking, at least from my perspective. There were kids at school, whose dads were in the National Front and they were fucking horrible people who programmed their kids to hate anybody who was different. It was pure ignorance and unfortunately I was caught up in the crossfire of all that.

I was chatting to Danny as we exited a classroom one morning. We turned left down this corridor and… CRACK! This bald head went straight into my face. I fell to the floor trying to protect my nose. Above me was this skinhead; he was at least two school years above me. I can still remember seeing the toecap of his oxblood Doc Martens before they marched off, clearly feeling that his work was done. I sat up, clutching my nose, dark blood seeping through my fingers.

I had a couple of incidents with this same kid who really had it in for me. Any time I bumped into him, be that in a corridor or the school playground, he would start on me. If I could, I would just leg it. The thing is, sometimes you need to run away from stuff because you know that if you stand your ground, you might suffer even more pain. This skinhead was a nasty piece of work and I later found out that his dad was in the National Front.

We used to go swimming with school at Bletchley Leisure Centre; a brand-new building back in those days. It was a lovely place with an almost tropical heat in there, complete with the 'no bombing' and 'no heavy petting' signs. I was in there having a nice casual time swimming underwater, and when I peered up while surfacing, I saw this thug rise up out of the chlorinated pool like a bigoted Poseidon. He then proceeded to hold my head under water for what seemed like ages. I was really struggling and panicking; I honestly think a lot of people don't know their own strength sometimes. I was properly panicking. Eventually, he let me go and I huffed and puffed to the side of the pool to catch my breath.

I really struggled at the start of high school. I just didn't want to go to school. Those painful memories come back to me even now whenever I see racism rearing its ugly head. The damage it does to your confidence and self-esteem is just horrendous, and there was nothing I could do to stop them picking on me.

There was another guy at school who took a dislike to me too and I can clearly remember thinking, 'That's it. I've had enough of this.' I knew I couldn't let these attacks carry on. And so I started doing judo as a result of all this bullying, which helped me so much. I got to my orange belt, which is four down from a black belt. I was now starting to feel confident and strong enough to at least protect myself. Now, if someone came at me, I felt I could hold and restrain them.

Then one day, a couple of these lads started picking on me again and got right up in my face. "We'll meet you by the school gates at ten-to-four! You're gonna get a proper fucking kicking!" I was thinking 'Jesus Christ. I'm going to be in a fight!' However, I felt quietly confident because of the judo. And so, come 3.50pm, there we were by the gates, as a crowd started forming.

I dropped my school bag to the floor and took my navy blue jumper off. Then the crowd separated, and this guy appeared. His face wore the expression of someone who was going to relish this duel. The crowd were excited too, shouting "Fight! Fight! Fight!"

"OK, let's go!" he shouted and he came at me like an angry bull.

As soon as his hateful face came within reach, BOOF! I knocked this guy to the floor. He just went straight down. I don't know if it was the power of the punch or complete shock, but he went down like a SACK OF SHIT. And then I was on top of him. I smacked him a few times more and then kicked the shit out of him until I was pulled away. He was howling in agony. I must have grown two inches in height. I had this overwhelming feeling of euphoria. I had stood my ground and taught this arsehole a lesson. This was one fight he couldn't brag about.

The guy was essentially a coward and it must have been awful to have parents who moulded their kids into such nasty bits of work, but I just wasn't going to put up with it anymore. And after that, nobody picked on me again. It was as simple as that. It's such a shame when you think back, as that is not how it's supposed to be. And it's not what you teach people now. But my ability to defend myself definitely worked. The law of the jungle, yeah? That's how it was. I found out afterwards that I'd broken two of his ribs.

# Toyah, Eddie Richards And A Very Long Walk

As a result of my legendary fight, I started to hang around with some of the naughtier kids. Not the bullies exactly, but mischief makers who awarded me a sense of protection, mainly due to the fact that no one would pick on them. The bullies wouldn't come after certain faces and so you just gravitated towards where you were safest. As the comedian Dick Emery used to say, "You're a naughty boy… but I like you!" These new friends were loveable rogues and their friendship stopped all this nonsense. Until you've actually been in that position, you don't know what it's like. You don't know what it's all about until you've been headbutted in the face by a massive skinhead. But if you can, stand up for yourself and fight back in whatever way you can.

I was getting a bit unruly myself by the age of 14. I ran away from home a few times and royally pissed Mum and Dad off in the process. When I say 'ran away from home', I essentially went to a mate's house for a whole weekend without contacting them. Which, on reflection, wasn't cool at all. But this was well and truly pre mobile phones and so my parents had no idea where I was. I'd spent years being a good boy – aside from the smoking incident – but now I was rebelling a little. I loved my mum and dad and so it wasn't all doom and gloom at home or anything, but I wanted to get 'out there' and have a good time. We'd always been really close as a family and my parents were so loving and giving. They've been so helpful and supportive to me and my sister, so

I can't paint too much of a bleak picture on that front. In fact, my love of going out and partying and the music and everything, all came from my parents.

As my dad was from Sri Lanka he had quite a few Asian friends from different parts of London. The Sri Lankan crowd, in particular, would get together for any occasion. And they loved to party! People often tell me that I am always smiling – 'The Smiler' yeah? – and look so happy and that's quite common amongst Sri Lankans. They're all like that and so I think it's partially in my genes. This positivity comes from my parents; my mum because she's Irish also has this jovial persona and loves to dance! But boy, Sri Lankans can party like nobody's business and I've been to loads of family gatherings, usually on Saturday nights, where there might be a house full of 50 people partying through the night until lunchtime the following day.

Sri Lankans like this music called baila, a jolly and rhythmic genre sung mostly in Sinhalese, but influenced by the Portuguese who colonised Sri Lanka. Baila has this really happy, upbeat Latin rhythm and this would have been blasting from the stereo at these get-togethers. Uncle Neville James was the ringleader of all the trouble. Uncle Neville was the master of ceremonies and he would get the whole place jumping. They were absolutely fantastic times. Sadly, Uncle Neville has passed away which was awfully sad as he was my dad's best friend and his partner in crime when he first lived in London. But my parents still meet up with his lovely wife Cathy and the others in that Sri Lankan gang, even though they're in their 70s and 80s now. Did all this partying influence me? You bet it did. We had some great times and that truly opened my eyes to the power of the party.

My newfound friendships with the 'cooler' kids, and with Danny of course, made my teenage years a lot more enjoyable. I'd become a pretty unruly teenager and was knocking around with these older lads who were punks. We went to a few nightclubs I shouldn't have gone to. We had already started getting into local clubs in Milton Keynes, even at the tender age of 13. I don't know how I got into those places, but I did. There was just a different door policy back then, and no ID, of course.

I started getting pissed when I was 13. I would drink the gin from the drinks cabinet at home and fill the bottle back up with water. I was a proper nightmare. I didn't mean to become one and I regret it now. In fact, I cringe when I think about what I put my mum and dad through.

I would go to bed and then climb out of my bedroom window, which involved me jumping onto the little ledge above our front door which protected Jehovah's Witnesses and the milkman from the rain, and then leaping down onto the front lawn to make off into the night when most other kids were fast asleep. Sorry Mum and Dad!

There was a night club in Bletchley's precinct called Brunells. I went there a few times with Danny and a couple of the unruly lads I knocked around with. Some of the older guys, one of whom had a Cortina, would pick me up from school. I didn't even think about any possible risks at the time. It just seemed like a good laugh.

Bletchley was only 60 miles to London and so we often caught the train to Camden Palace to attend Blitz, the new romantic night that Rusty Egan and Steve Strange were hosting. Blitz was a mad collection of bizarrely dressed hipsters who ditched the raw DIY look of punk and replaced it with a flamboyant sense of avant garde. Boy George and Spandau Ballet would be there and many other identifiable faces of the burgeoning scene. The music was Soft Cell, Blancmange, Visage, Spandau Ballet and David Bowie. Blitz at the Camden Palace was amazing and you felt like a rock star just being there.

As well as clubbing, my mates and I also loved going to gigs; mostly in Aylesbury, which had a decent venue or two. If we couldn't use the Cortina we would think nothing of walking as we were pretty skint. I was young and quite fit, true, but Aylesbury was 22 miles from Milton Keynes. The first time we walked to Aylesbury and back was to see my teenage crush, Toyah. We set off walking, early that afternoon. Sometimes we'd run for a bit and then walk for a bit. "Let's walk for 10 lampposts and then run for 10 lampposts to get there faster." But these were the formative experiences that shaped us, right?

I remember getting to the venue Friars Aylesbury just in time to see Toyah take to the stage. Once she'd finished, we were back on the road. Mental really. I remember being in a lot of trouble when I got back from that, though.

We also started going to a few things at a place called The Lakes Estate in Bletchley, Milton Keynes and some of those parties would qualify as being 'blues' with a little bit of reggae coming in here and there from booming sound systems. I'm one of those people that lets all those things soak into me, which is why I've got such eclectic tastes and why I play so many different styles now. I've always been a magpie picking up bits and pieces from all over. From the ages of 14 to 16 I loved

Blancmange, Thompson Twins, A Flock of Seagulls and early Human League before they became more commercial; tracks like *Being Boiled* and *Empire State Human*. And I was really into funk too. I was a big fan of Gwen McCrae and tracks like *All This Love I'm Giving*; I loved funk more than disco although I adored all the Chic stuff too. But I *loved* funk and soul. My favourite ever jazz funk track from those times is *Jazz Carnival* by Azymuth and I would spent literally hours dancing to this along with *Expansions* by Lonnie Liston Smith. The energy in those tracks is contagious.

From the age of 15 we started going to a night at the Rugby Club in Bletchley called The Gladiators Club, with a mixed crowd of gay people and straights. They played a lot of new music there. Danny and a couple of my other mates would join me for those nights. There was a DJ who would play all this really exciting new romantic material while also introducing new electronic sounds. He would also play videos on a projector. This guy was called Eddie Richards.

Eddie was also a Bucks lad, from nearby Amersham. Eddie was a few years older than us and was already a legend around those parts and beyond. Eddie would also play Camden Palace and some big-ticket venues.

At this point in time Eddie would play a truly eclectic mix of new wave, goth, indie all the way through to electro, disco and hip hop. Eddie would play all the local venues, moving from club to club as they invariably got shut down.

There was this place in the middle of Milton Keynes called Poppers and surprise, surprise, that was the place where I first encountered amyl nitrate. These were pretty, ahem, *salubrious* joints, but I loved that crazy hedonistic atmosphere. There was a healthy respect for diversity both in the clientele and the music and maybe for the first time, I felt I belonged somewhere. I was certainly not getting headbutted.

Eddie Richards was a huge influence on me and wherever he went, we would follow. Eddie just had this ability to make anything work within his set and he was as cool as fuck. Eddie would play all that alternative music, plus acts like Divine and Giorgio Moroder. I remember Donna Summer's *I Feel Love* getting played and Freeeze's *I.O.U.* alongside *Planet Rock* by Afrika Bambaataa And The Soul Sonic Force. We'd never heard *Planet Rock* before and Eddie was the person to introduce us to it; such a massive moment in our lives. *Planet Rock* would be played alongside Soft Cell and you could definitely see a correlation between the tunes. Eddie would play Kurtis Blow's *The Breaks* and *Hip Hop, Be Bop (Don't Stop)* by Man Parrish and all those early Mantronix tracks. Eddie had an encyclopaedic knowledge of music and was responsible for my first experience of being properly rocked by a DJ. Perhaps he doesn't realise just how many people he dragged across the dancefloor.

These were the days before mixing, when it was all about what you played next and that was a valuable lesson to me. You can be very technical with what you do, but what's really important is that the next track is an absolute winner. Of course, the art of DJing was to change massively, but that 'make the next track a banger' ethos was drilled into me very early on, by Eddie Richards.

## Eddie Richards, Camden Palace, Heaven

*"It was all down to a stroke of luck, really. I was doing a little party here in Milton Keynes at this bikers' pub called The Starting Gate. The bikers would be up one end of the pub, and I would be playing at the other. This was 1982 and Milton Keynes was dead at that point in time. There were concerted efforts to attract people to Milton Keynes, through various schemes, and so there was this mad mix of people from all over. I was playing all kinds of stuff at the pub: Killing Joke, Kraftwerk, Divine and early hip-hop to a mixture of straights and gays. The bikers didn't bother anybody and no one else went to the pub, so there was a mad mixture of people; some of whom would bring tracks for me to play. I remember one of them suggesting that I went to this club in London. 'Oh, you should go to Heaven. You'd love it!' I didn't really leave Milton Keynes very much, but I decided to check this place out.*

*Heaven was great. Like nothing I'd seen before. Had a real vibe to it. Colin Faver was DJing next door to Heaven in an adjoining club called Couples and I got speaking to him and invited him up to Milton Keynes to play at this little pub. And he agreed. I played some tracks that night too and he must have liked what I played, because when he was offered a job at Camden Palace, he asked if I wanted to get involved. So I went from just doing pubs and stuff around this area to doing one of the biggest club nights in London.*

*Our names weren't on flyers like they are nowadays, as it was all about the club, and the night. You needed to get word of mouth out.*

*This was 1982 and I stayed there for about five years as a resident DJ at Camden Palace for Rusty Egan and Steve Strange. Camden Palace had Rusty Egan playing all his Blitz stuff, you know David Bowie and new romantic tracks, then on another night it would be me and Colin playing up-front funk. Saturday night would be more of a mixture of stuff; more alternative than funk. I was buying quite a lot of music at the time too because the money wasn't too bad. I was mainly going to Groove Records in Greek Street.*

*And so I went from being a village boy playing in a pub, to working at one of the best clubs in the world at that time. It wasn't about fame or fortune then because neither of those things were happening, it was just about playing the music you liked."*

# CH. 5

## rob Tissera

# Drunken Drummers, A Glimpse Of Stardom And A Handbrake Turn

From 13 onwards, I had been gamely learning to play the bass when I wasn't out partying. I wanted to play bass because of the funky records I was listening to. I would think: 'Oh, right, I could play that bassline. I can slap bass.' It was my attempts with the bass that eventually got me into a band.

I was about 15 when I joined No Komment in 1982. Looking back, I don't even know how I met these guys as they were a few years older than me; more like 19-20. But it seemed like the next step for me, in terms of my love of music.

I must have met the No Komment guys at a gig or something and they asked me to play bass, so I said yes. The band already had a drummer and so sadly there was no space for my mate Danny. The drummer in No Komment was quite typical of a lot of that union; definitely the unruliest of the squad. He was also a terrible drunk and often failed to turn up to rehearsals at this studio in Milton Keynes called Peartree Bridge where they hosted some of these parties I attended.

These older lads worked with a guy who taught me how to play bass properly. George Webley was a pretty crazy character. A rock and roll session musician, George would tell us all these crazy stories about life 'in the biz'. A year later, he was working on Wham!'s *Club Tropicana* video in Pikes Hotel in Ibiza. I didn't have any knowledge of Ibiza at all back then. It was only a few years later that it properly resonated with me as to what Pikes actually was.

No Komment were a new wave style band. No keyboards, but definitely not punk or post punk. The songs were a little slower and the lead singer, Dave, looked not unlike Robert Smith of The Cure. We were heavily influenced by the likes of Flock of Seagulls, Thompson Twins and Tears for Fears. New Order were a massive inspiration too.

Danny (not my friend Danny) played the guitar and was pretty much the main guy in the band along with Dave, the curly haired lead singer from Manchester, who had moved down south; a lot of those involved in the building trades ended up working and living in Milton Keynes. The drummer was this complete nutcase also called Dave.

We actually got an audition with Polydor Records through George Webley and his connections to the music industry. The gig was at the Hammersmith Palais, which was pretty amazing. So, I skipped school to do this gig/audition, and true to form, Dave the drummer was so drunk we decided to use my mate Danny instead. We got one of the other band members to call the school office to get Danny the day off. They asked to speak to one of the teachers and told them that Danny's grandma was really ill and he had to leave school; luckily, she lived to a ripe old age. Danny had no idea that this was the plan, of course. Danny was academic and wouldn't have skipped school to do this. He had gone to school that day and was in lessons none the wiser. When he got the phone call, he genuinely thought his grandma was ill and dutifully went home. When he got back, I was stood there at the house. I told him he needed to come with us quickly for the audition. And so, Danny was now the drummer of the band and they fired Dave.

Unfortunately, the guy from Polydor didn't sign us up, which was a real shame. I would often think of that audition and what could have been a pivotal moment. We could have been the next big thing you know. It was so close, but it didn't happen. That said, it was an interesting experience. And you know, I loved working with those guys. I felt totally at home playing in front of a crowd. It just felt totally natural. I was at that age where you felt bulletproof and because I played football to a fairly decent level, in county cup finals I wasn't too overawed by playing live. It was a huge buzz to be able to play music to people from such an early age. However, No Komment were not about to embark on a Rolling Stones' style career path.

***

I remember the lads came around to the family home one Thursday night at about 9pm and announced: 'Right, we're going out!' I was thinking Jesus Christ, I shouldn't really be going out at 9 o'clock, bearing in mind I was still only 15 and had already done plenty of bad stuff. But they duly picked me up and took me to the pub. I drank about eight pints of snake bite in the Pilgrims' Bottle in Stantonbury. I was absolutely wasted. And then one of their mates gave me a lift home; I was in the front seat. Now, I don't even know what made me do it, but I suddenly pulled the handbrake on and the bloody car did a 360 on this dual carriageway and completely wiped us out. We were so lucky nobody was badly injured. But I had totalled the car. And as a result of that I was no longer in the band. My career had literally taken a handbrake turn.

Years later, around 2000, I went to see the manager of this club in Cardiff to get paid, and there he was, the owner of that car. I didn't recognise him at first, but he spotted me and gave me this pretty much empty envelope that just had a note in it saying: 'Do you remember when you met these people and we went to this pub, and you had a lot to drink and pulled the handbrake on during the ride home?' I don't know why I didn't pay for the damage at the time. Possibly, because I just simply couldn't afford to. I think they tried to sue me or something, but for whatever reason that fell through and then we lost contact. I don't have many regrets in life, but that was one of them. But that experience stood me in good stead. Let me tell you, there really is a thing called karma! I was mortified for being so bad. Another one of life's lessons learned!

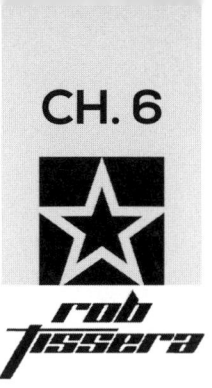

# CH. 6

*rob tissera*

# Shoe Shops, Ultravox And A Friend From The North

I left school in 1982 with bugger-all qualifications and so I signed up to the Youth Opportunities Programme; a UK government scheme for helping 16-to-18-year-olds into employment. Through that government scheme, I started working for a firm that delivered musical instruments to various studios and music shops including Chappells Of Bond Street, the music store in Milton Keynes that first alerted me to the idea of playing the synthesiser. We used to deliver pianos to all these big studios.

We had this one delivery of a grand piano and a huge Yamaha CS-80 analogue synthesiser – the Rolls Royce of all synths – to a London rehearsal room being used by none other than Ultravox. There were five workstations in this studio where they had all their modular keyboards, amplifiers and electronic drum kits and all that. It was jaw-dropping. I was 16 and into all this new wave music so this got me highly excited. A couple of weeks later, we delivered a baby grand to Elvis Costello's studio. Seeing these studios and the equipment up close, made it hard *not* to be inspired. I just knew I wanted to be involved in music. And it always stuck with me. I worked for that distribution company for about a year or so.

And then, following a brief spell flipping burgers at McDonald's in Milton Keynes – the first branch to open outside of London in the UK (1979) – I landed a job at the Faith shoe shop. It was while selling shoes one afternoon that I served this woman who was shopping with what certainly didn't look like the happiest bloke in the world. He was a bit growly. A piece of work. While she was trying the shoes on, I whacked a tape into the store's stereo system. It was a track by Everything But The Girl and as soon as it started up this grumpy sod cheered up a little and we started chatting about music. It's funny how music melts barriers and boundaries because this bloke and I just started talking about how we loved the chord structures EBTG used and its jazzy bossa nova style.

This bloke, Kev had a heavy Lancastrian accent and also played guitar. It turned out Kev had just moved to Milton Keynes from Manchester and the woman was his sister. He didn't know anybody in Milton Keynes and so his sister suggested we exchange numbers and get together. "Have a drink and talk about guitars?" And so that's what we did.

Kevin Walsh and I really hit it off. He was an amazing guitarist, a fact I found out during the first jam session with him. He could play a Joe Satriani track – that jazz and rock superstar guitarist who played with Frank Zappa among others – and instantly copy these intricate guitar solos. He also understood jazz a bit as well and could improvise like crazy. I didn't know it at the time, but that chance encounter was to play a massive role in my future.

Kevin worked for this millionaire called Tony Tartaglione who was married to Kev's sister. Tony's company produced shock absorbers for cars that would get your bonnet to open; brand new tech back then. Tony was a self-made millionaire from selling shock absorbers for cars, washing machines and office chairs. Tony owned a Porsche 911 Targa and he would often take us out for a spin in it. Clearly, my love of speed comes from my dad's driving, but also from going out with Tony and Kev when I was 16, racing down the A5 in his Porsche while listening to the *Ghostbusters* theme on the cassette player.

Tony was of Italian descent but with a German passport: "Now, I show you how to drive a Porsche!" It was a left-hand drive and being sat on the right while he was driving at 150 mph was a real eye-opener. 'Wow, this is living the life!'

\*\*\*

When I was 17 my dad left the firm he was with in Luton because he wanted a bit of a career change and so in 1984 we upped sticks and moved to Peterborough. Dad left the camera trade and started running this general store that had this really cool Italian deli counter. It was in the heart of this Italian community in Peterborough. I was 18 and still not ready to leave home and so I moved with them to Peterborough. I didn't quite know what I was going to do for a job, as I'd left school with virtually no qualifications, aside from an O-level in English. Then one of my parents' friends suggested the idea of joining the RAF.

I genuinely had no desire to do much job-wise and so the RAF seemed as good an idea as any and so I thought I'd give it a go just after my 18th birthday. I think my decision to apply to the RAF was a result of being a bit unruly, and not being able to sit still and do what I was supposed to. I don't want to be one of those people who goes on too much about this sort of stuff, but had they done some tests on me back in the day I probably would have been diagnosed with ADHD. I don't sit still for very long. I'm on with stuff all the time. I'll be doing one thing and then I'll be 'Oh, what's that over there?' and then get involved in that. ADHD is a good way of explaining my persona really and as a result of that, I didn't really do as well as I should have academically. I ended up with very few qualifications, whereas my sister Diane is one of the brightest people you'll ever meet. She's a genius. Basically she got the brains and I got the more creative side of things. I think that's the best way of putting it really.

I didn't get as many qualifications as I should have because I was always being a silly bastard. I should have just worked harder. I'm one of those people that once I apply myself I'm alright doing anything. However, I didn't get the grades to go to sixth form, and subsequently university. My mum and dad were probably a bit disappointed about that and so when one of their friends who was a flight sergeant in the RAF had a little chat with me about life in the air force, it definitely resonated.

When I was about 15 or so, I ended up getting really bad eczema and it bled through my trouser legs. It was awful. It turned out that some of my problems were allergy related. I'm allergic to cats for example and yet we had a moggy throughout my childhood, which probably didn't help much. It certainly made me a bit asthmatic for a while. When I did the tests for the RAF in 1984 they failed me on medical grounds and so I ended up having loads of tests done; thus uncovering the allergies. I had these dermatological tests at Charing Cross Hospital and this meant

I could get the correct ointments to drastically improve my issues. I think some of it might have been stress related; I have no idea, but I definitely developed this condition for a couple of years, really badly. But now I had the cure, I went back to the RAF for another shot, and they let me in. I was so determined not to fail that I must have impressed them. "Fuck, I'm in the Royal Air Force!"

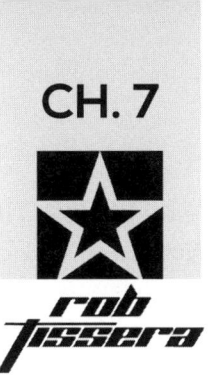

# CH. 7

*rob fissera*

# Hercules, Florida And A Round Of Golf

I will never forget being asleep in the barracks when the warrant officers came in on that first morning. They woke us by kicking the door in. "Get up! We're going out for a 10-mile run!"

The RAF taught me all sorts of stuff about being smart and disciplined. Even now, I can just get up anytime for anything and that's come from my military background. People are amazed that I can just wake up in the morning and that's it. Boom! I'm up for the day. I still do my own ironing and I'm neat and tidy. I learned all those things in the RAF. My time there was brilliant and I loved it.

I was quite sporty as well and so that life suited me down to the ground. I cannot recommend it enough to anybody in terms of the life skills and work ethic it has given me. It was absolutely invaluable and it will stay with me forever.

However, on that first day of the 12-week induction training in Hereford, I was thinking, 'What the fuck have I done here?! Why am I getting booted out of bed at 6am to do a 10-mile run while people shout at me?' It was absolutely mental.

I loved the physical element of that life, and the camaraderie was unbelievable. You just can't bottle that. A lot of people who leave the forces can't believe what an impact it has on you especially when you don't have that sense of togetherness anymore. These were the days before political correctness (PC) of course, and it was definitely the school of tough love.

I was stationed in Supply Flight which is not a particularly fancy trade to be in as it wasn't like I was a pilot or an officer or anything like that. I was in the supply trade and worked with the Hercules C-130 planes that did all the grain drops on Ethiopia and similar missions. They were massive planes. I was based at RAF Lyneham down in Wiltshire and our role was supplying those planes, used for Paratrooper and torpedo drop-offs at various RAF bases around the world, with all the logistics they required. We would move these huge trunks full of aircraft supplies: spares, attenuators, and water pumps and coolers for the engines, in these enormous trunks.

If anything went wrong, the engineer on the plane would say, "Right, I need this particular attenuator" and you would look through the spares and hand them the part; they would then give you the broken piece, which you would send back. We had to do all the customs forms and take the part to a local airport to have it imported or exported in or out of the country because you couldn't do it from base to base because of smuggling; it had to go through a civil authority. Essentially, I was in charge of logistics.

Sometimes we would go away for weeks on these missions to all sorts of places like Oman, France and Portugal to work with the Pathfinders and Paratroopers. I also helped with the mission training for the Desert Fox campaigns.

We would conduct parachute drops from 24,000 feet over the Alps and the Pyrenees. I would be up there, pretty much a spare part for most of the time because the planes rarely went wrong. I would also drive the SUV, with the pilots on board, backwards and forwards to the Air Force Base during the day. In short, I was getting paid by the government to go to all these amazing foreign countries.

I went to Florida for six weeks on a couple of occasions, which was amazing. We stayed at the Hilton in Cocoa Beach. We were also based in Fayetteville, North Carolina. I was 18/19 and getting paid £60 a day to stay in the Hilton; just sitting around doing absolutely nothing for six weeks in the Florida sunshine. And then because there was nothing wrong with the planes, I was just driving the pilots back and forth to the base, so they could fly off on their missions. I just had to come back and pick them up eight hours later, which meant that I was in an SUV with all this money in my pocket. I would go to Disney World, the EPCOT

Center and SeaWorld because I had nothing better to do. Absolutely marvellous. Thank you Queen Liz!

My dad was a massive golfer who used to play off an 8-handicap; he won competitions in Milton Keynes. He also taught me to play golf when I was 13. I was asked to play golf when I first joined the RAF, and so I must have mentioned it during my interview. And then one of the sergeants on this mobile supply flight said, "Oh, did you know we have a golf society where we travel off to other stations to play golf?" I didn't, but I was well up for that. I remember we flew down to RAF St Mawgan in Cornwall just to practise golf for the day before flying one of those C-130s over to Germany and back to Jersey for the match.

This golf course was enormous with a daunting links course where you were playing over the water. It was blowing a gale that day and I hadn't played competitively for a couple of years. I shot a disastrous 130 and cost them the match because I was so shit. However, that simply spurred me on to improve. No way was I having that.

I ended up playing golf for that entire summer at Ogbourne Downs Course down towards Swindon way. I played every single night until I became an 11-handicap. And then I played for the station every Wednesday or so. I would also get every Wednesday in winter off to play football at various different stations for the RAF Colts (under-21 team). I would also get time off for physio, but the real pleasure was being paid to play sport. That was an absolute privilege.

I met a squadron leader who knew I'd been playing football and he said he needed somebody to do the 100 metres in the athletics team. I was always pretty quick and so I started training with these guys. Sub 11.6 for the 100m, on grass, in football boots; a shade less than Theo Walcott. I was pretty quick, although I was raw. Dave Oakley managed the station's athletics team and he also got me playing football for RAF Lyneham and winning running events station to station; he even had me doing the 4x100m pretty soon after. We ended up winning gold for the Wiltshire AAA 4x100m. And every time I'd return to base from one of those events I'd go straight back into the football team. I even started playing for Chippenham Town; a semi-professional side. I was as fit as a butcher's dog back then.

My time in the Air Force was in between wars, during the Cold War, so it wasn't that dangerous. If I'd stayed on for four or five years more, I would have been in that first wave of people that went to Iraq. But I'm eternally grateful for my time there.

When I first moved to RAF Lyneham I was delivering parts in a three-tonne truck from aircraft hangar to aircraft hangar all day long, which involved driving on the runway, which had a 24-mile perimeter – it was absolutely enormous. Sometimes I would be driving on the airfield in a Luton van or the three-tonne truck and was always trying to get the thing to go sideways. I've always driven way too fast and I certainly used to ride that truck like a lunatic trying to get the thing to go sideways on the airfield as well as trying to get the Luton van up onto two wheels. I was driving forklift trucks like a lunatic as well.

I worked with this guy in the RAF who owned a security company on the side and he used to supply people like myself, who did the more ordinary jobs in the RAF, with work at events. He would take us to Aintree to provide security at the Grand National for example. I did the Grand National and the British Grand Prix a few times, as well as the Badminton Horse Trials. I would essentially tell guests where to go and check people trying to get into the VIP areas. I was actually in charge of the track area at Silverstone during the British Grand Prix.

There was a gate that led onto the track and I took my Fiesta round Silverstone one night. I managed to get it all the way round without actually getting done for it. I was convinced that the security would stop me, but... oh... hold on... we *were* the security. Ha ha! I'm sure you wouldn't be able to get away with that sort of behaviour now.

I remember sliding that powder blue Fiesta around like an absolute idiot. I even had a 1400cc Mini complete with a racing seat and a harness. I've always loved speed. If I could have my time back over I would pursue racing as it seems to be in my blood. Thanks Dad!

While working the Grand National one time, I stayed with my mate Kevin Walsh, the guitarist I met in the shoe shop, who had since moved back up north to Chorley, 28 miles from Manchester. I remember meeting one of his mates in Blackburn, Rex Sergeant, who had been the sound engineer for Joy Division and was currently working for New Order. Rex went to school with Kev and was now working as a roadie. It was a random chance that I bumped into Kev in that shoe shop, and now, through him, I had another useful contact, who would go on to open up another new chapter.

*\*\*\**

I split from my first girlfriend, who was back in Milton Keynes, soon after joining the RAF and I was gutted for quite a while. It was the end of my first serious relationship, and I was heartbroken. It was hardly a surprise, though. I just thought I could join the RAF and although we would be 100 miles apart from each other, everything would be just fine. But it soon fell apart. I was really depressed for a while because she was my first real love.

I met a couple of friends for life in the RAF, and one of the best was Tim Simmons. 10 years older than me, Tim was brilliant at racquet sports like tennis and squash. When you're feeling down you often need that mate who will come round and shake you out of your despair. "Get up, have a shave and a wash and let's get you back on the horse!" Well, that person was Tim. That was life in the RAF really, people looking out for each other. We're still best buddies to this day even though we've gone in different directions since.

Tim would knock on my door and take me out drinking. He was probably one of the most inappropriate people I've met in my entire life, but he was also somebody who gave me a sense of worth. He would come and take me to the gym to keep me active. I spent quite a few years keeping extremely fit and active as a result of his enthusiasm. This was very, very important to me and Tim was a massive influence on my life without a shadow of a doubt. He was just the wisest man and my go-to mate back then. What a proper geezer!

I really found my dancing feet in 1986 and would go out clubbing a lot. The music was becoming more high energy. I used to go to Papillon in Bristol every Friday and to Chippenham Goldiggers. I loved dancing to crucial electro, rare groove and some of the faster tempo funk and disco – tracks like D Train's *You're The One For Me*, *Jazz Carnival* by Azymuth and Chaka Khan's *Ain't Nobody*. I was rubbish at body popping and breakdancing, but I could dance. I was mad happy from the moment I got to the club until the moment I left and funk and rare groove were a huge part of my life. It was while clubbing that I met this girl.

I had a powder blue W-reg Fiesta 1981 XR2 with the extra XR2 wheels on it. My mum had given me this car and I loved it. I drove my Fiesta to this girl's house in Bath every morning and returned every night through these little country roads. I would always try to do it in the fastest time I could.

Now, this girl's dad owned some BMW dealerships in Slough and Maidenhead and it was through him that my life in the RAF came to an end. I'd had this amazing time with the Supply Flight, but when that ended, I found myself getting frustrated doing all the mundane tasks. I was getting extremely disillusioned too. At the same time my girlfriend's dad was looking for people to recruit into his business So they created a position for me at the BMW dealership and bought me out of the RAF at the end of 1987. Because I was good at logistics, my role was to manage the workshops and a new body shop down in Maidenhead. Bye bye Air Force and hello to a whole new chapter in the blink of an eye.

## Eddie Richards, Camden Palace, Heaven

*"I remember hearing this music coming over from Chicago around 1986 and I started playing it in the club, but some people didn't really get it, because there was no real melody there. It was really rough. 'It's just fucking drum beats!' But I really, really liked it, so I stuck with it. I was probably playing house music before a lot of people just because I had access to it. I was able to buy what I wanted at that time, and I was snapping up a lot of imports. That's how it started with house.*

*Initially the music was quite slow and you couldn't really pinpoint when it became house, because it was just based on what we were already playing: electronic music like Kraftwerk and disco. House music is disco really.*

*Then people started putting on a few warehouse parties. I think one of them was called The Dirt Box, run by Jay Strongman. He was more into funk and stuff like that. But there was this movement going on where you didn't have to dress up and that was also attractive to people. Then Shoom started and Colin (Faver) got some dates there. And then I hooked up with Mr C and Paul Rip at this night called RIP at Clink Street. It was me, Kid Bachelor, and Mr C as the resident DJs. Shoom was catering to those people that wanted that poppier, Balearic stuff and Clink Street was there for all the people that wanted that rougher acid music that was coming in. A lot of journalists wouldn't come to Clink Street because it was a little scary. It was really dark in there, and home to a lot of dodgy characters, but there was no trouble because everyone was on ecstasy now. Shoom was all bright and nice. So people didn't really write so much about Clink Street at the time, but it was one of the founding acid house parties in the world. Because after that, it spread around the world really quickly.*

*There was a club in Milton Keynes called The Point, and this modern building looked like a big pyramid made out of glass and it had this red neon around it. If you were in an aeroplane, you could see this red cross from the air. And this huge pyramid had a club inside it. It was a really commercial club, but I was doing the Tuesday there I think, trying to get things moving in Milton Keynes.*

*I bought a Jack Frost track on Trax Records, while I was at Camden Palace. It was only two minutes long, and I was complaining to Colin that it was too short. 'You can't mix it properly.'*

*–    'Why don't you do some edits or something at home, make it longer and then we can play it.'*

*I had a reel-to-reel tape machine and tried to copy the bass line on a 303, which only cost me £30 at the time. And so I made the track. But I couldn't get anything synced up – I really needed MIDI and everything. I didn't have a clue what I was doing. I had a drum machine and a 303, but I couldn't make them run together, so I had to mix them like I would as a DJ. But the samples would drift out, so when they did, I stopped the tape, and then I'd start it again. That way I could find the gaps, and in between the gaps, I'd put in a sample like 'Acid, man' from a Cheech & Chong skit called Trippin' In Court. I put some other samples in throughout the track, gave it to Colin, and he played it on Kiss FM, as he was one of the regular DJs when it was still a pirate station. And then Virgin got in touch with him and said, 'We like the track, we want to license it.' And that's how that Acid Man came about. I was shocked, because it wasn't even meant to come out or anything. It was done as a joke. Well, not as a joke, but you know, as something to do, just to extend the track.*

*And then Acid Man by Jolly Roger started climbing up the charts, and it got to a point where they asked me if I could be on Top Of The Pops, and I was like, 'What?!' It got to number 22, but there was another acid track released a week before mine We Call It Acieed by D-Mob Featuring Gary Haisman and they played that instead as it charted higher. And a week later the BBC, thinking it was about LSD (it obviously wasn't) wouldn't feature tracks with 'acid' in the title.*

*We decided to do some PAs anyway, and so I assembled a crew. There was a guy that used to go to Clink Street called Shakespeare and he was a crazy character. He once decided it was so hot in the club that he punched a hole in the wall. He was quite mad at times. And I thought he would be a great person to take on tour with me and Mr C who was good at rapping. I just came up with the name because Jolly Roger was a pirate, and that's basically what I'd done with that track. I wasn't trying to hide it either. It was entirely made of samples from my record collection. So, we made up this stupid story that Jolly Roger came from Iran and his parents had rejected him because he was into house music and so he came to the UK. Just some crazy story because it was all just a laugh. And they used that story in the press, and then we got coverage from all around the world, for a few months. It was mad. Mr C would be rapping with a bowler hat on, while I was on the turntables and the keyboard, playing samples. Shakespeare dressed up as an Arab and was jumping all over the speakers. Journalists were like, 'What the fuck is going on?' Things were just happening so fast, and we were just going with the flow and having a laugh. We didn't take it seriously at all. It wasn't like 'Oh, yeah, we're in a band, we can make more music,' we just didn't think about anything else. It was just all about the moment really."*

# BMW, Bracknell Town And A Little White Pill

Once I'd left the RAF I became a yuppie. I was having the time of my life at the BMW dealership. I was nearly 22 and driving around in a brand new M3 armed with a hefty Motorola 8500X brick. I was earning a lot more money than I had in the RAF and got myself an electric blue Escort cabriolet. That was a beautiful car. I used to drive it with the top down whenever I could. I was swanning around like a high-flying exec with a Ready Brek glow. I was bulletproof. But the thing is, the power had started to go to my head a little.

Whether it was due to my military background or not, I tried to introduce way too many new systems to the team in the BMW workshop and they really resented me as a result. I also ruffled way too many feathers with people who had been working with the same systems for many years. Then I came along and told them that they were slacking and disorganised. I wanted to make a mark on the company and save them money, but this was making waves with the staff, who basically hated me. Plus, I was earning way more money than them. I was a young upstart. 'Who the fuck does he think he is?!'

I was very annoying and quite unpopular with the workshop staff, but my attitude was: 'Who cares if I'm upsetting them?' However, my declining popularity with the team was making my job a lot more difficult, which in turn made it a lot less enjoyable. I had also split from the gaffer's daughter and was now dating another member of the team, and that created a lot of problems too. But the job was providing me with very decent money. In short, I was making every mistake in the book of growing up, for which I'm not entirely proud.

I was playing football again, for Bracknell Town, which was a great way of keeping fit post-RAF. This came about as a result of me seeing the floodlights beaming out as I drove home from work on dark February nights. I'd been desperate to find a new team, so I got out the trusty brass balls, so to speak, and drove down in my boots, shin pads and tracksuit to what turned out to be a training ground with a horrible muddy waterlogged pitch. There were nine lads and a trainer who was shouting and hollering at the top of his voice while they played 4 against 5 with a 'rush' goalkeeper.

I observed them from the side-lines for 5 mins to gauge how decent they were and then piped up when the ball went out of play. "I don't suppose you need a player to even the sides up do you?" The trainer said that would be really handy. And so I started playing. I really seemed to click with my new team mates. After half an hour of this, we got down to doing a bunch of shuttle runs. Bearing in mind that I was pretty nippy and had won the Wiltshire AAA 4x100 a year earlier, I seemed to be the fastest person on the pitch. The trainer pulled me to one side after the session had finished and asked if I wanted to play on Saturday. I was delighted and agreed straight away. I asked him the name of my new team and he said Bracknell Town who were in the Vauxhall Opel league, which was one league below the Vauxhall Conference. That was way above the standard I'd been used to playing at.

It turned out that Bracknell were having a mid-season injury crisis and I had turned up at just the right moment. It taught me a valuable lesson that sometimes you just have to be bold and back your ability and take your chances when they come along. I ended up playing for them for a year and every game I played I got £130. It was such a pleasure to get paid decent money for doing what I loved on a Saturday afternoon.

We were still in the days of wearing blazers, Oxford shirts, check trousers and brown leather shoes back then, and I would drink at Studio Valbon in Maidenhead with some of the lads from Bracknell Town. It was a happy period of my life.

1987 was an interesting time musically because soul music, funk, disco and what I referred to as 'machine music' were starting to morph into a more cohesive electronic sound. Initially, I couldn't get my head around it. I wasn't too sure about the first scoops of acid house itself and the stuff coming out of Chicago; it was a bit too syncopated and electronic. I was unsure of things like Mr Fingers' *Washing Machine*, *Phuture* by Acid Trax and *Love Can't Turn Around* by Farley Jackmaster Funk Ft. Daryl Pandy, but slowly I started to *get it*. My ears started to pick it up and I was tuning in.

Meanwhile, on a Balearic island, young Brits were starting to dabble with this new drug ecstasy while listening to early house tracks being spun by musical pioneers such as DJ Alfredo at Ibiza's Amnesia. Many other Brits had been introduced to ecstasy years before, in New York's gay clubs and bars. American house music and this brand-new drug filtered through to London and Manchester to create a new movement that would spread throughout the UK and beyond. Prior to this, acid house, an underground form of house in the US, featuring the squelchy bass from the Roland TB-303 bass synthesiser, hadn't really created much of a stir. But acid house, combined with the little white tablet, was creating pure magic.

***

Summer of 1988, Bracknell Town were to play the preliminary rounds of the FA Cup proper against Slough Town. It was during that match that I had an epiphany. 'Okay, I've reached my level here.' I was pretty rapid over 100 metres. However, I was not up to the job against Slough Town who had these two 6ft 5" centre halves from their local police academy. I think quite a contingent of their team were from the police academy and they were *bruisers*.

No matter how hard I tried I just couldn't get round them. If I beat one, his teammate just annihilated me. 'I may have reached my tipping point.' Football had been pretty much an upward curve all the way up to that match, but my interest was over. Lucky really, as a new obsession was just around the corner.

I had been working at the BMW dealership in Maidenhead for about five or six months when my mate Kevin Walsh and his friend Rex Sargeant went on a New Order tour of the States. They called me after New Order played in Los Angeles. It was lunchtime in the UK.

They called me from the top of this building, looking out over LA. "We've just taken this awesome drug called ecstasy and we're totally blissed out. We love you, man!" What the fuck! "It's AMAZING!" I was listening to all this on the work phone. They sounded so happy and ecstatic I couldn't quite process what they were saying, but it certainly placed a seed inside my mind.

My mate Danny was doing a post-grad course in Chelmsford, Essex and so it was easier to meet up in London during the week. Acid house had taken hold of the country by now and it was certainly preoccupying us. So much so, we started checking out some of those legendary nights in London.

We loved Soul II Soul nights and would go to some of their parties at the Fridge in Brixton. These nights were like massive blues really. What I loved about that time were the tempo changes going on, based upon the fact that it wasn't all about mixing then, it was what you played next and how great that record was going to be. And having been subjected to so much racism growing up in a predominantly white area of the UK, I finally felt I'd found my home. I was accepted. Everybody at those raves was there for the same reason and all the barriers simply melted away.

I clearly remember going to a party in April, 1988 and got home at about 12.30pm the following day. I watched Luton in the League Cup Final against Arsenal and I was so exhausted, it felt like a dream watching that on TV. Not least because Luton won the cup! That was one of the most beautiful days of my life.

We would go to the Astoria on a Thursday and a place called Busby's on Charing Cross Road, which we had no idea was actually the legendary Shoom. We just knew it as Busby's. We also went to Heaven for Rage; they were just phenomenal times.

Rage at Heaven was where we first heard Fabio and Grooverider and Trevor Fung as well; what a treat to hear those guys playing *Salsa House* by Richie Rich, *Sueño Latino* by Sueño Latino, Ralphi Rosario's *You Used To Hold Me* and *Tears* by Frankie Knuckles Presents Satoshi Tomiie. The piano playing by Satoshi Tomiie was just divine, it really was and hearing that being played by Fabio and Grooverider was pulling us further and further into that world.

I wasn't thinking about DJing just yet, but was collecting the vinyl because I had to own the records I'd heard while out and about. Obviously there was no Shazam then and so sometimes I would hum tracks to the record shop staff. But I was addicted to hunting down and playing these tracks. Acid house had taken my soul and music really was becoming my life.


## Eddie Richards

*"I was playing at The Point in Milton Keynes one night and this local lad came in. He lived in Milton Keynes and he was 'known'. He had a bit of an entourage because he was always buying champagne and stuff, and people would just hang around him. And he ended up being the guy that founded Sunrise. Tony Colston-Hayter had dipped his toe into these waters already with a night at Clink Street called Afters in 1987. And because Tony came from Milton Keynes, and he'd heard about me, being the local hero who got a job at Camden Palace, he approached me with regards to these plans he had. 'Hey, I want to put on an event,' he said. 'And I want you to be there.'*

*I've still got the sheet of stapled together papers with all the details mapped out. I was appointed Music Coordinator for the first Sunrise parties. My job was to find the DJs to play at the raves, and so I got hold of Carl Cox and all those people through my contacts. I gave quite a few people a bit of a leg up with that. And Sunrise became one of the biggest outdoor rave parties, followed by Energy.*

*Carl Cox wasn't well known at the raves at the time, but he became known for playing warm-up to Paul Oakenfold at The Project Club. Paul had just come back from Ibiza and wanted to put a night on, and Carl Cox had a sound system at the time. So Paul hired Carl to do the sound system as well as being the warm-up for him. And then Carl was working as the sound system guy at Shoom as well, and so he was around; people had heard of him and he was playing good music. And so I thought he would be good to put on at those nights.*

*When Carl first played, it was really early in the morning. The night had peaked and everyone was crashed out pretty much, just chilling out on the grass. So, Carl had to do something special. And that's when he started using three turntables because there were three decks available, as it was such a big rave. And Carl was so good, everybody picked themselves up, and got back out dancing again, and following that, Carl started getting more bookings.*

*These raves went from small beginnings of a hundred people when they started, to 25,000 within a year. And that was a whole other experience because that attracted the police. And then you got the gangsters who would come in because there was a lot of money involved. They would turn up at the door with shotguns and stuff like that. There was a scary side to it too. People would show up and threaten door staff and try to take the money. I saw quite a few people with knives and stuff, fighting each other. It was that horrible thing you didn't want to see when you were buzzing away at a party.*

*Obviously, there were other regional things going on such as The Haçienda, but the Sunrise parties were a big deal then. And then there were hundreds of them all over the country, from Scotland, Leeds, Manchester, all the way down to the South Coast, and then it became a worldwide thing.*

*I remember playing in a big grain silo at one of these raves. It was huge, and I think U2 used it for rehearsals. It was massive and the echo in there was just crazy. When a track dropped you could see a ripple effect of the sound going through that place because people would throw their arms in the air; the people at the front would be first, and you could follow the ripple down to the back. It was that big, it was massive, and we would climb up this little ladder, like 50 feet up in the air with a record box. It was madness.*

*Tony was always looking for something new, so he would bring in these mad displays, crazy lasers and big displays made out of LEDs just to make it a bit more spectacular. It was crazy.*

*I was on my way to a party going around the M25, and the police had actually blocked the road, which is crazy because people were going home from work and there were lorry drivers etc. We were told to come off the road at the roundabout and go back where we came from. I was like, 'Shit, this is mad.' I pulled off and there was a copper standing there, so I just went by the side of him and said, 'Excuse me, officer, what seems to be the problem here?' I knew they were just stopping ravers trying to get to a party. And he said, 'Well, sir, there's been a chemical incident. There's acid everywhere.' And he started laughing. A lot of the cops loved it, actually, and all the police I spoke to that were working the parties, on the periphery, were like, 'Yeah, this is great. We're earning overtime and there's never any trouble.'*

***

*The local Sharon and Tracey clubs emptied when the raves started, and a lot of the owners were desperate for business and so I started some nights in Milton Keynes. I'd had trouble getting into this club before rave as I was wearing the wrong colour socks or something daft. This is what they were like, they just didn't give a shit. You had to wear a suit jacket, because they thought if you wore smart gear you wouldn't fight. That was the theory. These clubs just pissed me off and so it was great that they got emptied because I could start some nights of my own.*

*We started a night at a youth club called The Joint and that was more about bands we'd hire. We brought in bands and dancers and stuff like that because it had a stage. And then when that got shut down we went to the Outer Limits and started a night there. I took over on the Sunday, and it had done so well, they gave me a Saturday and that'd done really well, so they gave us a whole week. I was putting on hip-hop days and one-off events at the Outer Limits.*

*It amazes me really that these things I've done have touched so many people because there was nothing going on in Milton Keynes then, and I was certainly a catalyst in bringing all these people together to show them stuff they probably wouldn't have had the chance to see, because I was bringing it all from my experiences in London and wherever I'd DJ'd. This little club in Bletchley, Milton Keynes was attracting people from Scotland, Manchester, Swindon and London. It was shocking.*

*It was one of those situations where I could just do whatever I wanted. 'This is how I'd like to do it,' and that's how I did it. And luckily, enough people liked what they saw. It was great because I could experiment and 80% of the time, we got it right."*

# Valbon, Sunrise And A Rave New World

*"Wow, this is well different," I muttered to myself as we waited on the side of the road. It wasn't long before there were about another 100 cars parked up. It was mad, really. You could feel this fervour, this bubbling atmosphere of the unknown…"*

I remember going to Valbon one Friday night in 1989 with some of the Bracknell Town lads. Valbon was the typical 'fucking and fighting' joint and we had some great nights there when we weren't out in London. I woke up on the Saturday morning feeling more than a little delicate and got a call from Dan. A mutual friend of ours, Rachael had started dating this guy called Tony Colston-Hayter and she wanted to know if we fancied going to his party that night. "OK, Dan, where is it?"
 – "That's the thing. It's a secret."
 – "C'mon stop screwing about. Where is it?"
 – "I don't know. We just have to meet at Milton Keynes bus station."
 – "Oooooooooooookaaaaaaaaaaayyyy."
 I didn't know who Tony Colston-Hayter was and certainly didn't realise the significance of the parties he was putting on. Our friend had been telling Dan about these parties she'd been going to with Tony and said they weren't club nights exactly, but 'raves'. I had no idea what a rave was. Rave was a term old people used. But Colston-Hayter had

witnessed the vibes at clubs like Shoom and had decided to take things to the next level.

I woke up, had some breakfast and forgot all about the evening's entertainment until it was virtually time to leave. I had bought some clubbing gear by now and so got my hoodie and trackie bottoms on for another night out.

I drove up to Milton Keynes and met Dan. We then took his red Escort estate to the bus station. There was a definite buzz around the place and lots of youths hanging around, car stereos blasting. "Wow, this is well different," I muttered to myself as we waited on the side of the road. It wasn't long before there were another 100 cars or so parked up. It was mad, really. You could feel this fervour, this bubbling atmosphere of the unknown.

The hair was curly permed for the ladies and some of the men, but mostly curtains for the blokes. Everybody was dressed in hooded tops, faded blue stonewashed jeans and Red Kickers or trainers. There were also bumbags and shellsuit tops. Dungarees with one strap loose. I turned to Dan as some of the cars started moving. "What do we do now?"

– "We follow them."

This huge convoy set off down the M1 in the direction of Northampton. We drove up a few junctions and then came off at a turning for Santa Pod racetrack. We were in the middle of a much larger convoy now as cars had joined us from other stretches of motorway.

Eventually, we entered some country lanes. I could see these security guards with Maglite torches, lighting the way in this huge open space. I could see some throbbing lights in the distance and what looked like a fairground ride. It was beyond exciting.

We carried on trundling down this lane until we hit Santa Pod racetrack; an old air airfield complete with a cavernous hangar probably 500 yards away; a laser was circling around inside. It was pretty basic compared to Goldiggers in Chippenham or Papillon down in Bristol, where they had enormous lighting rigs typical of the Luminar Leisure clubs. But you could see more lights flashing inside and the music was incredible. We parked up, got out of the car and I had a real *moment*. 'I think this is where my life is headed!' This was the beginning of a completely new era.

According to our friend, Rachael, Tony Colston-Hayter had told the people that ran Santa Pod that they were filming a video for Soul II Soul that required a party scene with lots of extras. And that's how he sold the idea to them. And then of course everybody just turned up mob handed and took the place over.

Colston-Hayter's pre-event advertisements would not state a specific venue. Instead, a BT VoiceBank phone number was given. The answerphone message was then regularly updated with directions closer to the start of the event and so you had to keep ringing it to find out what the hell was going on. The intention was to get as many ravers as possible to arrive at the party before the police so the authorities would be afraid to shut the event down without risking aggro. Colston-Hayter saw the rave as a business and ran it like one. He often had a barrister on site to greet the police should they try and shut the events down. It was quite a set-up.

We walked straight up into this warehouse that had a centrifuge fairground ride next door. About 300-400 feet ahead of us was a raised area where the DJs were. Adamski was doing a PA; he was brand new back then and we'd never really heard his stuff before. That night we heard tracks like *N.R.G.* for the first time, it was so incredibly edgy and fresh.

We didn't really know any DJs' names or anything. We weren't really privy to all that, yet. But the one face we did recognise was our old friend Eddie Richards who was now a definite cog in the emerging rave machine, popping up at a lot of things over the years. He was now known as 'Evil' Eddie Richards and had released the track *Acid Man* as Jolly Roger. Eddie was literally providing the soundtrack to our youth without even knowing it. We loved him.

That night – Sunrise – was incredible. We just spent hours dancing to acid house and Chicago tunes. It was a really eclectic night with all sorts of different tracks dropping in. Some of the raves would feature a section where they would play more downbeat stuff, like Izit's *Stories (Jackanory Mix)*. We loved this all-encompassing music from the funk and soul all the way through to the full-on machine music like Charles B's *Lack Of Love* and *Give It To Me* by Bam Bam. I also loved Tyree Cooper and Fast Eddie.

The hours just seemed to float by. We partied until the sun came up and then crashed on the grass for a bit. And my brain was forever altered. I just wanted this.

That Saturday at Santa Pod kickstarted a brand-new path for me. When could we go to the next event? I can remember the week after that me, Danny and a mate of ours called Geoff went to a party in my electric blue Escort cabriolet. We drove into this rave with the top down. It was a beautiful summer's day in 1989 and we were listening to *Three Is The Magic Number* by De La Soul. Just great snapshots of a wonderful time to be alive.

The other thing we were fully ensconced in was Green Apple Radio, the illegal radio station based near me in Slough. At The Centre in Slough was a good night as well. It wasn't on the grandiose scale of the Tony Colston-Hayter Back To The Future and Sunrise parties, but it was a good local shindig on a Friday night. And I used to go to that a lot. The Green Apple Radio DJs would play that night in Slough. Everything was changing, and the likes of Inner City and Technotronic were beginning to hit the charts. The raves springing up around the south at that time were known as the M25 parties and there was something on most weekends.

# CH. 10

**rob**
**Tissera**

# Sunrise: A Midsummer Night's Dream At White Waltham Airfield

One of the stand-out M25 raves was Sunrise at White Waltham Airfield, Berkshire, which was literally just three miles from where I lived in Maidenhead. That was the party *The Sun* called 'Ecstasy Airport'. They said there were loads of 'ecstasy wrappers' on the floor, but in reality it was confetti and tickertape released when the sun came up. That was the first time I heard *French Kiss* by Lil Louis. What a moment.

It was a beautiful summer's day and we were inside this warehouse full of people with a big podium in the middle with two tiers, both covered in ravers. When the breakdowns kicked in, everybody was just swaying as one. I'd never seen so many smashed people, and the music was synchronising them, as if they were in a trance. Some people were getting a bit horny from the effects of the pills. Hand on heart, we were just there for the music and so were many others, but you could tell that things had been *taken*, if you know what I mean. There were a lot of people gurning away. It was crazy. It was quite an honour to be a part of that moment.

When the sun rose they released these balloons, after all it was a Sunrise party, and so we were celebrating the sun coming up. It was the first time I'd heard Young MC during Carl Cox's set. I had no idea who Carl was at the time, but he stood head and shoulders above the other DJs that night. Carl played Young MC's *Know How* and all I could think about was listening to *Theme From Shaft* on my dad's Technics; the track that contained the sample. I was loving the fact that there were so many different styles being played at one night and so many different cultures and races coming together. We were still in a world where football violence was a big thing, but it wasn't long before that started to fade a little with casuals leaving all their inhibitions at the door.

I can remember hearing Rhythim is Rhythim's *Strings Of Life* for the first time that night and just thinking 'Jesus Christ! What is this?!' It was such an intense sound and I can remember people really pushing the boat out on the dance floor. It was great to be a small part of that crowd and that palpable change in attitude. It was absolutely beautiful. That was Midsummer Night's Dream, June 26, 1989.

***

I moved to Windsor during those M25 days. I was renting a room in an amazing Tudor house in Bray. All my early raving experiences would see me coming home at the same time as the milkman to this spooky Tudor house with its full-on coats of arms lining the halls. It was a mental place to come back to after a full-on evening. My new home was owned by a 94-year-old lady and it was so grandiose it had east and west wings. That said, I only occupied a small part of it, as the house was divided into bedsits. But it was well quaint. I was literally living like a lord through that Second Summer Of Love.

Weekends were spent locating fields along the M25 for the next stand-out rave. Every weekend was taken up with another crazy adventure with our new best friends. What a moment in time. What a time to be young and free.

It was August 26th during the summer of '89 somewhere in a Surrey field near the M40, and we were at this enormous Energy rave; 20,000 people or so. They were only expecting 5,000! It was absolutely mental and there was this searing heat throughout the night and into the morning.

Quentin 'Tin Tin' Chambers got up on stage at some point to deliver a little speech about something or other. As soon as he finished Black Box's *Ride On Time* came blasting out to 20,000 people. It was insane. It still feels like yesterday.

The whole event was out in some fields; there was no warehouse attached to it. It was just an outdoor party and better for it really. I can just remember how hot it felt lying on the grass. It was pure joy.


## Graeme Park, Haçienda, Cream

*"In the early 80s, a band I was in was getting a lot of interest from record companies. I sang and played saxophone and a few other instruments in a few bands in the East Midlands. I thought I had the best job in the world because I played in a band that was touring a lot and getting a lot of interest while also running the singles and secondhand department of Selectadisc in Nottingham. There were a few Selectadiscs in Nottingham and I worked upstairs in the Bridlesmith Gate branch. I got the job there by accident because I used to work in a record shop when I was a kid in Scotland on Saturdays and just got to know the staff in the Nottingham Selectadisc.*

*And then one day they said, 'Oh, you used to work in a record shop. You know how everything works. Do you fancy a job? Today? We're short-staffed.' I said, 'Of course, I will.' I ended up getting a full-time job and quite quickly, somebody left and they gave me the singles and the secondhand floor, which was amazing to me because I was able to get access to every new release that came in. I was only 18, 19, right, so 'My god, this is the greatest job in the world!' And being in charge of the secondhand department meant I was able to listen to everything. This was 1984.*

*People would come into the store with these old rock, punk, psychedelic or disco records or whatever. 'Can I sell them to you?' And I'd be going, 'Oh my god. I can't believe they're selling that.' So I would say, 'Not much call for these, or for these.' Ha ha. And I'm really thinking, 'I want them.' Then I'd listen to them in the shop while working and think, 'Oh, I'm definitely having this!' I'd get to buy them for pretty much what I gave the customer for it. And of course, the ones I didn't want, I'd put out for sale at a bit of a mark-up.*

*I've always had eclectic taste, so it was a great education and an efficient way of checking things out you might not necessarily have the time to discover, while getting paid to do it.*

*The owner of the record shop had his office on the same floor as the singles department. And his door was always open. Brian Selby (not with us anymore) had a bit of a history because he ran a northern soul record label. And he was very good at making trips around Europe to get lots and lots of what were called cut-out albums; European releases of stuff that hadn't done well in Europe. There were warehouses full of them. He'd get them cheap and sell them cheap in Selectadisc. One day he came back from lunch and said, 'I've just bought a nightclub!' And we were like, 'What? You bought a nightclub?'*

- *'Yeah.'*
- *'Which one?'*
- *'The Ad-Lib.'*
- *'The Ad-Lib? You idiot. That's a reggae club.'*

*Admittedly, The Ad-Lib was the only place you could have a late-night drink in Nottingham other than this gay club where you had to knock on this little window to get in. You always felt a bit of an edge in The Ad-Lib because it was a proper full-on reggae club with plumes of smoke everywhere; everyone was puffing weed. But it had amazing music and an incredible bottom end from the sound system.*

*And we were like, 'Why have you bought that?'*

- *'Well, Nottingham needs a really cool underground venue a bit like The Wag Club in London. And I'm going to relaunch it as The Garage Club.'*
- *'When are you going to do that, Brian?'*
- *'This week!'*

*This was a Tuesday lunchtime. 'Brian, that's not going to go down well with the regulars.'*

- *'Oh, I don't care about that, and Graeme, I want you to DJ at the club.'*
- *'What? No, no, no, no, I'm not a DJ!'*
- *'Well, I love the music you play in the shop. It's a real mix of stuff. You'll be great!'*

*And Brian pretty much blackmailed me into becoming a DJ. 'If you're not going to DJ in my club, then we don't want you here in the record shop.' I was 19, had the best job in the world, and so I agreed to DJ at this brand-new club.*

*I left work early on the Friday and went home to get ready. I remember going to the greengrocer around the corner and asking for some wooden crates, which they provided. I put as many records in those crates as I could and got a taxi to the record shop, to grab more vinyl before heading off to the club.*

*I'd never DJ'd in my life, but here I was, standing behind two belt-driven turntables and a mixer. The DJ booth was behind the bar and I had an absolute ball. I was essentially playing music I really liked and the people on the dance floor appeared to like it too. I thought, 'Hey, this is alright.'*

*I did the Friday and the Saturday, and the thing that struck me the most was, apart from enjoying myself, I got £50 at the end of the night and I didn't have to share it with four other band members. I didn't have to hire a van and set up a PA. I didn't have to pay the drummer's girlfriend to do the door and stuff like that. 'This is alright!'*

*Six weeks later, I was thinking, 'Actually, I think this is what I want to do for a bit.' I remember turning up to a band rehearsal and they said, 'Where's your saxophone?'*

*– 'Oh, right, lads, I've not got my saxophone with me because I hate to tell you this, but I'm out.'*

*This did not go down well because as I said, we were doing pretty well. And so, over the next 18 months, I was playing in Nottingham and clubs in Derby and Leicester. Those three cities have a very strong connection; they're very similar places all linked by road. People from all three cities would meet at the same clubs. I'm not talking about your big glitzy commercial clubbers, I'm talking about people who were into slightly different underground tunes. I played at the Bluenote in Derby, The Garage in Nottingham and then word got around about what was happening at The Garage and people from Sheffield would come down. Next thing, I'm getting asked to DJ in Sheffield for the Jive Turkey guys and doing a place in Leicester called Helsinki, which was an amazing place. That led to Rock City in Nottingham, the Powerhouse in Birmingham and The Place in Stoke. 'I'll definitely give this a go for a few years and see where it takes me.'*

*I was still working in the record shop in the mid-80s. I was playing stuff like Cabaret Voltaire, Human League, Depeche Mode, ABC, all those kinds of electronic dance/pop bands. They all had 12" dub mixes and extended versions which I just loved playing out because they mixed in old soul, funk and disco. It was a real eclectic mix.*

*There were two pivotal moments for me. Once a week I got on the phone at the shop to do the orders. One sales rep said, in 1985, 'Oh, we've got this new stuff from America called electro. Afrika Bambaataa and Jonzun Crew.' I went, 'Yeah, give me a couple of each.' And that was all the early electro stuff that eventually morphed into hip hop, like Big Daddy Kane, Roxanne Shante, LL Cool J and all the Def Jam stuff. Although this wasn't a dance shop and Brian Selby was never a fan of me playing that stuff in the shop, I was getting it and listening to it before playing it in the clubs.*

*The second pivotal moment was in 1986 and was probably bigger. One of the independent distributors said, 'Well, we've got all these 12" singles from Chicago. I don't know who these people are: JM Silk, Chip E.'*

*– 'Yeah, give me one of each.'*

*I remember playing JM Silk's Music Is The Key in the record store, but Brian was like, 'Fucking hell, what's this shit?!'*

*– 'Oh, no, no, no, this guy's amazing.'*

*And of course, they were all the early Chicago house records. This was still 1986 and I clearly remember Brian Selby popping his head out of the office going, 'Graeme, we don't want this stuff blasting out at the shop. It's fine in the club, but not in the shop.'*

*1987 was when Jack Your Body became the first international house hit and things really started taking off for me when I met Mike Pickering from Manchester's Haçienda club at an i-D Magazine photo shoot in London.*

*I'd been to Manchester for nights at The Haçienda prior to this. I was a Factory Records fan. I had pretty much every Factory record in every format possible: A Certain Ratio, Joy Division, Crispy Ambulance. I would get multiple copies on different formats of everything. I was such a Factory Records fan that when they opened The Haçienda, even if a band I liked was playing in Nottingham, if they were at The Haçienda before, I'd be on the train to Manchester after work just to see them there. And so, meeting Mike was a great moment.*

*Mike was aware of what I was doing and I was fully aware of what he was doing. And then I got the gig at The Haçienda with him. I had to go to Brian Selby at Selectadisc and say, 'Listen, you're not going to like this, but I'm going to hand my notice in.' And he was not best pleased, but that's when things really took off for me.*

*Mike and I did a night at The Haçienda in February 1988, following the i-D Magazine photo shoot in '87. The shoot was for an article about this new breed of DJs that didn't use microphones or speak to the crowd;*

Mum and Dad in the 60s

Me aged one

Mum and me aged two

My family in 1967

Me aged two mid-air shot

Me in my Luton Town kit in 1974

My lovely family in 1977

Me in my England kit in the late 70s

Me and my football coach Mick O'Leary from Bletchley Colts, 1978

The Tissera family, 1978

Me and my mate Paul in the RAF days. Tunbridge Wells, 1987

No Komment band in the 80s

The boy band look. No Komment in the 80s

My RAF days with Mum and Dad in the 80s

Danny James, Geoff and me on the way to a Sunrise rave, 1989

Me in the moment 1989 at Joy near Manchester

Blackburn rave, Chadwick St, 1990

Blackburn rave

Convoy Blackburn rave, 1990

Live The Dream, Blackburn, 1990

Warehouse party, Blackburn, 1990

Police storming acid house party, Nelson, Lancs, 1990

Police vans in Blackburn

The flyer for that fateful day in history

Hand-drawn cartoon image by Dave P from his regular Blackburn raves comic strip

Lancashire Evening Telegraph clipping after the rave

My first tape, 1990

My first gig at the mighty Ark in Leeds, 1991

Bliss at The Gallery, Leeds with Steve Luigi, 1992

Me with hair 1992

Ark and Orbit at Corn Exchange, Leeds. 22/8/1992

Circle City – *Moments Of Inertia* CD Warp Records

An old press shot from 1996

My studio partner and good friend Ian Bland (Dream Frequency, Quake and Dancing Divaz)

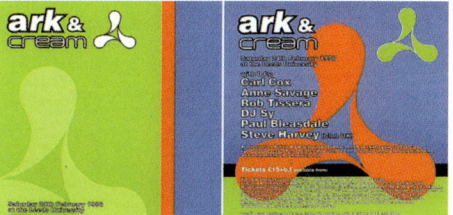

Ark and Cream 24/2/1996

Eden. My first Ibiza residency with Dave Pearce's Dance Anthems, 1998

Jacqui Ward from Minstrels in Blackburn

Picture from 1997

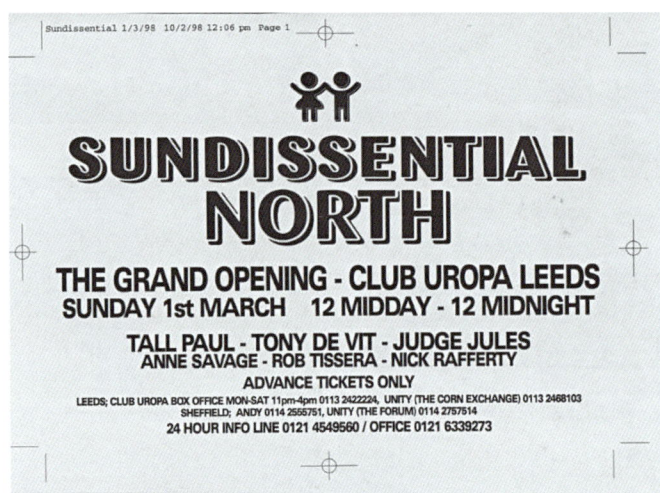

Sundissential, the grand opening, 1998

Blandy's Dreamscape Studio 1998. Where the magic happened - ha ha ha

Me and Ian Bland dressed as Batman and Robin in the Quake days,1999

*just played all this obscure music. Mike and I were the only DJs who weren't from the south east in this magazine article. And we hit it off and shared a taxi after. Mike was getting a train back to Manchester from Euston and I was getting the train back to Nottingham from St Pancras. We shared a taxi to Euston Road before going our separate ways.*

*We both agreed that a lot of the British media: i-D, Face, Blitz, NME, Sounds, all that stuff were all too London-centric in their coverage and that was a real bugbear for us because what I was doing in Nottingham and what Mike was doing on Fridays at The Haçienda weren't really getting written about. At this time, they were all still writing about rare groove, right? And so we thought, 'We should put a night on together.'*

*– 'Yeah, let's put a night on. We'll do it at The Haçienda. We'll call it the Northern House Review.'*

*We phoned all the press up and they were like, 'Fucking hell, this looks pretty good.'*

*– 'Well, get your fucking arses outside London and come up!'*

*Three months later, Mike rings me and says, 'I'm going on holiday for three weeks. I want you to cover my Friday night at The Haçienda.' I went, 'Yeah, that'd be fucking great.'*

*– 'But if you're going to do it, you've got to come up before.'*

*– 'Why? I've been to The Haçienda loads, we did that night together.'*

*– 'No, things are a bit different now. And if you don't come up, before I go away, then I'm sorry, you can't do it.'*

*Well, obviously, I'm like, 'Well, this is intriguing. What's going on?'*

*I went up to Manchester on that Friday before he went away. I walked into The Haçienda and I immediately sensed that things had changed. First of all, everyone looked the same. Everyone was wearing all the acid house gear: bandanas, bright colours, smiley faces and men in dungarees. 'What the fuck has happened?' This was '88, and so most clubbers who were into underground music dressed like they'd walked out of the pages of i-D Magazine, or The Face, but this was a whole new ballgame.*

*As I was walking through the crowd, I thought, 'Fucking hell, everyone's got this mad look in their eyes. What type of dancing is this?' I got to the DJ booth and knocked on the door. Mike let me in. He was wearing this same style of dress. He had his hair in a ponytail and he also had this mad look in his eyes. He gave me this massive hug which I found a bit disconcerting. I said, 'Fuck, what the hell?'*

‒   *'Right, this is why I asked you to come up.'*

*He put his hand in his pocket and retrieved a little white pill. He snapped it in half, and goes, 'You've got to take this half.'*

*I went, 'Oh, not drugs. No, no, no, Mike. No, no, no, no. I'll have a drink instead.'*

*Then the girl I was with at the time goes, 'I'll take the other half!' And necks it. I'm now like, 'Hang on a minute. If she's having it, I better have one.' Mike said, 'Right, here you go, fuck off and dance!'*

*20 minutes later, Mike played The Party by Kras's which has this nice little quiet build up intro before the piano comes in. When that piano hit, that's when everything kicked in for me. I was like, 'Oh my god, fucking hell! I get it!' There are loads of nights I've totally forgotten, but I remember that night vividly.*

*And then for the next three weeks, I did The Haçienda and totally understood why I had to come up because everybody in that club was taking E and now I was on the same level as everyone else. It was £25 for a pill of pure MDMA back then.*

*When Mike came back from holiday he said, 'Do you fancy staying and doing it with me every Friday?' And that's when that all began. It was a case of all the stars aligning. It was the venue and the people who ran the venue, Factory Records boss, Tony Wilson, Rob Gretton (New Order's manager) as well as the location: Manchester. Plus, you had all that great acid house and techno from Detroit, and the ecstasy, all those things combining just lit a spark that grew.*

*Lots of London-based record people would drop in to hear what we were playing. And of course, it wasn't till late 1988 that acid house really took off in the south. And even to this day, Mike and I often get annoyed by all that bollocks about how Paul Oakenfold and his lot went to Ibiza and discovered ecstasy and acid house and brought it back to the UK. Absolute bollocks, but it just proves that London-centric nonsense.*

*This was the first time that the people on the dance floor were a proper mixed crowd. It was the first time I'd witnessed teachers, bankers, doctors, nurses, football hooligans, hairdressers, plumbers, the unemployed, all dancing together, not giving a shit who everyone else was. Up until then, different nights attracted different crowds. The soul crowd were very dressed up. The Garage was more of a trendy crowd. It was a case of different crowds following different nights and DJs. It really struck us that acid house welcomed anyone and everyone because they were all off their tits hugging each other. There was a genuine sense of community."*

rob
Tissera

# Not So Grim Up North

Manchester was booming with the rise of Madchester and the baggy scene that delivered Stone Roses and Happy Mondays; indie bands that had funked their way over into the rave space – complete with onstage dancers Bez and Cressa. The rave scene was buzzing up there through 808 State and A Guy Called Gerald. Paul Oakenfold would go on to produce Happy Mondays biggest-selling album *Pills, Thrills & Bellyaches* and Stones Roses' *Fools Gold* featured a danceable bassline and drum track that 808 State would sample in *Tunes Splits The Atom*. For a while there, Manchester was the unofficial cultural capital of the UK and possibly Europe.

My mate Danny was now working up in the north west when I got a call. He'd done his degree in Manchester in the mid-80s and following the conclusion of his post-grad course down south, he'd decided to get back up north. "You know all these amazing raves we've been to? Well, scrub that, because you need to come up here to a club called The Haçienda. You need to experience this!" Danny made it sound so good, I just couldn't think of anything else.

At that time The Haçienda (catalogue number: FAC 51) was run and funded by Factory Records and New Order. The Haçienda was a venue on the southside of the Rochdale Canal in the centre of Manchester, that hosted a mix of gigs and club nights; the club nights starting to create a real buzz since the introduction of a certain tablet into the dance scene.

Greg Wilson, Hewan Clarke, Mike Pickering, Jon DaSilva and Graeme Park were the DJs that had helped create this stir.

Dan had been going to The Haçienda since 1984 when it was more of an alternative venue, but now there was something going on up there that I clearly needed to see. The vibes at that venue had clearly changed.

I was sat at work mulling over this piece of news from Danny and thought 'Fuck it! I'm going!' It was teatime on a Wednesday night and I had a few hours to get myself up north to 'Hot', the Wednesday night at The Haçienda. I grabbed the keys of a 5 Series BMW from work, because I was in charge of the compound, and drove that car straight up to Whitworth Street West as soon as work ended. It was to be one of the best nights of my entire life.

The red-bricked, two-floored Haçienda with its curved frontage was just INCREDIBLE! I couldn't get my head around it. The atmosphere was friendly and the sound in there was so intense and compressed. The ravers just seemed so much more into it and were not so concerned about standing around looking cool, which could be a feature of some of the London parties we'd been to.

The resident DJs that night were Mike Pickering and Graeme Park and they were brilliant. I'd never experienced anything like it and their sets were markedly different to the nights I'd been to in London; a little bit lighter in places, but completely mind blowing. They were playing tracks like Nicole's *Rock The House*, *You're My One And Only* by Seduction, Tony Scott's *That's How I'm Living* and *Dirty Cash* by Stevie V. Now, there was a lot of unity at the London parties, but there was just this one-ness in Manchester at that moment in time. I looked up at Graeme Park and just knew I wanted to be up there behind the decks. I felt this massive desire to be in control of the music. It was an amazing time to be alive and the way that music sounded in that club was like nothing else. It had that syncopated warehouse sound. Almost a hollow, cylindrical sound. The Haçienda had a relatively high ceiling and so the sound resonated around the whole club, giving off a warm vibe as A Guy Called Gerald's *Voodoo Ray* blasted through us. It was epic!

I drove straight back to work the next day having had no sleep. But that night was so good I was driving back up to Manchester again on the Friday for another night (Nude) at The Haçienda. Jesus Christ, it was amazing. I pretty much started going up every week.

The Haçienda might be the first place where I heard people like Jon DaSilva playing acapellas over the top of records, which I thought was very clever. Tracks like *Sueño Latino* with Ralphi Rosario over the top and Cappella with Loleatta Holloway's *Take Me Away*. Jon was doing stuff that really sparked my interest. The fuse had been lit. I wanted to be a DJ. Seeing Graeme Park, Mike Pickering and Jon DaSilva at The Haçienda had me completely obsessed with the idea of doing it myself.

My mate Danny and I were very much into hip-hop and we loved NWA, Mantronix and Grandmaster Flash and so we understood a little bit about DJ culture, but we had no equipment or skills. I had tried a few tricks on my dad's belt-driven Technics turntable that had a rudimentary pitch control to it. Instead of a minus 12/plus 12 pitch control, you had plus 3/minus 3. I managed to convince Dad that I should take ownership of the deck around the same time that Danny got one too.

I was now going to London as often as I could to buy records from Black Market Records in Soho just to get those tunes Graeme Park had been playing at The Haçienda. I also loved all those acapellas Jon DaSilva was playing and although I still didn't have a full-on set of turntables of my own, I was collecting all the records.

I had a fallout with my girlfriend in Maidenhead around this time and that relationship came to an end. To be fair, I was neglecting my duties at BMW driving up and down the country. I fell out with her on a Friday and so packed my car and bolted up north. I got to Northampton and phoned the boss and said, "I've left the south of England. And I've left my job." I did the same thing with my now ex-girlfriend and that was that. I was out of there.

I drove up the motorway to Manchester and went straight to The Haçienda and danced all night. It wasn't so much a rash decision, as more of a *calling*. I just knew I had to take a chance and make a new life for myself. I was trusting my gut.

Danny offered me a temporary place to kip at his student digs in Mold, north Wales, near Chester, which was great for a little while, but we soon decided we needed to be a bit closer to the acid house. We needed to be near Manchester. We ended up renting a house in Rochdale, just 15 miles north of Manchester. We got the house through Kev Walsh's mate Rex Sergeant, New Order's sound engineer.

The Suite 16 recording studio was on Rochdale's Kenion Street and the landlord of this house was none other than legendary New Order bassist Peter Hook. Joy Division, New Order and many more Manchester and Liverpool bands recorded at Suite 16. Tractor Music was downstairs at

Kenion Street and that was where a lot of the Haçienda's sound equipment was built and repaired. We sometimes got onto Hooky's guest list at his club too, which was a touch. Because I was the one who collected the rent, they nicknamed me Rigsby after the *Rising Damp* landlord.

I would sometimes go to Suite 16 with Danny, Kev and Rex after raving at The Haçienda. We ended up doing quite a bit of mucking around, recording bits and pieces in the studio. Those were interesting times and I was making some useful connections.

Through this mucking around in the studio, we actually formed a band with this other guy called Mark Pilkington. It was me, Rex, Kev and Mark and I can't even remember what the band was called. Now, Rex was a bass player and he had all the kit and access to the studio and so I was left as a 'minister without portfolio' so to speak. In fact, they wanted me to be the singer. Because I wrote poetry they even suggested I became a rapper. Now, I loved working with all those guys, but I just didn't fit into that scenario and those dynamics. I was a bit upset by that, but I didn't let on. But it was exactly at that point in time that I suddenly thought: 'I need to have a proper go at this DJ malarkey!'

I'd built up quite a record collection by now and we had two sets of decks between us in the same location, and so Danny and I spent a lot of time mixing. I went to Tandy, the home-tech shop that produced its own gear under the name Realistic and bought a mixer for £40 or something; definitely the cheapest in the range. I followed the instructions on how to wire it all up and put two tracks on.

My first attempts at mixing were moving the fader up on the first deck and then the second, before DADADADA! Disaster! It sounded like a wardrobe falling down the stairs. I thought Jesus Christ I must have wired it up wrong. I took it apart and built it up again and got the same problem. At which point Danny came in. "What are you doing exactly?!" I told him the mixer wasn't working. He said, "Mate, you've got to get that shit in time." I didn't have a clue.

Now, don't forget, there were no YouTube instruction videos back in the day. And so Danny explained that you had to get the records at the right tempo, but because I only had one deck with a semi pitch control, I learned to mix by turning the spindle of one turntable and then pinching the other to slow it down to get somewhere near to being in time. Then we would turn the next fader up on one and turn the fader down on the other and voila! We had a mix!

My dad was a bit of a proto mixer. He would record cassette mixes for car journeys on his tape-to-tape player. Dad would then splice the tape to remove the silences. He would put it on pause, then move the track forward and then take the pause off so that there were no gaps in the music. That's how I first learnt about continuous music. Although, when it came to the actual mixing, Danny was the person who taught me how to do that. And if only I had the skills he had because he was brilliant at it; he just didn't see it as a career choice.

I was like a dog with a bone from that moment onwards. Christ, DJing was all I really wanted to do from now on.

# Angry Punters, Rick Astley And The Joy Of Decks

Although I wanted to become a DJ, I needed money for rent and food and so I got a job at a Porsche dealership in Bury called Ian Anthony's, doing the same job I'd been doing down south for BMW. I would deliver the cars back to customers – at speed – while also being in charge of the service department.

I do have some regrets, and what have you, when it comes to my driving, but I had some fantastic times driving those amazing cars. I was never going to be able to afford one and so driving those 9-11s and Targas was an absolute pleasure. It really was.

I had a massive car accident on my way back from work one night, not in one of their cars, but my own – a ropey old Vauxhall Astra I'd had to downgrade to after leaving my high-flying lifestyle down south. I got hit by this drunk driver who was trying to overtake when he shouldn't have. He crashed straight into me and my car was a complete write off. I was off work for about three or four weeks. Unbeknown to me, the dealership was about to downsize its operations and so they sacked me whilst I was off sick. Which was very unfair; you wouldn't get away with that these days.

I ended up working for a Vauxhall dealership in Cheetham Hill called Sid Abrahams following that, which kept the money coming in while I was partying and learning to mix. Sid Abrahams was 600 yards or so from Strangeways prison and I can remember seeing rioting prisoners on the roof while I was at work. They were up on the roof for weeks in the searing heat. People would stand on Cheetham Hill Road cheering them on. It was crazy, and occasionally I would drive down there while undertaking a car demo for a customer as it broke the ice whilst I was desperately trying to sell them a new car.

Opposite the Vauxhall car dealership was this disco hire place run by a guy called Les Adams. Now, learning the trade on a home stereo was one thing, but if I really wanted to play out, I would need a proper set of decks and Les Adams hired out all the gear I needed. I went in to see Les one lunchtime and he hooked me up with a DJ console. The deck was in a flight case and it had the belt drive situation, but all in one console, so it wasn't that different to my parents' turntable to be honest. This set-up was not a Technics 1210 or anything like that, but it was enough to get me started as a DJ-for-hire.

I went into the shop one day to get some new needles and a slip matt and Les pulled me to one side. "Do you fancy doing some weddings? I can get you a few gigs, no problem." I jumped at the chance. Now, this was a very important first step to becoming a professional DJ. I was buzzing by the prospect of being paid to DJ.

My first gig was at a pub on a housing estate in Wythenshawe. I had a red Vauxhall Belmont CDI company car which was a pretty sweet ride for a youngster. I parked it up outside this pub and took my gear inside. The pub landlord didn't really lay out any rules or anything and I just set up the double decks and the PA system and got myself psyched for my first trip into the unknown.

The pub and the surrounding area were a little edgy, but coming from a council estate myself, I wasn't too fazed. It was a busy pub, and it soon filled up. It wasn't long before I had people coming up and asking for requests. "You're not from around here are you?" "And that's not a Manchester accent!" I started off playing some well-known chart stuff, but I could see some younger folk who looked well up for some dance tracks. It wasn't long before Technotronic's *Pump Up The Jam* and Inner City's *Good Life* were booming out. Feeling brave, I stuck some Frankie Knuckles on and A Guy Called Gerald's *Voodoo Ray*. The youngsters loved it and were banging glasses on the table. I had never experienced anything like this before. I really got off on the live feedback element of punters responding to what I was playing. It was such an adrenaline rush.

I played a good solid hour of dance stuff and then the landlord piped up. "Turn that fookin' shit off now!" Men in their 40s and 50s had started complaining about the "fucking boom boom shit!". I was told to stick some Rick Astley on. I guess I'd had my fun. Suddenly a whole bunch of ladies started dancing to *Never Gonna Give You Up* and *Venus* by Bananarama. That's just how that went really. So that was my very first gig, but there were definitely more positives than negatives. I was very invested now.

I took the gear back to Les Adams on the Monday and found out that the landlord wanted me back for the following Saturday too. I was elated. I was also booked to DJ at a wedding reception at another big pub. There were going to be 300 people at that shindig.

These mixed crowds, especially at the weddings, really highlighted the cultural split between the young and the old. You had the parents and grandparents who wanted The Beatles and ABBA and you had the youngsters who wanted acid house and techno. The youngsters started coming up very early on, wanting the tunes they'd heard at Haçienda, Thunder Dome and Konspiracy. "Have you got *Bring Forth The Guillotine*?" I also played Doug Lazy *Let It Roll* and a bit of hip house before moving into A Guy Called Gerald. I also mixed in a bit of Stone Roses and Happy Mondays, which were of a similar tempo. I did a good hour of proper thumpers, until the bride's father turned up with his angry red face. He looked just like an enraged tomato. "Get that fucking shit off now! If you don't switch it off now I will have you filled in!" He looked really handy and he was surrounded by his sons who also looked a bit tasty. I desperately flicked through the crate and found a 70s compilation and just let it play. Then I did a good hour of The Beatles. All these pub gigs were a learning experience and really toughened me up. I was booked to deliver a certain thing and so if you strayed too far outside the remit, you could experience a bit of turbulence. These weddings and local bars were in some pretty rough parts of Manchester; the kinds of places where even the cats carried flick knives and the dogs went around in pairs. I was literally learning on the job.

Now, I wasn't scratching or mixing or anything – I was still learning all that – but I quickly worked out how to work an audience. Quite often, the landlord or the bride's father would threaten to kick the shit out of you for playing the wrong stuff, which taught me an awful lot about knowing your crowd and not playing too much underground stuff during a wedding reception.

## CH. 13

*rob tissera*

# Sett End, Clitheroe Kate And The Birth Of Boomtown

**Tommy Smith, Blackburn Rave organiser**

*"I moved to Blackburn from my hometown Dumbarton to study in the mid-to-late 80s. I was 22, I think. I discovered travel not long after getting there, so I abandoned Blackburn and the academic life. In fact, I was living in Berlin when I first heard of acid house. I mean, I'd done acid before, so I wrongly assumed acid house was taking loads of acid; that certainly alerted me when I saw the posters going up around Berlin. 'Oh, acid house? What's going on here?'*

*I went to an acid house night in Berlin, but it made no sense to me at all, it was just this, boom, boom, boom, boom, boom. I came from a background of Pink Floyd, psychedelia, The Doors and stuff like that. So when I first heard that stuff I thought, 'This makes no sense whatsoever.'*

*I came back to Blackburn for a holiday around the time of the Second Summer Of Love. I couldn't quite work out what was going on. All the people I'd known previously, who were sworn enemies, were now drinking together in the pub. I thought, 'Have I missed something here?' There was this whole erotic love-in among these former enemies. 'What the fuck's going on here? Something has clearly changed.' It had changed for the better of course.*

*Everybody was talking about the music and the love they shared. There was no more violence and I thought, 'This is mad. Have I taken one too many trips? I've stumbled into Utopia here on some hallucinogenic trip.' I honestly thought I was imagining it. But no, it was true.*

*I went to this great party in Blackburn and had an epiphany with a capital E, let's put it like that. I was loving it. I was hooked on acid house. We started going to The Haçienda in Manchester, which I liked, but it was a different vibe; quite cliquey with the city people, and the doorman saying, 'It's not your night' and stuff like that. It happened to us one time, and I thought, 'It's not my night? It fucking will be. We're going to do it ourselves.' And we did.*

*We started putting on some nights in this small club in Blackburn called Crackers. The venue only held about 75 people, but we could cram 250 in there. It was a real sweatbox. The club was owned by this camp drag queen called Clitheroe Kate and he was the only one who would let us play that kind of music in Blackburn. And that was when the embryo started to form, if you will; plans started hatching. For me, the parties at Crackers represented a monumental moment in time, because you felt the energy in there, the sweat dripping off the ceiling, that pure vibe. Men stripped off, hugging and dancing together. It's quite common now, isn't it? But it was really alien back then. Anyone in Crackers could see there was something going on there. This was clearly the start of something colossal, something earth-shattering, really. That's when it all started for me.*

*And needless to say, we were soon outgrowing Crackers. And then we got another club called The Sett End; another legendary place in Blackburn. The Sett End was on the fringes of Blackburn on this big council estate. Run by an Irishman, the 'Sett' in the name referred to a badger's sett. A lot of badger baiters used to drink there. The highlight of that place were Saturday and Sunday mornings and the 'pie, pint and a stripper' events. So we were going from this euphoric dancing in the earlier hours to seeing these strippers turning up in the mornings. It was quite surreal, actually.*

*Needing ever bigger venues, my mate Tony and I started hosting raves in the many unused buildings around the town. There were a lot of abandoned mills in Blackburn, where generations of families sweated away in those huge places. We wanted to fill them with equally sweaty locals. Tony was quite a daredevil, fearless and nothing and no one was going to stop us from putting on these nights. The team was a combination of Tony and I and quite a few others. I will withhold the names for various reasons.*

*Initially, we had 75 to 100 people in these small events, but every week it would grow. We even had a party in a slaughterhouse and that was quite a memorable event. When the lights came up we were like, 'Fucking hell, what is all that on the wall?' That was quite bizarre. But soon, we were getting thousands of ravers rather than hundreds.*

*One of our greatest allies – unwittingly – was the local paper, The Lancashire Telegraph. The advertisement boards said things like 'Frenzied acid house revellers invade East Lancashire!' The slaughterhouse rave was reported as 'Half-naked girls in acid house romp!' The locals were seeing these headlines and then coming down to check it out. We were selling tickets for one event and sales weren't going especially well and then the local paper printed '30,000 set for acid invasion!' And that night was rammed! Joe Strummer, Boy George and New Order turned up because they'd seen the headlines. That night triggered even bigger events.*

*Remember the 'Can you feel it?' war cry? Well, our war cry was, 'Can you afford it?' It was like £10-25 for your usual club night. That was a lot of money, and the unemployment benefit was only £14 a week. It was only £3 entry or free if you had a dole card at our nights. It was all about access for everybody. We were anti-Thatcher, anti-Tories and all that stuff and so it was crucial that we let people in. For me, you can't charge people if they were skint and that's an important point. So, if people turned up we certainly weren't going to turn them away, and that helped numbers swell.*

*People were coming from Liverpool, Manchester, Leeds – all sworn enemies. Well-known football hooligans from back in the day were meeting up with rival fans from the terraces. It was good to see them hugging and all that stuff.*

*It was important for us to bring people together, so they'd come here as strangers, but leave as a part of the family. These were kids with nothing: no hopes, no dreams, no aspirations. And they were just piling in. And there'd be the volunteers and people getting arrested every week, but there'd be another 100 people queuing up to do their job at the next night. It was all about that spirit of the age. And the whole revolution, if you will. Soon all the townie clubbers were quickly converted to our way of life. The shirt was gone, the tie was gone and they were topless and sweating. It was clear what was going on, and I'm sure it wasn't that local Lancashire lager."*

## Graeme Park

*"Quite often in the winter, when I'd finished at Haçienda, you'd be bundled into a car, off to a warehouse in Blackburn. Blackburn, as a place, had already started to decline. The Thatcher government made it even worse. And there were lots and lots of spaces in Blackburn. I often had no idea who else was in the car, but I had my records in the boot, and was being sped up the M65 to Burnley and onto Blackburn.*

*Next thing I know I'm DJing in a warehouse 4-5am, always making sure my records were by my side, just in case the police came. And in the summer, it would be back of the car again, no idea where you were going and you'd end up in a field, anywhere in the north west or sometimes in the north midlands playing in a huge fucking tent. And then the sun's coming up and everyone's off their tits. Great days!"*

Whilst living in Rochdale I'd started going to a few parties up in Blackburn. I would work early on at the weddings and pub gigs before going on to Blackburn for the final hour or so at this bar called Minstrels. Once more I wheeled out the shiny brass gonads and asked the lady who ran the bar, Jacqui Ward, if she'd give me a shot at playing a few tracks in the bar. Luckily, she agreed after hearing a couple of mixtapes and just like that, I was in!

Once that had closed we would often go to these emerging raves in Blackburn with Kevin Walsh and Rex Sergeant. The van hire company Rex worked for was owned by his dad and based in Blackburn. Rex lived in the back office of this industrial unit. I went over to see him one night and there was a whole bunch of his mates chilling out with him, having a good time. They asked me if I wanted to go to this party at Pump Street in Blackburn.

Blackburn, the former mill town was full of empty industrial units and warehouses down these Victorian backstreets; pretty much ready-to-go venues for parties. Many of the legit locations such as The Haçienda closed quite early, especially if you were 'on one' and so Blackburn was emerging as a pretty lively place for an illegal get-together. A lot of it was centred around the Sett End. Tommy Smith was the face of Hardcore Uproar, who along with his best mate Tony, kicked off some Blackburn parties in the spring of 1989.

We approached this warehouse on Pump Street, which had all the windows kicked in, to find about 300 people inside. There was lots of what looked like asbestos dust on the floor and one strobe light trained on a guy doing poetry over a Joy Division track. It was mad!

They played a lot of Italo house at this Blackburn party, which was massive at the time. Tracks like *Pakito Lindo* and JT Company's *Don't Deal With Us* would be shoehorned in next to hip house anthems like Deskee's *Let There Be House* and *Don't Scandalize Mine* from Sugar Bear. I also heard a lot of stuff from Belgium by the likes of Modular Expansion and Liaison D. They would play Belgian hardbeat: Frank De Wulf and pretty heavy industrial tracks like *Acid Rock* by Rhythm Device. But the hardbeat was mixed in nicely with the more anthemic Italian tracks and then you'd get some acid house and the odd Joy Division record or Doors track. There would also be some hip house tracks like *Yo-Yo Get Funky* by Fast Eddie. It was a real eclectic mix and had a very different feel to The Haçienda and the London parties. I'd never encountered anything like it and when the bass dropped, it hit you low in the stomach. Boof! Smack bang in the abdomen every time the bass kicked in. Everybody felt it. It was absolutely awesome.

Unlike the London raves, there was no real organisation or sense of business to these Blackburn parties. There was no-one patrolling the venue with a clipboard orchestrating stuff or getting on the microphone to give a speech to the DJs. These parties were very organic. They'd have a DJ on for a while and then out would come the Blackburn 'shepherd's crook', and off they'd trot, as the next DJ started playing. DJ Shack was that shepherd, and he was enormously popular and one of the main orchestrators of those nights. It just depended on how it went for you, as to how long your set was. It could be three records or it could be 10, but that way it sounded fresh all the time. Shack was an awesome selector too. What a DJ and the energy he got out of the crowd was insane. He was also one of the hardest lads in Blackburn. Nobody messed with Shack. When he said your set was over, it really was over.

I met some real characters at the Blackburn raves. One such character was a girl called Amanda Michalak. We got on like a house on fire and she promptly introduced me to her brother Andrew 'Klak' Michalak who it turned out was supplying drinks for the parties. I'm so grateful to both of them, as their friendship gave birth to a tonne of new friends who I'm still mates with to this day.

There was this guy called John 'J' Jepson who was really popular back in the day. You would also have other guys coming along like the

Jam MC's from Manchester; two DJs and an MC. The Jam MC's were brilliant and everybody loved them. They were a bit more soulful and would often be playing as the sun rose. Quite often back then, the tempo would scope down a little bit with a slow section at the end of the night; known as the 'erection section' in townie clubs. Although, there was no slow dancing going on at these nights, there was just this soulful feel to the music. They would play Kariya's *Let Me Love You For Tonight* followed by *Snappiness* by BBG and *Natural Thing* by Innocence which were all down to 100-110 bpm, which was just brilliant in creating a new mood.

Those parties became a real phenomenon and went from 300 people one week to 400 the next and 600 following that. They just kept growing. Within six months there were 5-6,000 people at these nights. The punters would just drop the £3 entrance fee into a big plastic bag by the front doors. The warmth I felt from Shack, Tommy Smith, Joe, Jools and of course Amanda and her brother Klak was so important to me. I cannot tell you how much fun it was to go to some of those parties.

It was just this phenomenal moment in time run by a collective of like-minded people who all had their own specific area of expertise. For example, you'd have somebody who did all the lights and supplied the strobes and whatnot. It was a real family. It's fair to say that the collective known as Hardcore Uproar had bottled lightning at that precious moment in time.

## Tommy Smith

*"We had quite a roster of DJs: Gillie, DJ Shack, Kenneth and Kelly (two Jamaican legends) and John 'J' Jepson from Blackpool. They were the movers and shakers; the early DJs that helped move the scene along. One of our regular guests was a bit of a preacher who would read poetry. It was quite mad. Back in the day, if you turned up with records you were a DJ. Rob Tissera would often turn up to get a spot.*

*I remember this guy from Leeds came over one night, totally out of it, and he said, 'Tommy, I don't believe it, you've done it! You've actually fucking done it!' I said, 'What are you talking about, Andy?'*

*– 'You've taken over, your plan was to take over 'the system' and you've done it!'*

    – *'What are you going on about?'*

*This fella was on the motorway on the way to the party in this big convoy. Thousands of cars on the motorway coming from the Leeds side. The police stopped the convoy and asked, 'Are you going to the party?' He said, 'Yeah.'*

    – *'Great, follow us,' and they actually took him to the party.*

*The police didn't want drugged-up ravers on the motorway and so they decided to escort them to the rave. 'You've done it, Tommy. You've got the police working for you!' In his eyes, we'd taken over and had the police on security detail. Ha ha.*

*We thought anything was possible. That for me was the key of it all; we made people believe, we helped them dream again. And they had to believe, through the unity of it all, that anything was possible. And it was at the time.*

*The police soon started to crack down on the Blackburn raves and would often seize the sound system. And somebody, who obviously has got to remain nameless, found out where they were storing the equipment and broke into the warehouse and loaded the van up with loads of confiscated equipment. It was mad.*

*A lot of the old mills didn't have power. I remembered seeing temporary traffic lights outside this one venue and so we hooked up to that with the big batteries and cables. There was another party on New Year's Eve, and we got into a big mill that had no power, and so this guy ram-raided a plant hire business and threw two generators into the boot of a stolen car and drove up to the party. Nothing and no one was going to stop that night from going ahead.*

*One night on the Whitebirk Industrial Estate there was a massive fight with the police, who charged at us. Only the crowd charged back at the police and it was back and forth like that for a while. The police then abandoned one of the cars and it was turned on its roof and set on fire. And I'm thinking, 'Oh, my God!' because they knew who was organising these nights.*

*This was all happening in the days of Thatcher of course and because of the massive unemployment up there, they created stuff called Enterprise Allowance Zones. They built new warehouses and promised the North that people would invest in the region. We couldn't believe our luck when we saw these new units. We were used to these old sweaty, run-down cotton mills, that were really dangerous as well. And suddenly we're surrounded by these unbelievable brand spanking new warehouses.*

*So, we took that enterprise and made it our own. We thought it was an offer from Margaret herself.*

*One of the most important nights was at a place called Unit 7, which had never been used before. It had a beautiful floor, toilets inside, great light systems and huge emergency fire doors. If you were to design a warehouse for a party, you couldn't have designed it better. It was such a memorable night that people who attended still go and visit it today. Can you believe that?"*

***

There was one particular party held at the soon-to-be Post Office headquarters in Blackburn, which was crazy. The unit wasn't fully built, but it was on a brand-new industrial estate. We attended a night around the time the owners were laying the foundations of this building. It was still quite muddy underfoot, but there were planks of wood for you to walk on like a bridge into the first-floor window, about 6-7ft up. Inside people were standing at the sides collecting the money as you went through the window and down some steps into the main area or distribution centre; I guess the place where the trucks would turn up. You then went down the little staircase where you could feel the building throbbing. There were these corrugated iron panels that resonated and vibrated with the music. And then, when you walked in… boom! You would be greeted by tracks like Tony Scott's *That's How I'm Living*.

It was a slightly different sound up north compared to down south where there was a lot more piano and hip house like Lee Marrow's *Movin'*. The north loved the power and wanted to get busy to some darker stuff. Those Blackburn raves taught me a lot about light and shade and the different moods of music.

Inside the Post Office building they had a couple of diggers that were being used to build the warehouse. I can remember dancing on top of a JCB; in fact, I think there's some actual footage of it. I believe I was dancing to *Rich In Paradise* by FPI Project.

The DJ box at this party was on top of the foreman's hut; 10 feet above everybody else and it was just phenomenal. Everybody was hanging off the sides of the warehouse as the DJ played. Health and safety were certainly not front of mind back in those days. In fact, it was really bloody dangerous to be honest.

One particular night in Blackburn was held inside a warehouse where they fixed trucks. There were these bear pits that the mechanics would stand in to get underneath the vehicles that would drive over the holes. That night, people were running through the doors and into the warehouse, before plop! – they disappeared into the bear pit. Thankfully someone with a bit of a conscience decided to stand in front of the drop in order to prevent any further falls. We were young and carefree and just hadn't considered the dangers of people running blindly into a concrete pit.

One of the things I love about those early days was seeing things you would just never see anywhere else. I remember this one guy at a Blackburn rave who was absolutely smashed out of his face. He was a nasty piece of work who said he'd 'done more porridge than the 'three bears'. He was about 6' 3" and a very bad man. I remember him biting his hand until it bled, before running headfirst into a sheet of corrugated iron. He went straight through it like a cartoon Tasmanian Devil or something. His blood was all over these corrugated iron sheets that hung from the sides.

As I mentioned before, Klak ran the drinks at the Blackburn parties and he had three mates, Dave P, Jools and Joe who helped to build and install the PAs. And there was a real livewire called Preston Bob. Bob had a video camera and captured all the footage. Sadly, Bob passed away before any of his footage saw the light of day, which is a total tragedy as I'm certain he had some complete and utter gold in his vaults.

What I loved about the Blackburn crew was that they were so switched on to what needed to be done to get those parties to happen. They would have a couple of guys scouting for venues during the week and then they would approach security guards and see who was up for being paid off to turn a blind eye to 1,000 of our closest friends partying in an industrial estate.

They would then go back to the industrial estate every few hours to drop the kit off. They would buy these wood panels and cones for the speakers and the tweeters from Tandy. They would drop the equipment into the warehouse through a skylight so they could assemble the speakers in the warehouse during the week. Then they could come along on the Saturday with three amplifiers in an estate car or small van without bringing any unwanted attention to themselves. They were so inventive. Then they'd wire it all up and crack on come Saturday night.

The people organising events like Back To The Future would tell people they were filming a *Top Of The Pops* video as cover for why a good few thousand people were all bouncing in one location. Or they ran the nights as 'members-only' affairs. That's how they did it. Blackburn was a lot more underground. This was absolutely grassroots and pretty lawless, like an underground resistance movement. They were just making this stuff up as they went along.

One of the guys involved in doing all the electronics and getting the sound right was a guy called Joe Fossard and he was a right character. These people were Blackburn through and through. There was this guy Nathan operating the lights at one party and I can remember him attaching a strobe to a cable before ZZZZZZ!!!!! I thought he was having a stroke and when I looked a bit closer I could see he was being electrocuted. So, I just booted the wire and it stopped him from getting totally fried. I don't think any of the equipment would get through what they call PAT testing these days. Luckily, I'm still mates with Nathan D'Amour to this day.

One time there was no power in the warehouse they'd broken into, and Joe and his pal Jools 'piggy backed' the power from a set of temporary traffic lights that just happened to have been set up outside in the street. It was an actual stroke of genius by these guys. Bloody awe inspiring!

The Minstrels bar I played at in the centre of Blackburn, was often the meeting point you went to, to discover the location of the actual party that night, bearing in mind, there was a very small select group of people who actually knew what was going on. Once a convoy of vehicles had built up, we'd be on our way to the party.

I became the resident DJ on a Saturday night at Minstrels as well as doing a Thursday shift too. Quite a few of the people involved in the parties would meet in Minstrels and very soon I'd made some more useful new connections. There were two of us who played Minstrels. The other guy was a DJ called Mick Singh (his real name). You couldn't make it up, could you? I'm still friends with him to this day. Mick is a well-respected DJ who does high society weddings.

Amanda Michalak and her brother Andrew (Klak) ran the drinks van at the parties selling Lilt, Quatro and Vimto bought from the cash and carry. I went out with Amanda for quite some time and she played her brother some tapes of me DJing and that got me recognised by the Blackburn guys. I can't thank her and Klak enough for all the support they gave me. Without their help, I'd have never been made to feel so welcome. Around the same time I became friends with Tommy's brother George and his best mate Glen. These guys were two peas in a pod and the savage banter between us all created an unbreakable bond. I loved being around so many strong and incredibly funny characters. What a moment in time. We are all still in touch to this day. Not long after meeting them, they suggested I get involved in doing pirate radio. So, I would finish my set at Minstrels and then jump into my car and go straight to the pirate radio station BBC (Blackburn Buzz Corporation) with this guy Asim. Through this, my profile was getting raised in Blackburn, or 'Boomtown' as it was now known.

One of the characters I got to know from Manchester around this time was Adrian Luvdup who worked in the Vinyl Exchange. Vinyl Exchange was opposite the famous Eastern Bloc Records in Afflecks Palace, and had a section entirely devoted to Chicago and Ital house and Detroit techno and all that stuff. They would have so many eclectic sounds fused together through the main sound system such as Stone Roses, Young MC and Mr Fingers. They would sometimes drop a Bauhaus track too and it really reminded me of Evil Eddie Richards and his sets. It was landmark stuff and I was in awe of how clever they were.

I approached this guy behind the counter called Adrian Luvdup who was involved in the early days of the Madchester scene. Adrian was an influential character and somebody I consulted regarding the music I should be playing. Adrian was extolling the virtues of Dave Booth who had been DJing for a little bit longer than I had. Dave was one of the main DJs at a club called The Boardwalk, which was just across the road from The Haçienda. Dave was also resident at a legendary club called Pips in the early 80s playing Human League, The Cure and Blancmange. I used to hear these amazing cassettes that Adrian would play in Vinyl Exchange and one day I said, "Who makes these, they're the don!"

– "Dave Booth!"

I was instantly a fan. I would often play a mishmash of stuff too: Inspiral Carpets, Stone Roses and some Chicago house back then. That's just how it was.

Adrian had a little residency at Isadora's, below the Corn Exchange in Manchester, which was a Sharon and Tracy club on a Friday, but they were looking for something a little different on a Sunday, something more acid house and so Adrian and I ended up being residents for a few months on a Friday night. I got to know Adrian quite well and he was really pushing me to put some acapella tracks over the music, just like

Jon DaSilva was doing. So, I went to Vinyl Exchange with him one day and he introduced me to a little section of the shop devoted to acapella stuff. He then took me through the process of mixing acapellas. And I can't thank Adrian enough for that as the acapellas became a real weapon over the years.

I was still travelling backwards and forwards going to the raves and everything in Blackburn, but not so much The Haçienda anymore because I was too busy playing out at Isadora's and Minstrels plus all the wedding functions, bar gigs and pirate radio.

***

As well as the Madchester scene, there were also other things going on in parallel around the city. Moss Side had quite an active sound system culture and those blues would feature reggae, dub, lover's rock as well as hip hop artists such as LL Cool J, NWA, Public Enemy, Lakim Shabazz and The 45 King. Some of The Haçienda DJs like Mike Pickering would go to these blues to hang out after their sets. We would often go to all these different areas of Manchester to hang out at these smaller parties with maybe just 150 punters rather than thousands.

The police raided one of those blues nights while I was DJing. I had successfully blagged my way onto the decks. "Turn it off!" they blasted through a loud hailer. The police marched into the party and everything went quiet. There was no violence or anything. I think there were about five minutes of silence before the police left after giving us a stern warning not to turn the music back on. But the sound system boomed straight back on as I played *Fuck The Police*! Everyone was banging on the walls to NWA. It was such a moment.

I think what often gets lost in translation is how the government, through the police, tried to kill this all off. They actively wanted to halt people from being able to gather and dance after a certain time, and of course the police were there to implement it. There were plenty more incidents involving the police, but I guess we were riding by the seat of our pants by grabbing any opportunity that came our way. And this musical revolution was happening so quickly, you just got carried along by the wave.

I was rushing about all over the place trying to make a name for myself. I was DJing at clubs, bars and the odd wedding and still partying as a punter too. I had boundless energy and just wanted this so much, I'm amazed I didn't burn out. I'd finish my set at a wedding or a bar, get into the car and go over to Blackburn and then do the last hour in Minstrels. I would then go to the pirate radio station before finishing the evening at a warehouse party. That was my life. Music was everything.

I got to know some characters who lived in Cheadle Hulme in Manchester, and they hired a place that used to host quite a few parties after The Haçienda and so I started going to some of those. I remember leaving a hoodie at their place one night and went back the following evening to get it with my then girlfriend. "You're always rushing around, you're relentless!" she said.

– "Hey, that's my nickname. Rob Rush-head!"

As I was leaving I said goodnight to this girl who lived there and jumped over this small garden wall, not realising there was a 6ft drop on the other side. What a dickhead. I landed in what would have been the basement area of the house. Bosh! Straight down into the basement and all my weight fell onto my arm. "Jeezus! Well *that* fucking hurts!" I endured the suffering until the following day when I checked myself into A&E. I had broken my arm. That wasn't my brightest moment, I mean a DJ with a broken arm ain't much use. Luckily, I was back in action pretty soon after, but I must admit, that definitely made me think about slowing down. A bit.

# No Sleep Since Blackburn

I still attended all the Blackburn parties, taking my crate of tunes with me, just waiting for an opportunity to play. There were lots of times I stood there and the chance just didn't come along, as there was a long queue of people all wanting to do the same thing. "What about me?" But I played the waiting game and eventually got my shot.

**Tommy Smith**

*"I first met Rob in The Haçienda when we were doing parties in Blackburn. He was like, 'Listen to me, there are these fucking banging nights in Blackburn. You should check them out!'*

*– 'Wow, that sounds good to me, mate. I may see you up there.'*

*We bumped into each other at one of our nights and he went, 'Fucking hell, it's you, isn't it? Ha ha.' I said, 'Yeah.'*

*What first moved me about Rob was his passion and his love for the scene, his love for the music. It was his passion that really connected with us. Then he started coming to our parties. All my memories of Rob are beautiful ones. They're all positive stories and we all love him here in Blackburn because everybody knows him. He stuck out because of the accent. We called him Cockney Rob, but of course he's not a Cockney. But if you're south of Stoke you're a Cockney up here! But honestly, everybody loved him because of his passion and his belief."*

There was this one DJ who took me under his wing. DJ Shack (Neil Shackleton) the master of ceremonies at the Blackburn raves with the shepherd's crook often DJ'd with twin brothers Kenneth and Kelly. Kenneth and Kelly had soul music coursing through their veins and had clearly come through the hip hop and blues scenes, but boy, could they smash out the piano tracks too. What a dynamic and loveable duo. Shack was so important to me being accepted into the fold too and we got on like a house on fire from the off. They heard me play a few times and were kind enough to let me do one of their nights. And that gave me a place in the team. I think they saw something a bit different in me, which was nice. But truthfully, I was still building towards being a proper DJ at this point. I hadn't really evolved yet. I still classed myself as somebody who was aspiring to do all that stuff, but I wasn't going to turn down the chance to play at these incredible events. I guess my philosophy of playing winner after winner tunes was what made me popular, along with trying to create 'memorable moments' with leftfield tracks.

Toward the end of the night at Minstrels, I'd play Captain Sensible's *Glad It's All Over* which was this very downbeat track and then as it was fading out, I'd play the acapella of *It's Not Over* into it and then play Kariya's *Let Me Love You For Tonight*. People would lose their shit and it made me stand out for having the balls to try such a mental mix.

There was a party in the snow that winter, this time in a Blackburn woodyard. I went along looking for the opportunity to play, but I was also looking for a good time as well. I went to this party with my old school mate Danny and a friend of ours, Deb Hodgson. Deb was from Chorley and she was friends with some of the guys from Inspiral Carpets and Stone Roses. She went to The Haçienda and every single Blackburn party. I remember dancing to this absolute tune when a guy appeared out of nowhere, wearing a jester's tricorn hat. He then boomed in a broad scouse accent, "That track is Mr Monday's *Appreciate*. What a tune!"

- "Yeah, I need to buy this. I need this in my set."
- "So, you're a DJ. So am I!"

We really hit it off. That guy was John Kelly; years later a resident at Cream, Gatecrasher and the legendary Quadrant Park in Liverpool. As time went on John became a very significant character to me. He was just this lovely man from the off, an absolute joy. We used to go to quite a lot of these parties and he was getting to play out more than I was. John was a partner in an event in Liverpool called The Underground and he asked me to play there in 1990.

Now, we weren't doing any of this for anything more than petrol money, if that. Sometimes you didn't even get a single penny for it and I wouldn't have wanted anything for it. You just wanted to go out and play. These days people think of it as being something you might be able to make a decent living out of, but it wasn't really like that then. So, I went across to play in Liverpool and carried on that friendship with John. And then shortly after that some slightly more legal events started to happen. Clubs were now seeing pound signs in those little smiley faces.

Back in Blackburn things were booming. There was a fairly new stretch of motorway called the M65, which was a ring road that went off the M62 near Bury and went down through a place called Haslingden that leads you to Blackburn. This particular stretch was probably 25 miles of motorway and on one occasion there were so many people trying to get to a warehouse, one junction down from Blackburn (going towards Burnley), that there were three lanes of cars on the left-hand side of the road with another three lanes of cars on the other side of the carriageway going in the exact same direction. I'd never seen anything like it. There were people hanging out the windows and the sunroofs were down as *Meltdown*, *Quartz* and *Rich In Paradise* blasted out of car stereos. This was acid house and it was just as much about the fight against the establishment as it was getting to the party.

The police had cordoned off one junction – they had intelligence as to where the party was going to be – and so the ravers took advantage of both sides of the motorway. It was crazy.

## Tommy Smith

*"The last actual Blackburn party was in a place called Nelson and that was another Enterprise Allowance Zone. That was a valuable unit, and we had 10,000 there, maybe slightly more with the mass crowds outside. The moment the big shutter doors opened I kept thinking, 'Somebody shut that door. Shut that fucking door! What's going on?' A mix of the Beatles' Strawberry Fields was on and the DJ – lord knows you couldn't make this name up – was a Sikh called Mick Singh. A DJ called Mick Singh…*

*We had an office in the corner of this unit, where we put the decks. I think somebody had put something in my tea, but I was certainly in a whole other state of mind, shall we say. I was looking at this huge shutter door and thought, 'Oh, man, look at the sunrise. Look at that blue wave coming through! A fucking blue wave!'*

*It was a blue wave of riot helmets. It was the fucking police coming in. So here they were storming the place, and we were all in the office within the unit. I managed to jump down these ladders we got from B&Q and escaped. But Mick and a few others got a good thrashing on the spot and were arrested. I jumped down and could see all the police and police horses! 'It's a fucking Western. Is John Wayne going to come in?' Little known to us, but about half a mile up the road on another estate were four Portakabins where the police were detaining ravers. We had no mobile phones of course and so no one knew what the police were doing. The people leaving were either arrested or not allowed back near the site. Nowadays, you could phone somebody in the site and say, 'Listen, you'd better get out of there!' Of course, we didn't have that option. The police called it Operation Alkali, because you know what alkali does? It neutralises acid. Very good! Somebody in the police had a sense of humour. But we successfully escaped from there. And that really was the last of the great Blackburn parties.*

*We did Brave New World after that, which was held in Yorkshire, in the riding stables (The Equestrian Centre, Harrogate). That was the first time we had permission to use a building. And the police got in on that as well and stole the decks. We chased them out of the building, though. I remember one of the coppers falling out of the van as they were chased out.*

*Somebody went to a nearby house and got one of those old music centres, an Amstrad hi–fi, and we played some tapes on that until we eventually located some decks. And the show just went on. But that was the whole point of it, the show must, must, must, must go on. And it did. We had a fucking great night. That was 9th of June, 1990."*

The Blackburn raves had caused a major stir, so much so, that lots of similar parties started to spring up around Greater Manchester, Lancashire and Yorkshire, mainly because the police had started to get the upper hand in Boomtown.

I went to this warehouse party in Leigh just between Manchester and Wigan and there were about 400 people there. It was snowing and the warehouse only had three sides on it. One part of the warehouse was totally open and so the snow was coming in from outside. Obviously, there was nobody in that bit.

The guys who were running the party put the decks on the back of a Luton van. Luton vans had an area on the top where you stacked blankets and stuff and that's where they put the decks. The DJs had their backs to the crowd when they played that night. There was a whole bunch of people listening to you, but you weren't facing them.

I remember DJing while standing on two crates, on that little flat area, mixing Roxanne Shanté's *Live On Stage* with *Phantom* by Renegade Soundwave when someone started tugging on my sleeve. I couldn't turn around, but just dug my elbows out and hoped they'd give up. Then the tugging started again. "For fuck's sake!" I was starting to lose it a bit as I was concentrating hard on making sure the beats didn't drop out, but this idiot just kept tugging at my sleeve. And so I elbowed him with a proper "Fuck off!" But he carried on. I eventually turned around and elbowed him again and realised that this hand belonged to the Chief of Leigh Police complete with that hat that had the scrambled egg braiding on top. "Turn that fucking shit off! You're nicked!" Okay, fair enough.

They took me away in the back of one of those Mariah police vans and that was the first time I lost my liberty so to speak with 24 hours in the cells. I missed a day of work at Sid Abrams Vauxhall dealership the next day, which didn't go down well. I was just on an out and out mission to make this work.

The police took my box of vinyl and confiscated the lot. I never saw my records again. And the thing back in those days was that there was no back–up. No memory stick. No hard drive. No online record shops. And so I had to try and hunt down and buy every single track again, which was absolutely terrible as you can imagine. A lot of those records were extremely rare. And so I was back to square one. And so I had to rely on mates like Adrian Luvdup to try and recoup all the tracks I'd lost.

Record shops were competitive places for DJs back then. It could be quite an unhealthy experience going into a record shop. Don't let anybody tell you anything else. You had to gain the confidence of the people who worked in those shops in order to get the good stuff. Rival DJs didn't want you to know which records they had and would cover the names of the tracks with stickers etc. and that went back to the northern soul days. You might hear a song on a show like Jeff Young or particularly Stu Allen and you just had to have it. I first heard Stu doing his stuff on Key 103 and I would hear the tracks he played at Eastern

Bloc, Spin Inn and Manchester Underground; the three biggest stores in Manchester.

Eastern Bloc was established in 1985 by John Berry and Martin Price from 808 State. Back in the late 80s Eastern Bloc helped to launch bands such as the Inspiral Carpets, while also hosting in-store signings with The Stone Roses and Happy Mondays. The shop was also responsible for breaking much of the new dance music at the time, being one of the only shops in the UK to import dance music from around the globe. Eastern Bloc also had a heavy involvement in the early career paths of A Guy Called Gerald and K Klass. Many famous faces worked behind the counter or had been regular customers in the shop. Local DJs and globe-trotting super DJs would use E Bloc as their first port of call to get their hands on the latest vinyl promos.

Some of the people that worked in those shops were DJs and there was definitely an old boys' network; they did not want you to have those tracks. Some DJs would come in and the staff would have a plastic bag ready for them. And they'd be like, "OK, there you go." 'How do I get a plastic bag like that?' I would sometimes be in those shops waiting to get served for absolutely ages. And once I'd finally got served I'd say "I want the Mr Fingers track which sampled *Can You Feel It?* with the Martin Luther King 'I have a dream' speech on it?" They must have sold me five different tracks over the course of the week. "No, no this is it, this is the one!" And you'd get home and it wasn't that track. And so you'd go back again. "This is definitely it!"
  –  "Can I listen to it first?"
  –  "No, this is it, mate!"

You'd get home and of course you'd been stitched up again. The staff at Eastern Bloc would sometimes go off into the back room to get my record and just never return. And because the counter there was particularly long you might, after 20 minutes, go to the other end, which would have been seen as a bit of a stroppy move at a time when you were trying to build trust with them. And then I'd see the guy talking to someone else and he'd turn around and say, "I haven't got it, mate."

If I went in there with someone who was known, like Adrian Luvdup, I was more likely to get the nod. There was this change in attitude. "He's alright, he's done a couple of gigs with Adrian." Quite often back then you had to buy what *they* liked before they'd sell you what you actually wanted. "Dug out some real specials for you. You're going to love these." And you'd get home and think 'Jesus, this is shit.' But you'd always pass on positive feedback when you returned, just to get on their good side. I always felt you had to really work at it to shine and get a lot of things to align in order to get an opportunity. So, to me, it's all about the networking and biting the bullet and going out and doing stuff when you don't really want to do it, knowing it might lead somewhere. And a lot of famous names shopped and worked at Eastern Bloc, so there was a good chance you might get an opportunity to play for half an hour at 2am somewhere just to rub shoulders with the right people. It was just something you had to do. And we all did it. Everybody did it. That's probably why I'm so grounded and humble because I understand work. It's been graft all the way.

\*\*\*

I borrowed some money off my dad and finally bought some Technics 1210s from a free ad in one of the Manchester papers. I had to pay him back week by week. I can still remember the excitement of bringing those decks home. Now, I could *really* learn to mix with a set of direct-drive turntables. However, I was making so much noise at home I started to receive a lot of complaints from next-door.

Tired of the angry thumps on the walls from my neighbours, I hired a tiny little unit in a mill in Manchester's Chinatown; it was just big enough to get a set of decks, speakers and a chair in there. I would go there every night after work and mix and mix until I couldn't mix anymore. Then I'd crawl into my sleeping bag for a while, before driving back to Rochdale at 6am for a shower. Then it was back to the Sid Abrams dealership to sell cars all day.

Part of my role at Sid Abrams involved fleet sales, essentially selling cars to businesses. Because I was so desperate to get to my 1210s, I would often make a load of false appointments to say I was going to visit all these companies and then simply nip off back to my unit to practise mixing. I would return to work the next day saying I failed to get any leads. The problem was, I wasn't selling any cars and after a while I was rumbled. The thing is, I'm a very industrious person, and a real dog with a bone when I have a 'mission', and sadly, that obsession didn't involve selling cars. Mind you, by the time I left Sid Abrams, I had my decks, a replenished box of records and some gigs under my belt.

I was in my studio one morning when I bumped into these two guys from a neighbouring unit while I was making coffee in the communal part of the building. These two characters ran a company called DAT To DAT in Manchester that copied digital audio tape for the music industry. They said they loved the music coming out of my studio and would I do a mixtape for them. We became quite chatty and after a time they said they knew someone who was staging a fashion show in Manchester – and they needed a DJ! Last minute! "Do you want to do this gig?" they asked. I nodded. "Well, it's tonight!"

- "Shit! Yeah, absolutely, I'll do it, where is it?" I was born ready.
- "Haçienda."
- "No fucking way!"

So, this was Thursday 4th July 1990 and I was going to play The Haçienda. I was told that a few of the regular Haçienda DJs were also going to be there and so I was buzzing.

I was on early doors straight after the fashion show and I only went and broke one of the golden rules of DJing as a 'warm-up'. I played all the most massive Haçienda tracks at 8pm. I didn't have a clue. But you should never do that. A real schoolboy error and I pissed quite a few people off by doing that. Oops.

I played this bootleg track of *You've Got The Love* by Candi Staton called *The Love And Rock* bootleg (cost me £30 and that was a lot of money back then). That track was pretty much the biggest tune of the moment and it still sticks with me today as being one of the standout, pivotal moments of playing in The Haçienda.

In terms of DJing back then, not everybody could mix as we would get to know the craft; it was a bit of a free for all in some respects. Not an awful lot of people had full-on skills. It was all about what you played next. Your choice of music. And that covered a multitude of sins. But I had a big pair of brass balls on me and I wasn't afraid to ask a question bearing in mind I'd been working in the car industry, which taught me that sometimes you had to wear your heart on your sleeve and actually ask people for favours in order to get what you wanted. I was quite well known up there due to my conspicuous accent. I was known as Cockney Rob or Cockers.

Through doing that gig I met the guys behind the fashion label Gio Goi; a real acid house/baggy fashion label run by a right couple of characters: the Donnelly brothers. I'm quite a friendly person and will talk to anyone and I'm sure that has stood me in good stead over the years. I'm a smiler!

You never know who might help you out in the most interesting ways. The Donnelly brothers seemed like good people to get in with.

I remember walking on air as I left The Haçienda. I parked myself at a bar on Canal Street and watched the England/Germany World Cup Semi Final. Neither the tragedy of that game nor Gazza's tears couldn't dampen my mood. I was absolutely buzzing.

I ran into the Donnelly brothers again during that summer of 1990. Anthony and Chris were so certain that Gio Goi was going to become a big deal they were on the look-out for a sales rep. Yet another opportunity. Anthony and Chris knew I was a salesman and offered me the job. So, I finally stopped 'working' for Sid Abrams, which had become a little bit untenable. After all, the wedding and bar gigs were giving me pretty much the same income I received trying to sell cars all week. And Gio Goi was much more in keeping with what I wanted to do. So I binned off Sid Abrams and joined Anthony and Chris Donnelly, who took me right under their wings. They were just brilliant to me. They made me feel at home right from the off.

Gio Goi had a warehouse unit and designed all the stuff on site. Everything was stored in an old mill in Great Ancoats, central Manchester. They showed me these fantastic designs of this high quality clubwear. 'Wow, this is shit hot!' They had really cool baseball jackets with embroidered logos on them, which was quite a rare thing. Gio Goi was quality high-end fashion and they wanted me to go out all over the country, to the coolest clothes shops and spread the word. Gio Goi was being sold in Afflecks in Manchester and a couple of other shops, but they wanted to get into the best shops of *every* town. Be that Huddersfield, Leeds, Liverpool, you name it. "Go find the coolest outlets and see if you can sell them 15 T-shirts."

I'd go to Birmingham for example and the shop would sell all the products in five minutes flat. Then they'd be on the phone asking for 15 more. It got rolling really quickly. I was their first sales rep, a fact I'm massively proud of.

The Donnelly brothers were also very involved in the Manchester club scene. They put on a party called Joy, which was something I went to the year before I moved up north. So that would have been about 1989 when I still lived down south. I drove north to go to this party, which was just outside Manchester in a place called Haslingden, not far from Burnley and Blackburn. It was an awesome party where the sun just shone and shone during that Second Summer Of Love. It was phenomenal. I didn't know the Donnellys at that point in time and it was only when I was working for Gio Goi I realised that they were responsible for Joy. I said, "Wow. That was one of the best days of my entire life. It was so hot and so beautiful. The music was perfect." *The Independent* did a piece on acid house and that particular party and the front-page picture featured me dancing, in the prime of my life, 22, with a bloody six pack. Totally in the zone, if you know what I mean. *Wink.*

The Donnellys' father was a guy called Jimmy The Weed – so called because he grew on you – who was the boss of the infamous Quality Street Gang who were about as *connected* in Manchester as it comes to be honest. Channel 5 featured them in a documentary about Britain's most notorious gangsters. This was a whole episode solely dedicated to Jimmy Donnelly and his band of brothers. These guys were the Manchester version of the Goodfellas. They were lively characters and it was definitely good fun working with them.

Gio Goi was smashing it. Lots of ravers and football casuals were wearing the label and it was being featured in all the hip magazines.

The guys from Gio Goi started doing a night called Club Shaboo in Blackpool and they kept insisting I play there. I was suspicious and kept thinking to myself 'This is a test. If I go and play there on a Thursday night and I'm not in work the next day then there will be hell to pay.' I would tell them I'd be in Liverpool selling some of the products, you know, and they'd be like, "OK, all right, fair enough. But you need to come down because we've got this new kid called Sasha!" This was before anyone knew who he was. I'd met Sasha at Joy the year before, with his then girlfriend and he said he wanted to be a DJ. It was only a couple of years later that I realised that the person I'd been talking to was actually *Sasha*; he became an enigma very quickly.

After working for Gio Goi for a bit I started to travel further afield to some satellite towns. So I did a run into Birmingham and then went down to Cheltenham. I got to Cheltenham shopping centre and it was this lovely place; spa town of course. Cheltenham didn't have an edge like Manchester or Leeds. I went into the main shopping precinct in Cheltenham and there were a few lads hanging about. Now bear in mind, at that point in my life, I was bulletproof. I did not have a single hang up in the world. Not a single care. I would talk to *anybody*. So, I asked this guy, "Where's the coolest clothes shop in Cheltenham?"
  – "What's in the bag?"

– "I'm a sales rep. Just got some samples."

– "Let's have a look."

I opened this ski holdall that had all the Gio Goi gear in it. And he's like, "Wow, that's well cool." He tells me the name of this clothes shop and I thank him and head off. I rock up to this menswear place and agreed a pre-order with them because ordinarily I didn't like to sell the samples; I needed them to be able to show at the next shop. So, I did a deal, came out of the shop and this lad from before was there. "Man that stuff is wicked, can I show my mate?" Bearing in mind they were both cool as cucumbers, I opened the holdall and started to pull a tee out when eight geezers appeared out of nowhere. "Just leave the bag there and fuck off!"

– "What?!"

The bag had about 35 bits of kit in there and so that was a good £600 worth of stuff I would have thought because even then they were retailing quite high. Gio Goi wasn't cheap. Shit. I now had to walk off and leave the holdall. That had to be one of the lowest moments of my life up to that point.

I rang Anthony and Chris and said, "I don't know how to tell you this, but I've just been mugged."

– "Where have you been?"

– "Cheltenham."

– "You what?! Fookin' Cheltenham?!"

– "Yeah, I've been mugged in Cheltenham."

– "Tell you what. Do us a favour. Drop everything and get right back up here. Just come in and see us *now*!"

'Oh, my actual God. I've got to go and see the Donnelly brothers because I've lost all the kit!' And in Cheltenham of all places. It was quite late when I arrived back at the unit, but they waited for me. As I walked into the office I was thinking, 'I don't even know what to do.'

They sat me down and said, "Tell us the story." So I told them what had happened while they stared at me. After a brief pause, they said, "Right. That's fine. We just needed to look into your eyes. And what you said is exactly how that went down. Your eyes are telling us the truth. It's all good. No problem. We'll crack on." That was one of the scariest moments I've ever had. I'd been mugged and I just needed them to see, hand on heart, that there'd been no funny business. I'd been had over and they knew it. They knew I wasn't pulling the wool over their eyes and I'm so glad they were cool about it. With regards to Cheltenham, I wouldn't have messed with any one of them. They were proper characters. And you completely forget sometimes that not everyone's as cool as you. And just because it's a smaller town, you still get some bad characters who probably try that little bit harder to prove themselves.

# CH. 15

## rob Tissera

# The Love Decade Party

We drove to Birch Services, on the M62 between Manchester and Leeds; pretty much just as you come out of Manchester, and quite close to Rochdale. There was this massive convoy of people who were all going to The Love Decade, rumoured to be in Yorkshire.

The service stations were a massive part of the rave scene as they were often the meeting place where the ringleader, the 'pied piper' if you will, led the convoy off to the party in a huge procession of hatchbacks and vans.

I had been DJing at a wedding in Manchester and so I packed my gear away in the car after and drove to Birch Services. I arrived at the Services, went into the gents and got changed into my hoodie and tracksuit bottoms. After a while, the engines started revving and the convoy set off in the direction of Leeds.

The police had absolutely squashed it in Blackburn. The pivotal moment that ended the raves in Blackburn was the Nelson party, just outside Blackburn; the party was known as Strawberry Fields. That police raid completely decimated the party scene in that area. There were more police than there had ever been. They were drafting in police who'd been dealing with the miners' strikes and still had all the riot gear to hand. These riot squads had broken up the parties in Blackburn and then the final nail in the coffin was this rave in Nelson just a few weeks before. And so we were off to Leeds.

The convoy of 500 cars or more trundled off to Leeds, stopping at Hartshead Moor Services, about 40 miles away. We all parked up there and met a whole new bunch of people: the West Yorkshire contingent. The Pied Piper in the lead car that night were our friends Jane and Tracey and a couple of other lively characters. They led this convoy of thousands in the direction of Leeds.

We eventually came to the M621 about six miles outside of Leeds. We came off at the Gildersome Intersection which is very close to a town called Morley right on the outskirts of Leeds. The team had done their due diligence and found an industrial estate that was just off the motorway, without having to go into the city centre. The building was an old disused Sony warehouse on Treefield Industrial Estate on Gelderd Road, Gildersome.

I liked to get my car right to the front of the convoy if I was playing. I remember looking in the rear-view mirror thinking 'Wow!' There was this army of people. The organisers were still building the amplifiers and the speakers in the venue while the revellers were amassing outside. It was like a military operation. After all, they couldn't hire this equipment because the gear was getting confiscated by the police and so they bought and assembled these massive speakers at breakneck speed. It was mental. Eventually, the party started.

On this particular occasion my mate Shack was playing and just as they'd done on previous nights, he had the decks in a long Rossignol ski holdall. The decks were laid out on a surface so they were still inside the sports bag, but unzipped, so if the cops got in you could just zip the bag back up and run off with the decks. There were about 1,000 people in there, but at least 4,000 more outside.

There I am, playing out at this packed warehouse in West Yorkshire. Everything was going great and I was loving every single second of it, playing *LFO* by LFO, *Casanova* by Jazz & the Brothers Grimm and Seduction's *(You're My One And Only) True Love* because it was a real mishmash of music. I remember playing *Technotrance (Yaah)* by D Train, which was a real belter.

Then one of the guys who ran the event came in from outside to have a chat with me. "Things are looking a bit dodgy out there," he shouted, over the booming music. "The police are out in force." The police had successfully broken up so many parties recently, but once we were on it, we always fancied our chances due to the sheer numbers in our favour and the fact that most of the ravers were off their nuts. But the situation was worsening with the introduction of a new clampdown on raves by MP Graham Bright and the successful takedown of the Blackburn parties.

The crowd inside that Gildersome warehouse were starting to bristle as word got out that the cops had assembled outside with 4,000 revellers who hadn't made it into the packed venue.

The music stopped. We could now hear the police dogs and the helicopter circling outside. I plugged the headphones into the back of the mixer and used it as a makeshift microphone. I could see thousands of ravers packed into this warehouse. I raised the headphones up and tapped them to make sure they were working. "Oi! Oi! Listen!" I now had their full attention. "Look, if you guys want the party to continue, we're gonna have to fight the bastards!" A roar of approval went up and the atmosphere started to get very dark. Very quickly.

The party was now a riot. Ravers started breaking up wooden pallets bordering the industrial unit. KERRRRRRRUUNCH! The planks of wood were now being launched through the windows; the smashed glass shattering onto the police in the street below, like crystal rain. Anything close to hand was being lobbed through the windows to keep the police from entering the building.

I left the DJ booth and climbed up onto a container that some of the ravers were using as a vantage point from where they could peer through the broken glass. You could hear the shouting first and then once I'd popped my head up over the ledge I could see a blurry fog of torches and police car headlights lighting up the Yorkshire evening. Another strafe of light was coming from the helicopter circling above.

There must have been 300 Old Bill in riot gear, with batons, shields, the lot, and even more ravers making a run for it. The party had 1,000 ravers inside, but possibly another 4,000 outside and we heavily outnumbered the police. But any thoughts that our greater numbers would force the police into retreat were soon extinguished. Because when I looked out that window and surveyed the devastation below I could see there was no way these guys were going to give up. Not in a million years. What the fuck had I done?!

I could see all the partygoers that didn't get in thinking 'Fuck this, we're out of here!' The police, in full riot gear, were chasing them with dogs. As I looked out of the window I was thinking 'I started this! What have I fucking done?! There's gonna be hell to pay!'

Some of the guys who were selling drinks inside the venue had a Luton van, which they used to barricade the front entrance right up against the main shutters. There was a spy hole you could see through if you stood on the bonnet of the van. The police were on a forklift truck trying to break through the barrier. But our guys had the van in first gear butting up against the shutter which was going backwards and forwards in a full-on Mexican standoff. This was war! It was mental.

Now, my intention was never for it to go this pear shaped and some people were being out and out naughty and were pushing pieces of wood through this hole and trying to hit the coppers. So once all that started to go off I knew I'd fucked up by waging war on the police. It was absolutely horrendous and I regretted the entire situation. What the fuck had I done?

Anyway, this stand-off went on for hours with the music blaring out once more, after all, there were a thousand people still in the warehouse. Everybody outside had left, but the police were still there. But many of the people barricaded inside were still dancing as the DJs kept playing.

Eventually, the police managed to break into the unit next door and then found a way of smashing through into the Sony warehouse. All hell broke loose then because they were really pissed off having been kept at bay for so long. And now they were mad and had their batons out. They were hitting people left, right and centre. It wasn't pleasant. They even hit a pregnant woman. They were out and out nasty.

When the police broke through, Shack zipped up the decks inside the ski holdall. The police had a 50-60 metre dash across the warehouse and so Shack had time to put the shoulder strap on and ran for it, but the decks were still plugged into the bloody wall. It was almost like a cartoon sketch where the legs were still going, but Shack was going nowhere. And so I booted the wire to release him and off he went. Unfortunately, he got smashed up by the police. The music had obviously stopped by now and the police were in control.

There was this caged area down one side of the warehouse which would have been for V&A (valuable and attractive) goods: the most expensive stuff the warehouse had. And so the police managed to herd all these revellers into this caged unit. We were trapped. The police then started removing ravers, 20 at a time, in order to whisk them off to a police station inside their riot vans. We were thinking that this was going to take ages and that they would soon get bored, or that there would be too many people to process and so we disappeared to the back of the crowd. However, they just kept taking people away and it eventually got to a point where we were in the last round and there were definitely a few characters in there who were much more involved than anyone else.

I had started talking to this one guy called Huggy. Huggy was a proper Yorkshire legend and a very respected DJ. We were in a state of shock, I think. It was mad, because even in that caged area people were picking tablets and gear off the floor, such as a matchbox of drugs, and so they were properly leathered by the time we got into the back of these police vans. I was in that last van taken to Halifax Police Station.

There were some ravers with a handheld VHS video camera inside the party, which was quite a common sight, but upon arriving at the police station I could now see that these were not ravers. They were undercover police gathering evidence. I even hung out with them for a while at the party and we were like "Wahey!" as they recorded us.

They cautioned everybody at these police stations all over West Yorkshire. I rolled out of the cell in Halifax at about 11am and got the bus back to Rochdale because I'd lost my car keys somewhere along the way. I don't know whether they confiscated them or what. I remember going back to get the car keys before giving up and having to get the train back to Halifax, thinking 'Oh my god, what have I done?' I remember having no money or anything at that point too. 836 people were arrested in the end, but surely they couldn't charge everyone. We thought we'd got away with it, in terms of just a caution, which was still terrible. And so I eventually returned to the warehouse to pick up my car. I hoped that was the end of it.


**Tommy Smith**

*"And then on the 21st of July, 1990, was The Love Decade. We went down in a blaze of glory with that one. When you look back it was inevitable that that was the only way it could end. But the point is, we were done fighting.*

*Of course, Rob played that legendary Love Decade. And that was my abiding memory of him, because I didn't see him for a while after that. The police were storming the door and the people in the far end of the warehouse were beating them back. And Rob was on the mic giving it the clarion call to the people, such was his belief, such was his passion for the whole thing. Rob was the last man standing on that ship of the last 'Blackburn party', albeit it was in Yorkshire, that went down in a fucking blaze of glory. 836 arrests. And Rob stood on the bow of that ship, that great ship of freedom, belief, hope and love, and went down with it. We were all fighting and Rob was there with that passion; it was totally infectious. That's why people loved him and still love him to this day. I can still see him there in the corner of that warehouse, 1990, giving it some. Fucking fight for your right to party. What a man. What a fucking man! As the truncheons rained down, Rob was still playing. What a memory. The truncheons thrashing to the beat of Rob's rhythm. I loved it, I absolutely loved it. You can't make this up, honestly, a memory you will die with. I was blessed to have been there and seen it.*

*I thought, 'He's going to end up in trouble.' But did he care? No.*

*He was just consumed by belief and love. And for me that, in a nutshell, is Rob Tissera. Legendary enthusiasm and an infectious spirit. Always smiling.*

*836 people were arrested that night. That was the end of it for me, in that sense. All the people that had done the Blackburn parties had been imprisoned and I was the only one left. Last Man Dancing, they called me.*

*The police were lining everybody up in the warehouse, and I heard the inspector saying, 'Anybody from Blackburn with a Scottish accent, we have to keep back because the police are coming over from Blackburn.' They'd been looking for me for ages. So, I thought, 'Fucking hell.' So they took us to these cells all over Yorkshire. I got talking to this guy from Huddersfield called Warren, and I got his name and asked him if he had a brother?' 'Yeah,' and he told me his brother's name. Of course, I also knew where he lived. I gave the police a false address and got released.*

*When the Blackburn police turned up and opened the cells they were quite miffed apparently. They knew I was gone, and it was all over. I'd got away with it. Or so I thought.*

*They caught me about six months later. I was driving this car and there was a drug dealer in the back who was a friend. I've never dealt drugs, everybody knows that. And so I turned around and said to the guy, 'You got any drugs on you?' He says, 'No, no, no.'*

*   – 'Because there's fucking plain-clothes police behind us!'*

*Anyway, they pulled the car over. 'What's going on? You got any drugs?'*

*   – 'No, I don't have any fucking drugs.'*

*I heard someone on the police radio asking, 'Is it a strike?' And the plain-clothes guy said, 'It's a double strike!' I'm thinking, 'What the fuck?'*

*– 'What do you mean?'*

*– 'You will not believe who we've got driving this car. You will not fucking believe who we've got driving this car!'*

*They took us to Blackburn Police Station and there were about 12 of them in there. They said, 'Is that him? Fucking hell, I don't believe it, where the fuck did you find him?'*

*– 'I haven't done anything wrong.'*

*– 'Yeah, yeah, yeah, we know you've not done anything wrong, but you're still getting 12 years.'*

*– 'What!?'*

*The guy who was with me was immediately arrested as he had imported some drugs and what have you. But I said, 'I'm innocent.' The copper who arrested me said, 'We know you're innocent, but you're still getting 12 fucking years. You didn't think you could go to all those parties and those fucking riots and just walk away did you?'*

*I got charged, but on these trumped-up charges, which meant I couldn't go back to Berlin. They falsely charged me with importing LSD, and I was on remand for a year in prison, which I didn't like at all.*

*I was that naïve I thought I could just walk away. I did nearly 11 months on remand, which I hated of course. Because prior to that I was on top of the world. My fucking brain and soul were wide open, my wings were spread. I was at the top of my game, flying through the universe. And then bang, I'm in a fucking prison cell with two other people, facing 12 years. 'I don't like this. I don't like this at all.'*

*And so the police got somebody to say they'd seen me at this drug stash over a period of two months, apparently some innocent bystander, but I now know it was a friend of the police.*

*Luckily, in the interim when the parties finished, and before I got arrested, I went to America for a month-long holiday. So, when they said in the trial, 'Why would this innocent member of the public lie to get you arrested? He's seen you at this stash house on these dates,' I produced my passport. We kept that quiet from the police and so when my solicitor pulled it out at the trial he said, 'What dates did you see Mr Smith in this stash?' And he repeated the dates. And he said, "Well, I've got Mr Smith's passport here, stamped by US Immigration and they cover those dates.' You should have seen the faces of the police. The blood just drained away. That was it. They knew it was over and*

*I knew it was over, although we still had to carry on with a two-week trial.*

*In the end the guy standing next to me got 12 years and another got 17 years, one got 16, and I got not guilty. I never heard the word 'guilty', I only heard the word 'not', and I collapsed in tears.*

*Everybody jumped up screaming and shouting. 'Order! Order!' There was no order of course. The judge disappeared, and it was only when calm was restored that he returned and said I was free to leave.*

*Within a couple of weeks I was off to India."*

# CH. 16

rob
Tissera

# The Long Arms Of The Law

BOOF! The door was kicked in at about 6am. Suddenly there were eight policemen in my bedroom like something out of *The Sweeney*. What the fuck!

I was with a girl, who I'd only met the night before while playing out in Manchester. The girl stood up, protecting her modesty with the quilt, which left me stark bollock naked. "Get your fucking clothes on! You go in the other room (to the girl)! And keep them separate!" They then raided the house looking for the clothes I'd been wearing at the Gildersome party, which of course were there. What an idiot. Then they chucked me into the back of the meat wagon and took me off to Rochdale Police Station. CID from Halifax were waiting there to take me to West Yorkshire.

I was rubbing the sleep from my eyes in the interview room, when they said: "Right, we've got a video nasty to play to you!" I thought 'Oh my god, here we go.' They put the video on and freeze-framed a scene from the party. "Is that you there?" And of course, it was me, absolutely no question about it. It was me on the microphone shouting, "Right guys, if you want to continue partying, we're gonna have to fight the bastards!" I was charged with Incitement To Riot.

So, this is the period where it all goes very wrong. A dark period in my life. The 1990 Bright Act (set up by MP Graham Bright) was clamping down on illegal parties and they now had the chance to make an example of us. They gave me bail conditions so that I now had a curfew, which meant I couldn't go out at certain times of the night. I also had to report to the police station every day (in Leeds) to stop me from going out and doing more warehouse parties. They completely clamped down on me. I was no longer working for Vauxhall either and so I was just on my own in terms of trying to make it work as a DJ, and so my income was effectively frozen. It was really hard trying to keep a lid on everything.

I had to wait six months for the court date, but I still had to sign in at 7pm every evening, which involved going from Rochdale to the Central Police Station in Leeds every night; the police station in Chapeltown had been shut down. It was all a complete ballache doing that every single day.

I was a lot less law abiding back in those days and so I would sneak into parties wearing a baseball cap or with a bandana around my face, which was a thing back in those days before it became a proper gangster look. I knew I was breaking my curfew, but I was desperate not to lose touch with the clubs.

My mum and dad took me away on holiday not long after because my bail had been lifted, now I had a court date. They knew nothing regarding the arrest whatsoever. And they took me on holiday to Sri Lanka to meet my granddad for the very first time. But all the time I was there, I had this black cloud hovering over me.

Meeting my grandad for the first and last time was a beautiful, but intensely sad moment, that I will treasure forever. He and my grandma, who I never had the fortune to meet, had been school teachers. My granddad was overjoyed to meet me and my sister. We spent ages trying to communicate, even though he didn't speak English. He was 94 at the time. I can still feel his touch as he affectionately stroked my face. Saying goodbye to him knowing that we would probably never meet again was a really heartbreaking moment for us all.

I returned to the house in Rochdale when I got back to the UK, only to find that my front door key didn't work. I went to the local payphone and rang the landlord. "You've been evicted!" Apparently, these other guys that had been living there hadn't paid their portion of the rent. Not only that, but all our stuff had been confiscated, including my records. I eventually got them back, but that house was history.

Over the previous year I'd become good mates with another aspiring DJ who lived in Leeds. Drew Hemment would often come over to my place in Rochdale for days and weekends and myself, Drew and Mick Singh would have these long mix sessions. DJ Drew had been doing promotional stuff for events associated with the Blackburn movement. And when things started getting difficult for the Blackburn crew, Drew found Hardcore Uproar a location for Brave New World at the Equestrian Centre on Ilkley Moor.

I left Drew at my place when I packed my suitcase to go off to Sri Lanka. I called him from a phone box to tell him of my plight when I returned. He said he was there when the bailiff turned up. Luckily, he'd managed to rescue a bunch of my belongings and that I was more than welcome to move to Leeds to stay at his. And so I ended up moving to a student house on Mexborough Drive in Chapeltown.

It was really kind of Drew and he introduced me to his girlfriend Nikki Hainesworth. Nikki was an actual living, breathing angel and still one of my best friends to this day. Although life for me was pretty bleak back then, Drew and Nikki were great company. Nikki is the kindest person I know.

Shortly after moving in, there was a knock on the door and these two lads turned up. One of them was Nikki's brother Justin and another guy called Adam Falkingham and we all just hit it off like a house on fire.

Drew had decks set up in the dining room of this house and we would have some great evenings in, and out. Those guys would be my constant raving companions for donkey's years. They also served as my sounding board when I did mixes, just trying to work stuff out on the decks and picking the right tracks. I loved them all dearly. Adam has never been afraid to say if he likes something in the mix and also, more importantly, when he thinks something doesn't fit. My advice to anyone is to surround yourself with proper mates who don't just blow clouds of smoke up your bum. I see it so often in the DJ world. It doesn't half help to have mates who keep your feet firmly on the ground.

As soon as I got to Leeds, I felt right at home. I'm one of those people who believes that some things are just chapters in the book, but they're not the whole book. I'm sure we all have periods in our lives that we thought would go on for a long time, but end up just being a couple of years in your life, but when I moved to Leeds, I truly felt at home, even though I'd loved it in Blackburn and in Rochdale. And I'd loved it down south too. But I was made so welcome in Leeds I suspected I might just stay. Meeting up with those guys that I dubbed 'The Diamond Posse' was a real revelation to me. I just knew I could depend on them and vice versa. People like that are solid gold.

Once I had a court date, I was no longer on bail and so I started playing more at KU Club in Huddersfield on a Friday and Saturday night. They were getting 1,000 people through the doors there and it had this fantastic atmosphere. I loved DJing with this guy, DJ Tom.

I'd started knocking around with a whole bunch of people from Huddersfield back in 1989, and one of those guys was a resident DJ at the KU Club. It was one of those places where when you played certain tracks you would get thousands of hands in the air. I always remembered hearing Alison Limerick's *Where Love Lives* for the first time in that club and when the piano dropped that place just exploded. These were just breathtaking moments. I started going to this club when DJ Tom asked me to play there. DJ Tom was a bit of a social climber and a talented DJ, but just a shade murky. Tom hit the decks with me a couple of times, and of course you tended to look through each other's collection to get some inspiration. I knocked around with Tom for a while. Huddersfield's KU Club was fantastic – and Sasha went on to play there quite a bit.

\*\*\*

I managed to get a connection, through Beat Street Records in Bolton, to a set of people running events in Kavos in Corfu. They asked me if I'd like to go out there and DJ for the summer, which sounded amazing! This was when Kavos was a Club 18-30 destination. This trip would involve me going over there with all my records. Now I definitely needed to take somebody else with me in order to make the trip work, because I couldn't DJ every minute of the day. I invited my then DJ partner, Tom from KU Club to join me. So, we made this plan to load up my car on a ferry to Greece, and then from there to Corfu. We had to get a huge number of records over there one way or another.

Meanwhile, back in the UK, my solicitor put me in touch with a barrister. The barrister seemed confident that I would get a suspended sentence because I'd been talking with the police. "If you turn up to court with some money for the fine I should be able to plead your case and that might lessen the severity of what's coming your way." Seemed fair enough, so I got everything set up so that we would leave for Corfu straight after I got out of court. But just in case anything went wrong, I left my records and £500 with Tom.

The day of the court case had me quietly confident that I would evade any truly damaging sentence. The only people to be taken to court were me, and 11 or 12 others who they had down as the main players at this party; one of whom – a guy by the name of Lockie from Wigan who had somehow joined forces with the Boomtown crew – turned up in a panama hat and a beige linen suit. He might as well have been lighting cigars with £20 notes; talk about bold as brass. Bearing in mind I wasn't the organiser and I made absolutely no money out of it, my barrister seemed to think they would view my part in The Love Decade as a passion project.

The Graham Bright Bill was the beginning of the Criminal Justice Act and unbeknown to me, this was the test case. My nerves jangled a little when I noticed that MP Graham Bright was actually there in court with the prosecutor. "This doesn't look too good, you know. Jesus Christ." But my barrister was super confident I was going to get off and it would all be fine.

They eventually read out the charges and the magistrates told me that because of what I'd done, and because this was such a landmark moment in time, they had no other course of action, but to give me a custodial sentence of three months. What. The. Fuck.

I was sentenced as part of the biggest mass arrest since the Peterloo riots in 1819. I was found guilty of Section 2 Violent Conduct, one below Incitement To Riot.

I turned to the barrister. "Are they fucking serious?!" My eyeballs were actually shaking uncontrollably. I have never ever experienced anything like it before or since. He just nodded. Before I knew what was happening they were taking me down the steps and off to HMP Prison Leeds in Armley. I was in a state of total shock, shame and fear. I just hadn't seen prison as a viable outcome of all this.

# CH. 17

## rob Tissera

# The Darkest Hour

Armley was a proper prison, just like the one in that old sitcom *Porridge,* and I was bricking it. The front entrance had these two imposing turrets either side of the giant doors. It was like some castle from a vampire movie. I was allowed one phone call, which I made to Drew Hemment just to let him know that Tom was going to come around to pick up my records; he was going to have to go to Kavos and wait for me. "Hey Drew, I'm in jail."

Armley was no bed of roses. I think my military training helped me a little because nothing could be as bad as those first few weeks in the RAF. But was I really prepared for what was coming? I remember that moment walking the yellow line with my bedding and getting changed into my prison clothes. Talk about humbling. I was in fucking prison!

I walked into the main hall, carrying my blanket, and looked up at the staircases and landings. It was eerily quiet save for the odd slam of a cell door and the jangle of keys echoing through this cavernous hall. I was led up the stairs to a landing right outside what would be my home for the next three months. I was petrified.

Inside the cell were two beds, an exposed toilet (or bucket), and Ray from Barnsley. I sat down on the edge of my bed, and for the first time heard the door being locked by the departing wardens. I was 24 years old and locked up inside a cell just like a… well, a criminal. The feeling of shame I had rushing through me was not healthy. I'd never sunk this low before.

I don't know what was worse. Going to bed inside a prison cell and hearing that door being locked or waking up and realising where you were. I felt so scared and ashamed. I was desperately hoping my parents wouldn't find out. That would be the worst.

Ray took me through everything I needed to know – in the broadest Yorkshire accent. Ray was really nice and was genuinely interested in how I ended up there, and he was really curious regarding the acid house scene. In fact, once word got out that I was a DJ that had gone to jail for acid house, it earned me some respect with quite a few inmates when it came to going to the gym or anything else that was communal. It wasn't like I'd been murdering kids or anything so I didn't have anything to worry about in that respect, but you just didn't know what might be around the corner. But Ray was a godsend.

We were on lockdown at least 22 hours a day. That's just how it was. Whether that might have been because they were understaffed or not, I don't know. Once a day you'd get out and have some food and twice a day you got to walk around the yard. Of course, I'd never been anywhere like it before. "Stick with me, kid," Ray instructed. "Follow me and don't go anywhere else," he told me, as we paced around the yard. The inmates would stroll around the exercise yard in little clusters, rather than in a line. You would get some nasty looking blokes just pacing around on their own, plus there would be some intimidating gangs.

It was very early on in my stay at Her Majesty's Pleasure that Ray warned me to never go into the communal bogs. I could guess why he said that, but it wasn't until I saw a guy come running out of the toilet with a fresh slash across his cheek, that the penny dropped. Seeing things like that brought it home that I may have made a real error at that rave. 'Oh my god, what have I done?'

Most of my time was spent in the cell of course. There were no PlayStations or televisions and so I would spend hours talking to Ray about all the things he'd done in his life. Ray was covered from head to toe in prison tattoos. And these weren't inkings of Japanese figures or celtic bands. These were proper prison tatts, including the 'love and hate' knuckles. You get to know your cell mate really well, and thankfully Ray was about as good as I could have wished for.

Ray was a car ringer who'd been in prison and other institutions for longer than he'd actually been at liberty. Ray had spent his childhood in youth detention centres and borstal before upgrading to full-on clink. Ray would be in and out of jail every few years for various offences, but his main vice, as it were, was car ringing; the process of flipping stolen cars with legitimate number plates. So, at least my cell mate wasn't an axe murderer! He had been inside for so long and had shared with God knows how many different cellmates, he had nothing to prove.

Prison food was shocking, as you can imagine. Really horrible stuff. Ray got the shits really bad one night and we had to make up jokes to cover the sound of his emissions. But having been to the bog (a bucket) for the ninth time we ran out of gags. These were pretty humiliating situations. And then you'd have to 'slop out' in the morning.

It was just a really difficult situation and without Ray's help, humour and guidance and a little bit of my military training, I would have really struggled. The RAF stood me in good stead to be honest, and I started to view prison as just another institution with a strong sense of order to it. As long as you worked within the parameters, you *should* be absolutely fine. Just keep your head down.

I ended up being put to work, like all the other prisoners to earn a few quid that I could spend on the weekends. The job was putting ball bearings into stuff like casters for sofas or metal runners for doors. Hour after hour of packing little ball bearings into these wheels was somewhere between inane and mind numbing. And the only thing that made it any more interesting was listening to everybody's plight of how they hadn't done whatever it was they'd been found guilty of, with the exception of a few people who openly admitted they deserved to be there. There was this one guy, sat across from me, also feeding ball bearings into casters, who had a deep scar snaking across his face. He was an armed robber who'd shot a postmaster in the face. This brute was not to be messed with and he absolutely deserved to be inside. He was a real livewire and deeply horrible. He took great joy in telling me what he did and it was sickening. I just smiled and nodded and wished he'd shut up. How could he be laughing about the truly disgusting things he'd done?

Bearing in mind I was still a gullible youth, more or less, I was quite nervy around one particular inmate who had apparently shagged a horse. I know now that this was almost 100% horse shit, if you pardon the joke, but 2-3 people told me that story and so I certainly didn't want to meet him in the showers.

In the background, my barrister was working away trying to resolve my situation that he'd completely underestimated. "Turn up to court with £500 and you'll be fine," he'd said. Oh well. The original plan was for me to get a slap on the wrist before jetting off to Corfu with Tom for a summer of fun, but now I was trying to avoid horse shaggers and homemade shivs. It was just unlucky that the Love Decade party was used as a test case for the Criminal Justice Bill. And I was the chief scapegoat. In fact, the people who got off lightly, namely Lockie from Wigan, were the ones who profited from it. I was done for Violent Conduct - a public order offence - plus, a charge for dishonest abstraction of electricity, because the decks were plugged into the warehouse's power supply. But three months inside seemed pretty harsh. "I will get that brought back to court," my barrister told me as I was being led away.

rob Tissera

# What Next?

When you're in jail, you have no idea how long you're actually going to be in there, especially having watched a few prison movies like *Over The Top* where Sylvester Stallone's character, the trucker Lincoln Hawk, gets put away for something really minor and then never gets out. I'd only seen that film a year or two before I got put away. You can't help but think about stuff like that. Plus, the days all just merge into one and time becomes meaningless.

I was sat in my cell one afternoon reading the Kevin Keegan autobiography, because there was nothing else to do but read or talk to Ray about ringing cars, when there was a knock on our door. "Tissera, you're coming with me." And I'm thinking to myself, 'Here we go. This is just like the Sly Stallone film.'

I'd got done for driving somebody's car without insurance a few years back, but hadn't mentioned it when I arrived at the Big House. "Anything else you want to tell us in case it crops up while you're in here?" I filled the form out to say 'no' that I hadn't done anything else. So, when I got to the Governor's office I was now convinced that things were only going to get worse for me. 'Please don't lengthen my sentence! I need to get out!' I had all this shit hanging over my head. Was there new footage from any other parties? My mind was racing.

I entered the Governor's office and he peered up from some papers he was studying and said, "Right, Tissera, it appears that you can leave today. Your case is going to a retrial to see if they can get the charge quashed."

– "What?!"

I was so shocked, but in a good way, obviously. I felt my body go limp. Was I dreaming?

I felt this rush of euphoria run through me. Unless you've been locked up in an institution it's hard to imagine how it affects you. In some ways, you completely lose sight of who you are/were. You become a number and everything you've known is taken away from you. It was an awful chapter in my life, but now it had come to an end. Within an hour, I was back in my tracksuit and walking out through those forbidding doors. It was a bright summer's morning and I was free!

Now, although I was out of jail, I was back on bail, which was still a major naus. The main police station in Leeds at the time was Bridewell and that was where I had to check in every day.

Now, originally I had left that envelope of money with Tom as well as instructions on what to do regarding our Corfu residency. But when I came out of nick, I couldn't get hold of Tom. The money was to be saved for getting the ball rolling once I was out and would help pay for the travel costs to Kavos. But I couldn't locate the money back at my digs.

I contacted the people who got us the gig, a lady called Pru from Beat Street Records in Bolton and she said that there had been some issues with Tom over in Kavos. Tom had not been super reliable apparently and had got involved with some drug dealers. In fact, the club fired Tom and banned him from the venue. I had no contact details for Tom either. I'd started my adulthood as a young yuppie with a cabriolet and a brick phone and now I was a former con, and skint. It was a pretty low ebb and I felt like I was back at the bottom of the ladder.

Two things happened in the 'real world' whilst I was in jail. My mum got into contact with my ex because I hadn't told them what I was doing or anything – I certainly didn't want them to know about my little break from society. Mum was obviously worried by the deafening silence coming from Lancashire. This was before most people had mobile phones and let's face it, lads are often not the best at keeping in contact with family. I just didn't want to put them through that stress and shame, but I also felt bad for blanking them. However, my mum got really worried that I might be dead and sent a letter to my ex-girlfriend in Maidenhead who promptly phoned my mum back.

"Oh Mrs Tissera, don't worry, Rob's not dead. He's in prison!" she explained. She pretty much dobbed me into my mum out of spite. Which was a shame, as she needn't have mentioned prison; she could have said I was DJing in Cyprus or something. Obviously, I'd pissed her off a great deal and so she took delight in twisting the knife. And so Mum started sending me letters to the prison wanting me to seriously think about what I'd been doing. I was in no doubt as to what they thought of the acid house scene. I remember putting the letter down on the bed and just sitting there, in the jail cell, staring through the bars at these back-to-back houses in Armley and the industrial estates of Leeds. I just sat there looking through the window thinking 'I've got two paths ahead of me. I either do what my family wants and knock this shit on the head. Or I'm going to go for it.' I made a decision. 'I'm actually going to make the whole thing work to my advantage and move forward.'

Bearing in mind that there's very little in the way of illegal stuff going on in the dance scene at this point because it had been driven overground and into clubs that viewed raves and acid house as money spinners, forging a career as a DJ now had some promise. It sounded like a 'thing'. Venues now *wanted* dance music in their clubs. All of that had been falling into place before I went to jail and so if I could wash my hands of those illegal parties, then I could still make a career from DJing. It was a definite epiphany. 'I'm gonna make this work!' I then sat in my cell, looking forward to my summer in Kavos. Little did I know.

I rang Mum and Dad when I got out and had 'the chat' with them and they said, "You're going to have to knock this on the head and come home to Peterborough." From their point of view I'd gone from being in the RAF and the BMW dealership to acid parties and prison and they just wanted to get me back on the straight and narrow. I'm not proud of putting my family through that kind of anguish, especially when their friends found out. But I took a deep breath and told them that I was going to crack on. "Give me a bit of time here and trust me. I'm going to make this work. I know I can do it."

My next phone call was to try to find out what was going on with the missing-in-action Tom. I spoke to Pru at Beat Street Records and got all the gen on the situation with this tit. I also needed somewhere to live because my six months were up at Drew Hemment's place and so that was also seriously worrying. And that's when you need great people around you to help you out.

My friend Nikki Hainsworth's dad, nicknamed Skinny, was this notoriously crazy guy from the heart of Chapeltown, Leeds. Skinny was a real character and a proper night owl. He liked a drink or two, let's put it that way. Skinny said: "I've got a spare room at home. You can come and stay at mine if you want." And that was one of the kindest things anyone's ever done for me. After being in such a difficult spot I could now move what was left of my dwindling possessions into the spare room at Skinny's. I still had my turntables and vinyl and that was all that mattered. I set the decks up in his bedroom and got straight back into mixing.

I was now partying with Nikki and her friends: Adam Falkingham, her brother Justin Hainsworth, Aaron Sanders and Nikki's boyfriend Drew Hemment who had kindly put me up at his place in Leeds. Drew had helped to put on this Brave New World party the year before in an Equestrian centre in a beautiful idyllic Yorkshire village called Ilkley, close to the Lancashire border. Brave New World featured another running battle with the police who once again managed to confiscate the decks. However, there was a load of people still at the party once the police had left and somebody had managed to locate an Amstrad tower unit, which they wired to the main PA. And so 1,000 people partied at this rave not knowing that the music was coming from a home stereo hidden behind some scaffolding. Because it was dark they were shining a torch on the Amstrad tape player to see just how far along the cassette was. "Still got five minutes on this one." When it got right to the very end, the MC would pipe up so they could flip the tape to Side B. It was mental! But that's how inventive and committed they were to the party. They were absolute troopers. The things they did for the cause of acid house were truly remarkable.

Anyway, Drew had a bit of history working for events like Brave New World and he was now talking about his ambitions to do some stuff in Leeds. He knew a couple of characters at university in Leeds called Tuin and Mick who had a bit of money, which they wanted to put into doing a party. And so Drew and these students and I started a Thursday night in Leeds. It was called Audacity Presents Creation at the Phoenix Club in Chapeltown, right in the heart of the red-light district. I was now a promoter!

The Phoenix Club had a real workingmen's club feel to it and the people who ran it gave us the Thursday night. Now, in Leeds there were good parties on a Friday night and there were good parties on a Saturday night, but nothing happened on a Thursday, and so we decided to be the best Thursday around. If nothing else, it gave me the opportunity to go out and play again.

# Diamond Posse, Sheer Audacity And A Three Deck Wizard

My first foray into promoting wasn't even the result of a desire to put on nights of my own, it was just something I fell into. It felt really good to be working with these guys, while still trying to reassimilate myself back into society. I was just so relieved to be out of Armley.

Audacity was a sluggish start with 15 people on the first night at the Phoenix Club, but that doubled to 30 the following week. But we didn't care and just kept going. And then a few more people started coming and the funny thing is, some of the first people that started coming on a Thursday night included the infamous Leeds legends Dave Beer and Huggy who I'd not seen since being locked up with him at that Love Decade raid. They just rolled in one night. They were just this crazy crew from Wakey (Wakefield). There were about eight or nine of them and we had some mutual friends who started coming on a regular basis too. This tiny crew of me, my new girlfriend Lis who was at nursing college along with Nikki, Adam, Justin, Mick, Drew and Tuin ran that night for about four months.

Audacity started at the back end of '91 and ran through to the winter of '92. We got to the Easter bank holidays and the club owner said, "Instead of doing the Thursday, do you want to do the Sunday?" Drew jumped at the chance. Let's face it, it couldn't get any worse than Thursday.

The problem was, we just couldn't get anybody to come into Chapeltown, which was a pretty rough area. Had we been in the centre of Leeds, it might have been a different story. We realised we were going to need to have more lighting and a smoke machine to make more of a spectacle. We hired the equipment on Tuin's driving licence and got all the stuff delivered on the Saturday. Because we'd hired it on a Saturday we ended up installing it in one of the other guys' front room. And we ended up partying all night with the smoke machine puffing away. We then slept for most of the Sunday.

Sunday afternoon we got ourselves to the club to assemble the equipment. It was about nine o'clock when the club owner dropped by. "We need to get those doors open!"
–   "Why?"
–   "There are about 1,000 people outside!"

I don't know whether it was because nothing else was going on in Leeds or just word of mouth, but by the time we opened the doors it was heaving outside. We knew we'd turned the most massive corner. It felt so special and was to be the gateway to some really good stuff. In fact, we stopped doing the Thursdays and just concentrated on the bank holidays going forward. The next few parties we did were all like that and that was a real pivotal moment for us all. And for it to have gone so well between all of us close friends was brilliant. A very special time.

Audacity ended in the autumn of '91. Tuin, Mick and Drew were students and they moved away and so I started doing a Thursday night in a ropey old pub in Crossgates, Leeds with a friend called Martin. The night ended up being packed out every single week with folks cruising in the car park in Vauxhall Novas and Ford Fiestas; Italian piano tunes blaring out on this rough old estate three miles from the city centre.

Often, when our parties finished we'd go to this legendary blues place in Leeds called Sonnys. We used to pile round to Sonnys to listen to DJ Mikey, a true Leeds legend who came out of the funk and soul times before he got into playing house. Sonnys was one of those places where you could cut the atmosphere with a knife. The owner, Sonny, would take the money at the front door dressed in a full-length trench coat. It was a crazy place. There were definitely some unsavoury characters around the edges at Sonnys, but in the middle of the dancefloor was a huge dollop of love. It was an absolutely brilliant place and we got to listen to Mikey and another DJ called Task. Task would do things like play Mariah Carey's *Someday* acapella version with the piano bit and then stop the track. He would then play a bit more and then stop the track again until everyone was shouting and banging on the walls for more. And then he started it back up again, but with the piano drop. It was awesome! He played Patti Day's *Right Before My Eyes* when none of us had ever heard it before. The atmosphere that particular record created was special with people banging ashtrays on the walls and just roaring. Absolutely amazing times.

I met this young lad at Sonnys, who would have been about 17 at the time. Marc Leaf or 'Leafy' was just cutting his teeth as a DJ. He got a break to play in Sonnys and he lit the place up. Meeting Leafy and his then partner, Tracy was a beautiful moment. I also met a scratch DJ called Graham Dixon; the only one amongst us who could do all the DMC stuff. He used to play the acapella of *Brass Disk* by Dupree while scratching Leftfield over the top. Dixon ended up doing loads of events in Leeds and is a real OG up there, and his brother Steve Dixon would also go on to make a name for himself under the name Stefan Groove. Stevie is 100% solid gold. Anytime you ever needed anything, day or night, Steve would be there. He is definitely part of the Diamond Posse.

We made contact with a guy called Phil Easy from London around that time. Like me, he had moved up north and we soon became kindred spirits. Phil's mate Tony Walker was another legendary character in the Leeds scene and Tony and Phil wanted to put some gigs on and asked us if we wanted to be part of it, based on what we'd been doing at the Phoenix Club. He wanted us to move about 500 yards from the Phoenix Club to a place called the Trades Club. Now, the Trades Club wasn't licensed and was a little bit lawless and edgy, but they had some ambitions to put on acts from down south as well as some from up there to become the biggest live party. They asked me, Leafy and Drew to become residents at this new night along with another DJ called Tony Walker from London. Tony now runs a legendary night called Love To Be and tours the globe to this day.

We started up by booking Utah Saints who had just put out *What Can You Do For Me*. They duly came along and smashed it. They were awesome. Jez and Tim are true gents and our paths have crossed on tonnes of occasions over the years.

Phil was connected to some guys who were setting up a pirate radio station in Leeds called Dream FM and the plan was to broadcast from the top floor of the Trades Club, but for whatever reason that didn't happen and so it was set up in a rundown house between Chapeltown and Chapel Allerton. Leafy and I used our decks to kickstart Dream FM. We were the first two people to play on the station which was quite a thing back then and another gateway to getting back into the scene.

The Trades Club nights were booking people from down south like Trevor Fung, SL2 and Carl Cox. I'd seen Trevor play loads of stuff, including the Back To The Future and Sunrise parties. I'd seen Carl Cox at Back To The Future and The Midsummer Night's Dream that became known as 'Ecstasy Airport' near Maidenhead. That was an amazing party and Carl Cox was a brilliant DJ. The night Carl Cox came to Trades Club, he wanted to play on three decks and so I took two of my decks and Leafy took one of his and we set them up for him.

Leafy played first and I played second. I was hanging around after my set, when I spotted this guy walking through the club with one of his mates and two big boxes of records. He made a beeline into the DJ box and gave us the biggest smile. "Hi mate, I'm Carl."

– "Hi, I'm DJ Rob."
– "Looks like a brilliant night!"

Carl was just the nicest bloke you could ever meet. At one point he said, "Will you do me a favour? Can you get a light because I can't see what I'm doing?" I got this desk light from the office and plugged it all in. Carl was busy taking all the records out of their sleeves. He had one of those old black vinyl record boxes, where the lid split into two halves. So he put the discs in one half of the box and the sleeves in the other. And then he was firing the records up onto the three turntables. Once he'd finished playing them he was putting them back into the sleeves to make it quicker to get to the tracks. While he was playing, I noticed that the plug cover on the desk lamp had fallen off, which was dangerous and so being careful not to touch the live wire I pushed it back in before ZZZZZZZZZ! I fried myself for a few seconds. Having thousands of watts of Carl Cox coursing through my body was a wake-up call. It was a moment I'll never forget. If that didn't make me a fanboy, nothing would! But at least Carl was off and running.

Carl was playing this breakbeat music that we'd never really heard before. And all of a sudden it was like 'Oh my god, I'm a breakbeat addict!' It was a real change in direction. My dad used to have the

*Apache* records with the famous break in them and the *Shaft* album and all that kind of stuff, which was then procured by Young MC and so hearing breakbeats in Leeds for the first time was quite a moment and a gift from the gods. Leafy and I were just mesmerised by this guy's energy and enthusiasm. What he was getting out of the crowd was mind blowing and that remains to this day the best thing I've ever seen behind the decks. I've never seen anyone close to that and he was just so experimental. He played two copies of Moby's *Go* and it was going "Go! Go! Go!" with one beat behind the other, hip hop style. Carl was playing these big chunky breakbeats and SL2 *Music Takes Control* and *Way In My Brain* and Blapps! Posse's *Bus' It (It's Time To Get Busy)*. The place just erupted.

We got a thousand people into those particular events on the Saturday night, which was ridiculous. And it was amazing to see Trevor Fung again after hearing him over the years at Heaven and Rage and all those seminal events. I spoke to Trevor after and just let him know how much he'd influenced my journey to becoming a DJ.

***

Having heard the breakbeat tunes Carl Cox was playing, I made a concerted effort to get down to London for new vinyl. I'd go down on the train or in whatever banger car I had at the time, with Marc Leaf and a few other mates or I would just go solo. My mission was to go get the crispiest biscuits I could from the various record shops in London, Black Market Records in particular. They were fantastic times, picking up these records and trying to implement them into my set. The dance scene around 1991/92 was fragmenting like mad and there were all sorts of new genres and subgenres springing up. British acts like KLF, Prodigy, Altern-8 and Bizarre Inc were getting to the top of the charts, which really helped to popularise the whole thing and took it to a new commercial level, which was fantastic.

The Trades Club had a huge wooden dancefloor upstairs that would hold about 1,000 people with a stage at one end. They held trade shows there in the 60s. It was this huge working men's club on steroids. Anyway, I was walking up the stairs there one night, with my box of vinyl, when a guy came up behind me with one of those lights that has the chattels on the front. He followed me up about two flights of stairs and into the main room. "So, you're the DJ?" he said. "What's your name?"

-   "DJ Rob."
-   "I'm Rob, too. I'm Rob Tyrrell, one of the silent partners in this event. You know what, I like what you do."
-   "Thanks very much. That's very kind of you."
-   "I've seen you play quite a few times, although you won't have seen me. I used to go to Audacity at the Phoenix Club. And of course I've heard you play here as well. Well, I run another night in Leeds called Ark. Do you fancy playing there for me some time?"

rob
Tissera

# All Aboard The Ark

Ark was pretty much one of the biggest deals going in Leeds. There was also Kaos at The Warehouse run by Tony Hannon; they were the two big ones. Ark was at Leeds Polytechnic and they were getting 1,000 people every time they did it and so being approached by Rob was another big landmark moment. Rob Tyrrell was a successful businessman who had seen real opportunities in the rave scene.

And so I went to do a party for him at one of these Ark events. It was me, Dave Seaman from Brothers In Rhythm, John Kelly and local legends Gary Norman and Mark Holliday. And the night could not have gone any better. I was the third person on and it was rammed. Because of what I'd learned from working with Adrian Luvdup, I now had a couple more strings to my bow. I played a couple of acapellas over some Italian piano tracks and that overlaying was something a little bit outside the box at that time and really enamoured me to the crowd. As a result of that set, I spoke to Rob and his business partner, Tom Edge, the next day and they just said, "That's it, you're our new resident. So, Rob, what's your surname?"

– "It's Tissera."

– "Why the fuck are you not using that? From now on, that is your DJ name. You can't be DJ Rob. You're Rob Tissera."

And so Rob Tyrrell was the person responsible for making me see the light on that. After all, he was a marketing guy and he knew how to sell his products. The images on the front of his flyers were the strongest I'd ever seen. They used a lacquer finish, which was a new thing back then. And bear in mind, when you think of rave culture, you think of flyer culture. The ravers know how important it is to have something that looks 'the don' and Ark was really effective in that regard. And so thanks to Rob Tyrrell, Rob Tissera entered the scene.

Ark booked everybody: Smoking Jo, X-Press 2, Carl Cox, Faithless, Felix, SL2, Grooverider, Dave Angel, Frank De Wulf, Baby D and many, many more. As soon as DJs became popular, Ark would book them. It was a proper business and bringing the best of the best every single time. I would play after everybody as 'the closer'. Marc Leaf and I were residents for Ark for quite some time. And going on after all those people meant you really had to bring the fire and taught me a huge amount about being flexible with styles. You had to be able to change it up and know when to get to the next level. You also had to know how to finish without a dry eye in the place.

In the autumn of 1991, I started playing for these guys who ran Bliss at The Gallery in Leeds. The Gallery was a great club and had been a Leeds institution since the 70s. Bliss at The Gallery was one of the last bastions of rave and was run by Steve Luigi from The Listening Booth record store in Leeds and another guy called Shakey. I ended up being a monthly resident for those guys. There was literally sweat dripping off the ceiling in that place with people hanging off every fixture and fitting. The Gallery was on two levels, so you're DJing right in the top level, right up in the sky of this ornate club with its wooden dance floor. There was also this wooden balcony all the way around it. The atmosphere in there was electric and we had some phenomenal times playing alongside Steve Luigi, Dream Frequency and Prodigy. What a time to be alive.

Late '91/early '92 and breakbeats were my newfound passion. In fact, several other people in the Leeds clubs had developed a love for breaks too. This new genre hadn't got a name yet; people just seemed to be playing breakbeats rather than playing within a genre. Some of my strongest influences over the years have been David Bowie, Madonna and those musical chameleons. I absolutely love people who try out new things, or who maybe fuse those styles together with older material. That's something I've always loved and always will. I love the science of making people go mad. What it is that makes people jump up and down. If I was playing a massive rave with people like Kenny Ken, Top Buzz and Carl Cox, I wanted to make sure that I absolutely hit the spot with everyone around me, so I very much got into the breakbeat thing. Tracks like *Take It Easy* by Cedric Winkelburger, all the Rabbit City Series and Bass Construction's *Dance With Power* were some of the best along with the SL2 stuff and of course, Prodigy. Back in late '91, Italian pianos were still huge too, and had massive respect from the people putting on those types of events. I regularly played Zone in Blackpool, which was pretty much 'Piano City' and you were encouraged to drop all of those Italian tunes there.

That massive rave sound that mixed in breakbeats was getting big. Altern-8 had got into the charts and Quadrophonia were kicking off as were Praga Khan and Dream Frequency who were absolutely enormous back then. I used to play a lot of Citybeat Records such as *Higher Than Heaven* by The Badman Presents N.D.X. and tracks like that. They were phenomenal and what I would call 'switch tracks', that flicked from piano happiness and into the darkness and I loved that contrast. I loved this big mishmash of stuff, which was making it really exciting to play out. I was covering a good, broad spectrum of stuff, certainly for the Ark crowd.

Ark was at the Polytechnic in Leeds, which was a big venue regularly getting 1,500 people in who definitely picked up on the breakbeat thing. Because I was playing the last set as well, it allowed me to explore those genres, plus it gave me an extra gear on some of the other DJs if everyone else was just playing house. That made a huge difference and stood me in good stead for a number of years without a shadow of a doubt.

I started playing at Wigan Pier, that massive iconic club from the Northern Soul days, as well as some pretty big raves in Scarborough and Bridlington because it didn't matter where you went, there was always a huge pocket of ravers. It was booming. I did some big raves with Carl Cox in Bridlington and Scarborough. Those parties were pretty significant and the next time I met up with Carl I was watching him play at SPAR in Scarborough, which was a huge complex. Watching Carl Cox and Kenny Ken playing those raves were inspirational moments. I was also meeting with some of the MCs for the first time and getting a bit of a rapport with guys like MC Natz. I just loved the way he toasted stuff by not riding over the top of the lyrics. He left the vocal alone and then delivered his message in between. Natz had an amazing energy and fast became one of my favourites. I met MC Natz through the Bridlington and Scarborough connection, Fraser Barraclough, a white guy with really long dreads and a million prison tattoos who was putting on massively successful parties in Bridlington called Lick. I became a resident DJ for those monthly events and they were awesome.

I also managed to get the landline number of Mike Knowler who booked the DJs at Quadrant Park and drove over to Liverpool to hand deliver a cassette I'd done. I went in and handed this tape to Mike Knowler who gave me the opportunity to play on the Friday night at Quadrant Park, which was another huge landmark moment for me. Even though Quadrant Park was known more for the Saturdays than the Fridays, it had become so good and busy that they started Friday nights. Even on a Friday night you still got a huge contingent of people that would also go on a Saturday as well. So again, it was a very, very significant moment in time and one more opportunity to get the old fingers into the rock face, to pull yourself up just one more rung.

# CH. 21

**rob tissera**

# Blandy, Crate Digging And Baby D

I was out DJing every weekend and still going down to London on the train to buy records. Because back in those days it wasn't all about playing the same tunes. It was the complete opposite. You had to have the new stuff. And it had to be good! These were the times when people covered the names of the tracks with stickers or sometimes wrote the wrong name on the record sleeve to confuse rivals. It was a competition. That was just how it was. And if you didn't compete, you lost out. And so everyone wanted those individual bullets and the only way you were going to get them was to travel a bit. And that meant travelling to Liverpool and Huddersfield to Fourth Wave Records and Beat Street in Bolton and all these places where they had different distributors rather than just going into Eastern Bloc the whole time.

By this time, I had a great connection with Eastern Bloc, because my friend Huggy was working there; our paths constantly crossing. Huggy had just become a resident at the house music institution that was Back To Basics in Leeds. When the authorities started clamping down on the warehouse scene in Leeds, Dave Beer decided to do his own thing. Along with old friend Alistair Cooke, Dave started Back To Basics on Saturday, 23rd November 1991 on the top floor of The Chocolate Factory, later renamed The Music Factory, a three-storey gay club on

Lower Briggate in Leeds. Knowing Huggy and some of those Back To Basics guys was to prove most useful.

Through knowing Huggy, I was now able to walk out of Eastern Bloc with a bag full of the crispest biscuits. They even let me go downstairs to listen to the records. I was getting some fantastic treatment from Huggy, John and Mike Eastern Bloc, who was part of an act called E-Lustrious. They looked after me and for that I'm eternally grateful because it was those records that really made you stand out. I loved the chase for the precious vinyl and I pursued it to the ends of the earth. I was a major vinyl hunter.

I made my first trip over to Amsterdam to buy records in 1992. I went over there with Rob Tyrell on the back of his motorbike. I ended up buying so many records I had to buy a backpack to bring them all back. We spent four days over there in Amsterdam buying tunes and forging relationships with some vinyl connections over there, which would stand me in good stead over the years. I would end up visiting Amsterdam two or three times a year, just to get something a little bit different.

I was now busy with my residency at Ark, plus all the other bits and bobs that came up. Having those important contacts and getting in with people was a massively important part of the job. I made a good contact in Power Promotions simply by chancing my arm. I went down to London one day to go record shopping, and thought I'd pay this company Power Promotions a visit. They were hugely influential back then. Sometimes I would talk to other DJs and ask them where they got their tracks from. Quite often they'd say Power Promotions. Power, run by Paul Gotel and Terry Marks were the leaders in their field, but I'd had no contact with them whatsoever. I didn't know who they were, but a friend of mine who worked in a record shop had given me a blurb sheet that came with one of their promos. And so I decided to be as bold as brass and go knock on the door of their offices in Shepherds Bush.

It was 11am on a Tuesday morning and I just rocked up and asked if I could get onto the Power Promotions mailing list, in order to get those precious promos, completely unaware that there was a process you had to go through. DJs had to fill in a lot of forms and had to get references from companies and clubs in order to get on the mailing lists, but I just knocked on the door and asked for Terry Marks because I'd seen his name on this blurb.

It turned out Terry was also from up north, Newcastle, and when I told him I lived in Leeds we instantly clicked. He said that for being so cheeky and just turning up, he would put me on the promo list. Terry was this really warm and friendly 6ft-6" giant of a guy and he really looked after me. And from that moment on, I was receiving amazing new vinyl every single week and that was making a huge difference to my sets and to the audience's enjoyment of them. I couldn't thank them enough really because they were so kind to me.

When you received promo records, you fulfilled your side of the deal as the DJ by completing the reaction sheets that came with them. The record companies wanted to know everything about how the records were received by the punters; information that could make or break the release of a tune. I kept in close contact with Power Promotions and would phone them quite regularly. I think they really liked my upbeat character and valued my opinion. A lot of establishing yourself in the music industry is through who you know. It might sound obvious, but simply concentrating on your craft is not enough. You need to get out there and make those connections. That contact was to create a real boost to my DJing at a particular Ark party.

Ark was on the up and had moved from the Leeds Polytechnic to the Refectory in the University which held 2,500 people. Ark was selling it out every single month. Rob Tyrrell then decided to do a one-off in Leeds at the Corn Exchange; a beautiful ornate dome-shaped building split into three levels of shops with balconies on each floor. Rob organised this night at the Corn Exchange with a stellar bill: Paul Oakenfold, Dave Angel, Huggy, DJ Sy, Grooverider and me. Putting on a party at Leeds Corn Exchange was mental really. It was this bizarre, amazing space. I was to play last after Oakenfold and all those guys and so they were pretty big boots to fill.

22nd, August 1992, on the morning of the gig I'd been sent a package by Terry Marks from Power. I opened it up and popped this promo onto the decks. Wow! Jeezus, this is a big record! There wasn't much info on it, but I knew this was the first track I'd play. It was a test pressing of Baby D's *Let Me Be Your Fantasy*. I made my way to the Leeds Corn Exchange, with this absolute weapon in my record box.

The Corn Exchange was buzzing, as you can imagine. So many top names on that flyer. I sat on my record box in the DJ box, just soaking it all up in this amazing place.

The reason they'd chosen the Corn Exchange was because Ark was leasing a shop in there, which sold their merchandise. The decks were up on the top level and you wouldn't be allowed to get away with that now as it was a commercial space. So, the DJs on the top balcony were looking down on two levels of ravers below. It was stunning. I sat on my wooden record box all night long thinking 'I've got Baby D. It doesn't matter what anybody is going to play, because I've got this absolute banger.' Baby D fitted in perfectly with my DJ philosophy of starting big, and just trying to get bigger and bigger. Finally, it was time to unleash the beast.

I can still remember the astounded look of the clubbers and DJs all around me as that track dropped. That was a landmark tune for me and one of the finest moments of my career. Just having something as big as that was a game changer. And of course, as well as having that tune I had all the Ark tracks that everybody knew, alongside Felix's *Don't You Want Me* and tracks like that. But *Let Me Be Your Fantasy* set me on this amazing trajectory. It really did.

***

I played a huge rave at Ripon Racecourse in October 1992. 8,000 attended Galactica featuring Shades Of Rhythm, Dream Frequency, Felix, Sun 3, Hyper Go-Go, Joey Beltram, Jumpin Jack Frost and a huge number of others. I was playing after Kenny Ken and Top Buzz at Ripon. I can remember standing to the side of the stage in this big top marquee staring at thousands of people going mad to Top Buzz, thinking 'Wow, these guys are good! I'm gonna have to pull my socks up over my knees on this one.' There was only one way to go there and so I kicked off with a banger. I dropped *The Horn Track* by Egyptian Empire at a time when nobody had heard that tune. There's a bit in the song where it goes 'One more for the foghorn!' and it then bursts into this crazy kind of woodwind riff that sounds like it would be perfectly at home in a Moroccan souk with a tonne of reverb on the riff. It's out-and-out bat shit crazy and really catches the audience by surprise. It went down a storm in this sea of white gloves, glow sticks and dummies; the air thick with the smell of Vick's.

That was another hugely significant moment in my career, realising the power of music and creating that unified connection. There was nothing else like it. Backstage at Ripon I was introduced to these guys who were friends of friends of Rex Sargeant, who went all the way back to the Rochdale days. I instantly clicked with Ian Bland from Dream Frequency; we got on like a house on fire. I told him I loved his music, especially the EP *Live The Dream*, but said I wished it was a bit more mixable. "Because none of your tracks have got the beats at the front and the back, it means it's very hard to just pick them up and mix." Bearing in mind it was just vinyl in those days, you needed some early beats to be able to create a neat mix. But Blandy's tracks made that really difficult. We kind of laughed about it, but I think it touched a nerve with him, even though there was no animosity whatsoever. I was just giving him some advice from a DJ's perspective. Anyway, we exchanged phone numbers and about two weeks later he gave me a call.

Ian said he'd taken on board what I'd said about making tracks more mixable, and that it wasn't something he knew that much about, but could I come to the studio to explain it. Of course, I jumped at the chance to spend some time at Blandy's studio while he was making a track. That was quite a moment for me although it was a bit embarrassing in some respects that I'd questioned the mighty Dream Frequency! Ha ha!

**Ian Bland, Dream Frequency and Dancing Divaz**

*"Cheeky fucker, critiquing my records! But yeah, he had a point. One of my tracks even had a tempo change right at the start – ha ha. So, Rob had a point. But yeah, no offence taken."*

# CH. 22

*rob fissera*

# We Are The Music Makers

1992, I started making music with Ian Bland from Dream Frequency. I was now a musician, DJ and promoter, and so things had moved on quickly from my days playing the wedding gigs.

Blandy was a joy to work with and we made a decent pairing. I loved the stuff he'd made with Dream Frequency and was so lucky to have connected with him. We met at Blandy's house in Leyland, Lancashire and started playing around with some Italian house sounds. After a few days of mucking around we ended up with the track *I've Got The Vibe*, which had this real feelgood factor about it; an Italian house sound twinned with a big DX bass line. We were to revisit the Yamaha DX bass on loads of tracks and it would become our signature bass sound.

Blandy wanted to make his tracks more mixable and DJ friendly, having taken onboard my constructive feedback. Blandy was so nice about it all and was great to interface with. This was a guy who had worked with Laurent Garnier. It was a breath of fresh air for both of us and initiated a gateway to something special. It was nothing but belly laughter every single time I spoke to the man. My life was enriched no end by knowing Blandy. We recorded at Blandy's home studio in Leyland and so I was driving back and forth from Leeds to Lancashire as often as I could.

Being so musical, Blandy could easily interpret the ideas I came up with – just like a mad professor. He would unravel all the samples and ideas I had and transform them into a thing of beauty. He was great on the keys too and I always referred to him as The One Fingered Riffmeister. It was like he had one magic finger that could create pure magic on the keyboard. You may remember the 80s comedian Kenny Everett who created an American character that had these giant white gloves that pointed up into the air. That was Blandy. The One Fingered Riffmeister. Blandy's riffs just raised the room. The music we were making was a real mishmash of house and the harder, faster stuff that was beginning to sound a lot more epic.

Making music was starting to become a real focus for me outside of the work I was doing with Blandy when Rob Tyrrell at Ark told me that he wanted to start up a record label. The Ark brand was growing and Rob was also scouting for a shop from which he could sell official merchandise, because he was selling thousands of tapes from the events. He wanted to get a shop in Leeds so he could sell tapes, record bags and bomber jackets from his shop. Plus, he wanted to start this record label. He wondered if I had any contacts who could help him out and so I put him in touch with my old mate Kev Walsh, the guitarist from Chorley. And from there we embarked upon starting up a record label.

Rob was this madcap character; very gregarious and referred to himself as a 'ginner' on account of his fiery red hair. He had the best of personalities and everybody who met him loved him and the events he put on were magnificent.

In order to start a record label, we needed material, which meant that myself, Kev Walsh and his mate John Farrell started writing music together. We recorded the debut Ark track *My Feelings* under the name P.P. Orange on Ark Recordings.

The first stage of recording was getting the ideas together. We had this Italian piano melody together with a few little breaks here and there, but it was mainly a house track.

We recorded the track in our old haunt, Suite 16 in Rochdale. The executive producer was Stuart James who worked as an engineer for Joy Division, A Certain Ratio and many more. Working in that kind of exalted company was an amazing thing. The recording involved a couple of all-night sessions in Suite 16 with its proper 24-track mixing desk. We acted like we were bloody Led Zeppelin or something. It felt awesome to be involved in something like that; to actually be recording your first track, in Suite 16, as an artist.

Once it was finished, Rob Tyrrell set about publicising it in some of the music magazines that were around at the time, using all his marketing skills to make it look as sharp as it possibly could. Rob wanted to make all the record covers look like works of art that worked together as a design ethos.

Even though the track didn't amount to a great deal and didn't duly bother the pop charts or anything, it was a hugely significant moment for me. That P.P. Orange track led to a second single: *Better Daze* by L-Dopa also on Ark Recordings. Rob's vision was to put out four releases in that first year that all had very similar artwork so you could put them all together as a collector's piece; you could actually frame them, I guess. The second single wasn't as good as the first, but it was definitely more on a breakbeat tip and keeping in with the Carl Cox and Trevor Fung vibes. Now we had two singles under our belts, we were off on this mission. Suddenly my troubles surrounding my incarceration at Her Majesty's Pleasure, were starting to fade away inside this cloud of creativity.

I was still doing quite a lot of work with Zone over in Blackpool and I bumped into these two characters from Huddersfield there one night. It is quite a common theme where you meet people in clubland who have almost been walking in parallel lines with you over the years, with mutual friends and experiences. And then you finally meet and intertwine with each other. I was playing massive piano anthems from the day like Techno Age Ft DJ Phil Anthony's *Moving On* and Meeting Place's *House From The World* and JT Company's *Don't Deal With Us* and tracks like that. I was playing out at Zone when these Huddersfield lads came over and spoke to me. "We're an act called Flipped Out," they said. Now, I'd heard one of their tracks before and they were mutual friends of the guys who ran events in Huddersfield and so we struck up an instant rapport.

Mark Hindle and Vic van Dyke were very funny. Vic was an absolute lunatic and a beautiful man; probably about eight to ten years older than me. Flipped Out asked me to remix a track for them. The track was *Love Bomb* (*Love Will Take Us Higher*) on Fourth Wave Records. I jumped at the chance. And a week later I was working with them in this studio in Huddersfield. We had some of the best fun I've ever had in a studio. Those two were absolutely mental characters and so full of joy. None of us had that much in the way of production/studio skills in terms of making electronic music and using samples and so we had to rely upon engineers who actually knew the technology. Some of the stuff we were asking them to do was simply impossible, but we were learning the basics of how to sample as we went along. We would turn up with a bunch of records and work with the engineer to try to get these ideas down. But that would involve maybe six or seven shifts. We would turn up every Wednesday to record and eat our own body weight in chocolates and sweets, while in the studio.

James Reid, our engineer, was also one half of Blue Amazon, which was impressive. We worked with James every Wednesday until we nailed this *Love Bomb* track. And then once we'd finished it, Rob Tyrrell from Ark made it the third track on his new label. My mix of *Love Bomb* had this big piano riff that owed an awful lot to those guys. And that *Love Bomb* mix got me more and more attention as a DJ too and the bookings started to boom. I started playing for people like Maxime's in Wigan and a legendary place in Manchester called Bowlers.

Bowlers was this huge venue used for indoor cricket and they would get 5,000 ravers in there every single week. Howzat?! I started playing for Bowlers on a monthly basis and the queue was unbelievable, just like when we first went out raving, snaking around the block from 7pm. The Bowlers crowd loved the power as well as the piano stuff and straight-up house. They also loved a few breakbeats in there too, but definitely leaned more towards the pianos. The North West loved the likes of Bassheads' *Is There Anybody Out There?* and boatloads of big piano tunes. They were very special nights. Absolutely phenomenal!

I was also getting booked at this place in Rhyl run by these guys I'd played for in Middleton, Manchester at a night called Hippo's. Hippo's was held at the Hippodrome (hence the name) in Middleton and was full-on techno with a couple of resident DJs: Moggy and Jay Weardon. Jay Weardon and business partner Colin Boulton started Hippo's with just £100 borrowed from the latter's father and due to its success at the Hippodrome, they decided to branch off and start a Friday night in Rhyl, North Wales. 130 miles from where I lived, it was no biggie to go and play there when Colin asked me and Marc Leaf to go over as residents, playing techno every Friday night in Rhyl.

And so we embarked on this great run in '92, when I bumped into the Flipped Out guys again. Of course, I'd made some tracks with them and James Reid the studio engineer: the *Love Bomb* track was followed by *Basstab*; both engineered by Stuart James in Suite 16. Those tracks sparked the interest of a promoter in Northern Ireland, we'd never met before, but whose girlfriend at the time was studying to be a doctor at Leeds University.

DJ Mark Jackson was a pioneer of the rave circuit and was integral in bringing house music over to Northern Ireland. Mark was quite a bit younger than me, but an absolutely lovely bloke. He came over to see me play Ark and was obviously impressed because he went back to Northern Ireland and mentioned me to this promoter Billy Dunseath or Billy D as he was known locally. Billy was a maverick promoter who was putting on events at a place called Circus Circus, in Banbridge, Northern Ireland. Circus Circus had a great reputation and he invited me over to DJ, plus Flipped Out who would perform PAs at a couple of parties. I mean, Northern Ireland was in a bad state, but we were young and didn't think too much about any of the consequences. It sounded like a proper adventure.

# CH. 23

### rob pssera

# Glocks Across The Irish Sea

Northern Ireland was a country at war. The evening news often featured footage of bombed-out shops, armoured tanks and petrol bombs. It seemed to us, back in England, as an otherworldly place. And not in a good way.

My main concern was that someone over in Northern Ireland might find out about my military background, although it was something I never spoke about and so I didn't honestly expect that. But it was in the back of my mind as we prepared for our jaunt over the Irish Sea. I guess we thought that music transcended all that sectarian violence and was bringing the next generation of Northern Ireland very much together, and that this was just a fantastic thing to be involved with. Accentuate the positive, yeah? Plus, the idea of playing gigs outside of England was a pivotal and monumental moment in my career thus far.

We drove from Huddersfield, where I hooked up with Vic and Mark from Flipped Out, all the way to Stranraer to get the Sea Cat ferry to Belfast. The party was being held at the Point Inn, Londonderry, but the people we were playing for would have called it Derry.

We took my car on the ferry and once we were in Belfast we set off on the 70-mile drive to Londonderry. Once we were out of Belfast we hit the countryside and travelled through several towns before deciding to take a break.

We rolled into a little town after a half hour on the road just to get some water and sweets. There were signs on the shop windows announcing items that were on sale 'due to bomb damage'. It was now sinking in that we were in a country at war. A few of the locals were giving us hard stares and seemed to be aware that we were from out of town. Anyway, we piled back in the car and drove about another 45 miles down the road and stopped at a pub to get some food. It was a little like that scene in *An American Werewolf In London* at the Slaughtered Lamb pub when everything just stops as the Americans walk in. We ordered some pie and mash and some drinks and started to look forward to the evening ahead. We just kept our heads down.

When we got to the Point Inn, Londonderry, we told Billy Dunseath where we stopped for lunch. Billy's eyes rolled back and he coughed in shock. Apparently, those towns we stopped at were Catholic strongholds and there we were in my little white Golf GTI with UK plates. This car had a massive bass bin in the boot and an expensive Alpine head unit that shook your whole body to the core. Fair to say, we stood out like a sore thumb. We might as well have had targets painted on our backs. And I don't say this lightly, but we were not popular over there with that particular community. But luckily, we evaded any real heat and because Vic and Mark were such clowns I don't think we posed much of a threat. But Billy didn't see it as anything other than completely fucking mad. "What were you doing? Are you mad? Are you fucking mad?! You could have got yourself bloody done!" You live and learn, I guess.

The Point Inn was located at Quigley's Point, Donegal, a couple of miles out of Londonderry and it had this massive car park. It was a great little venue and one of those places that was so hot, you would burst into flames if you wore red. But it was brilliant with 350 people in there going nuts to harder-edged house and techno. It didn't matter what you threw at them, they would roar when the bass came in and hit them with a low punch to the guts. It was absolutely beautiful and I would definitely put that in the top 10 feelings I've ever had in a club. Just hearing that noise from the crowd pushed you to get tougher, and the tougher you got, the louder the roar. It was a dream come true. And those guys from Flipped Out certainly made it eventful.

We went to the hotel afterwards and I can just remember us jumping up and down on the bed like kids. Flipped Out were likely lads and the northern banter was savage. Nothing was off limits. Those lads had no sense of danger at all; I guess it was quite funny. But we were lucky not to get into any bother there. I remember they were egging on some of the locals in the hotel bar, yelling "C'mon, you Irish bastards!" Total silence greeted their call, and then, after a few very awkward moments, all the locals burst into laughter. The cheeky little tykes had gotten away with it.

The Point Inn gig was the start of what became a Northern Ireland gravy train and I was in and out of there quite a bit; playing at least once a month, sometimes more. I was playing places like the Met in Armagh and the legendary Kelly's in Donegal. Plus, The Coach in Banbridge and I became resident at the Network Club in Belfast not long after, so massive thanks to Billy Dunseath and Steve and Mark Jackson. I used to play Kilwaughter House too.

Kilwaughter House was a little hotel in Larne and the event was held in a function room at the back of the hotel. Kilwaughter was run by Marc Dobbin and his younger brother Gleave Dobbin who was also the resident DJ and a pretty fine one at that. It felt great to be recognised for doing what you did, in a different country.

\*\*\*

I once played at a club smack bang in the centre of Belfast. After the gig I was shown up to the office to collect my money. The owner of the club opened this massive safe and said, "Close your eyes and hold out your hand." I duly did as I was told, expecting my fat envelope full of cash. However, instead of my lovely dough, I felt a weighty metal object. It was a glock pistol. Jesus! What a scary moment and a stark reminder that I was in a community at war with the British. Being a DJ kept me safe however and needless to say I covered my surprise with a hearty laugh whilst cooly trying to remove any trace of my prints from the gun!

Another time I played in the Catholic stronghold of Londonderry and stupidly ended up going to a party on my own with a couple of new best friends. I eventually sobered up a few hours later and came to my senses. I phoned Billy D as my flight was leaving early from Belfast. "Where in fuck's name are you?" he barked. I asked the two people I was with for the address. "I'm on the Shantallow Estate." There was a sharp intake of breath followed by the words, "See you? You're a fuckin dickhead! Stay where you are. Don't move and don't get in a cab. We're sending someone to get you. You're a total dickhead!"

I didn't return to Ireland for a few months after that just to give Billy time to calm down. Not my brightest moment by far.

*\*\**

On a happier note, I became godfather to Marc Leaf's daughter Denver in 1992 and that was quite a significant thing at the time because it just came out of the blue and was such a lovely thing to happen.

# Bowlers, Angels And Karma Is A Bitch

1993, I'd moved into a back-to-back terraced house in Harehills, Leeds with my then girlfriend Lis. We lived a few streets away from Nikki Hainsworth and just up the road from Adam and the rest of the Diamond Posse.

These were very happy times where every day was bringing more bookings. It was gravy all the way. It was about this time that my compensation claim came in from the nasty crash I had when I first moved to Rochdale. I got a decent pay out, which allowed me to buy a red Escort that I drove everywhere at breakneck speed.

I got a call from an old pal in Huddersfield not long after getting the Escort and he seemed quite excited. "I know where Tom lives..." Now, Tom was the arsehole who stole my £500 when I was inside, and the same prat who cocked up the residency in Kavos. "He's living in Glasgow and is a resident DJ at a club there."

I didn't even hesitate. I jumped into my motor with a huge monkey wrench I'd found abandoned on the pavement just a few days earlier and set off to Glasgow. I couldn't let this go.

I drove up there as fast as I could and pulled into this housing estate flanked by high-rise flats and a load of narrow alleyways. It was a dank, drizzly November evening where you could see your breath. I checked the address to make sure I'd definitely got it right and paused by the front door. I could hear music pouring out of the window. I banged on the door a couple of times and eventually Tom surfaced. I had the wrench in the side pocket of my cargo pants and to be honest I don't even know what I was going to do. He was so shocked to see me all he could do was beg for my forgiveness. I was steaming mad, but I kept composed and simply said, "Let me in and give me every single record you own, you shitty twat!" He didn't argue.

In short, I cleaned him out. I took all his records too as part payment for the £500. It took a few trips to the motor to get all the records into my car. I'm so glad that that matter was settled without spilling any of his blood. I guess he might have thought twice before doing anything like that again.

***

Paul Gotel and Terry Marks at Power Promotions were sending me some pretty elite records in '93. If Power Promotions had 25 test pressings of something special, I would get one. Terry sent me a copy of this track called *Dreams* by Quench, which was pretty much one of the forerunners to trance. Now, this track was a total weapon and I got it on the morning of New Year's Eve, 1993. I had already played a set in Hull that evening and was on the way to Manchester to play Bowlers when we stopped on the Humber Bridge and opened a bottle of champagne. We had a little drink and then drove to Bowlers. Don't worry, I wasn't driving... I never ever do that.

We came in, round the back exit of Bowlers with about 10 minutes remaining until midnight. I stepped up onto the stage and I could see that the place was rammed to the rafters.

Now, this Quench *Dreams* track has bells in the middle and of course I wanted to drop that in on the stroke of midnight as a moment. So, I played a *Space Odyssey* type intro, complete with a countdown before mixing in the bells section of *Dreams* at the stroke of midnight before it smashed into this massive trance riff. I saw thousands of pairs of Puma and Adidas trainers going mad on the floor and there must have been thousands of holes in the ceiling too where everyone was launched through the roof by this killer of a sawtooth trance riff; they'd never heard anything quite like it. The building just exploded and that is still probably my best ever memory of Bowlers. It was spine tingling! Playing the Quench track during that period was a little risky, but it definitely struck a chord with everybody. There was no doubt about that.

I was still doing lots of stuff with Bowlers as well as playing for Zone in Blackpool, and Maxime's and Wigan Pier, plus some new rave events in Hull. Wigan Pier and Maxime's wanted that Italian piano, but Hull and Bridlington were more connected to the breakbeats. But I have to say that was the point where I began to grow a little bit tired of that particular scene. I felt like the scene wasn't as fresh as it had been a couple of years prior and it was beginning to get very laddish and the atmosphere changed and I just started to loosen my grip on it a little. With all forms of music, you get acts that come along and pioneer and then you get one or two years of people making similar stuff. And then you have another wave of people making downgraded versions and that's where I felt it was getting to unfortunately. Although, Slipmatt's label SMD really knocked things back up again, I was just not loving a lot of the new hardcore stuff coming out.

Progressive house had been making a name of labels like Hard Hands and acts like Leftfield, DOP and Fabio Paras. These acts were doing some great stuff and I really started to fall for that sound. The only problem was that not everybody liked progressive house. Often, when a DJ falls in love with a sound, it's easy to take your eye off the dance floor a little bit and you stray into educating people rather than entertaining them. It's a risk. And I definitely boxed myself off in playing more of this slower, proggy sound which didn't necessarily fit in with the parties I was playing at the time, especially if I was playing the closing set. I probably made the mistake of playing a bit too much of that at Bowlers and Ark. I don't think it was necessarily the right turn, but I just loved the music. Although when I played for Angels in Burnley I stuck to the breakbeats because that was another full-on rave, and you definitely knew what the parameters were there. You did not want to drift too far out that bandwidth at Angels, and so I played much more of what I would have played at Zone: some good old anthems.

Angels was run by a DJ called Paul Taylor, who was quite a bit older than me and he had a lot of experience of playing in the disco era. Paul had an encyclopaedic knowledge when it came to music and he taught me the importance of knowing your crowd. You had to please your punters. I remember he came on after me at Angels one time and I stood back, open mouthed, because he was awesome! I was in awe as this massive lighting rig descended to kick off a full-on laser show. The lighting rig had a globe of flashing lasers on the top and the volume went right up a good couple of notches. It was just a brilliant piece of theatre and it really struck a chord with me that was to return in the not-too-distant future. Turn the sound right up and get the lights working. It was breathtaking. I was standing there thinking 'Fair play, Paul, you flicked me off like a fly!' Ha ha. I really can't thank him enough for that lesson.

# CH. 25

rob
Tissera

# Moments Of Inertia

My record shopping had now found a great new haunt in Leeds. The Listening booth was run by Steve Luigi, the promoter and resident of The Gallery. Steve is a proper Leeds superhero of a DJ and a real legend in the northern soul world going back to the early 70s. Steve was a few years older than us and a wise old owl. Steve was a font of knowledge on all music and had been importing vinyl for donkey's years. The Listening Booth was in the Leeds Corn Exchange, where I played for Ark that one time, which had a lot of amazing independent shops in it selling wacky clothing and arts and crafts; loads of really cool boutique shops. Once I'd discovered The Listening Booth, I was in there all the time getting to know Steve and his assistant Rich Simpson.

For me, Steve Luigi is the godfather of rave in Leeds. Nobody can hold a candle to him in terms of his knowledge. His ability to work a crowd is second to none. They really looked after me and gave me loads of great promos, which made such a difference when playing at all these different events.

Rich Simpson was making some tracks with this genius producer Carl Finlow and he asked if I would be interested in coming into the studio with them. Carl was a student from a town between Runcorn and the Wirral and he was an educated guy with a slight Scouse accent. Carl was a ninja at laying down tracks on his Amiga computer. He knew this Amiga inside out, whereas all the stuff I'd done had been on the Atari 1040. The Amiga was completely foreign to me, so I didn't really have a great grasp of what he was doing. But Carl worked so intelligently, he could transform your ideas into reality just by listening to what you were saying or by the reference track we brought in. "We want to sound a bit like that, Carl." Carl would then interpret the ideas like nobody I'd ever met before. And so the three of us embarked on making this track called *Moments Of Inertia* under the name Circle City.

As with all the tracks we made in those days, nothing was done in a day. I mean, I don't know how other people worked, but we did it as a hobby. We would just go in and eat as much chocolate and as many sausage rolls or plates of pasta as we could and just mucked around making music. This Circle City track probably took us at least five or six sessions to be able to say it was right. We also did multiple versions with daft titles like *Final Ever Ever Ever Version 2* and *More Bass Version*. These sessions were really fertile and acted as a window into making trance, which was bubbling up. *Moments Of Inertia* was more like progressive house at 130 bpm with a soundscape that contained a chilling orchestral part in the middle.

We directed that recording by standing on the chairs in Carl's student house in Headingley as if we were conducting an orchestra – bringing everything to a rousing crescendo. Carl was like, "OK, cool. Let's power some more orchestrals down." He was a whizzkid, he really was. Steve Luigi kindly pressed up a couple of hundred copies for us and started selling them through his record shop. I played it to a couple of people and then played it out myself. Soon after I got a call from some guys at Warp Recordings.

Warp was flying off the back of tracks from Tricky Disco, LFO, Nightmares On Wax and Sweet Exorcist that had kicked Warp into orbit back in '90/'91. And so we were pretty chuffed that they wanted to sign *Moments Of Inertia*. Warp covered a lot of that more cerebral dance music, from Sheffield bleeps to prog house and techno and I guess our track fell somewhere within that. We ended up doing all right with that single and shifted around 8,000 units, which was quite good for an independent label. And so that track added a different string to our bow.

***

1994, and I was still working with Ian Bland when he asked me to remix a couple of Dream Frequency tracks, one of which was *Kushinada* which had a nod to rave/trance at 132 bpm. It was a bounding epic and a little more left field compared to some of the other stuff I'd done; I was really enjoying making that kind of music.

I also remixed this track *The Dream* by Dream Frequency in '94 just as there was another major fragmentation to dance music, with new genres popping up all over the place. On top of doing all the breakbeats and the straight up house, I was beginning to get a penchant for the techno. After all, I'm a bit of a chameleon and do get turned on by different sounds and the science of making people go mad. I am curious where music is concerned.

Circle City opened a few doors to clubs that wanted me to play, one of them being Orbit in Morley, West Yorkshire playing alongside Joey Beltram, Huggy and John Eastern Bloc, who was also one of the residents. I remember playing Orbit one time and I was in the top office with Huggy. Now, bear in mind that Huggy's got the broadest West Yorkshire accent; he's from Wakefield. So, we were in the office and Sean, who was running Orbit said, "I want to introduce somebody who is a really big force on the techno scene, meet Sven Väth." Huggy stood there with a bottle of Bacardi under his arm, and he looked across at Sven Väth and said in the broadest Wakey accent, "Sven Väth… [long pause]… have a bath!" Sven just stood there in this leather cape thing, looking at Huggy as if he had ten heads or something. It was absolutely comical. But it was the pause that got us. "Sven Väth… have a bath!" Huggy is one funny fucker.

Club culture was undergoing massive changes by '94 as many overground clubs were now getting late licences. This was great news for DJs, as this extended our working day (night) to make multiple gigs possible in a single night. Every big town had a club that would now go on until 6am, which was a dream come true for me. A lot of my work was in the north, which meant I could go do my business in Manchester, get paid, and then I could play out in Leeds or Wigan. Or I could go back to Leeds and go clubbing at Back To Basics which was pretty much the best night in the country at that time.

At the back end of 1993, I got residencies in London at the Leisure Lounge and Club UK, plus I was playing Bagley's. I was playing Leisure Lounge with people like Judge Jules, Steve Proctor, Lisa Loud and all those guys. They were great times, plus being in London meant I could shop for records at places like Zoom Records, Pure Groove and Black Market. Pure Groove was on Holloway Road, Archway and Zoom was also in the same manor. Nick Worthington, Tarik Nashnush and Ziad Nashnush ran Pure Groove and they introduced me to a guy called Steve Hill who was an absolute diamond! Steve is a wise old fox and if I ever need any advice on anything business related, Steve is my go-to man. His wisdom and his friendship means the world to me. Over the years, we have worked in the studio tonnes of times and done various gigs all over the world. Steve Hill and my mate Tim Simmons are the best!

Now clubbing in the UK was something that went on beyond 2am, I was often doing three sets in an evening. I remember finishing my set at the Leisure Lounge one night at 4.30am, and Ziad, Nick Worthington and Tariq took me to a night called Trade at Turnmills on Clerkenwell Road. There were 2,000 people in this place. "We've come so you can have a listen to this DJ. He's a bit special!"

Trade was a gay club, and there were about 1,800 blokes in there and 200 women. We were playing pool in the bar area when I heard this intro start. It was this rumbling, rising *whoosh* like an aircraft taking off, and it built right the way up, and then came back down. Then the sample dropped in, and it kicked off with this track I've never heard before. It was like a cross between CLS' *Can You Feel It* and *The Nighttrain* by Kadoc. "Who the hell is this?" I shouted to Tarik. "It's Tony De Vit!" I just remember thinking, 'Oh my God. Wow.' Tony took the roof off the place. He was on another level.

Tony started with this tough handbag-y house and just built it up and up over the next two hours. The bpm got up to at least 145 which was really quick for those days. It was really tough house. It was just phenomenal. He was also playing stuff from the Reactivate label and giving a big old nod to the old skool with rave samples. Tony's set had a really stabby *Dominator* sound and it was a real eye opener to see the level people could be taken to. Again, it was another inspirational moment just like watching Carl Cox for the first time. I was completely plugged into that moment. Tony De Vit was brilliant.

Three or four weeks after hearing Tony De Vit at Trade, I spoke to Rob from Ark and said, "Mate, I saw this guy Tony De Vit and he is fucking ridiculous!" It wasn't just me singing his praises either, he was making a real name for himself. "Rob, you need to check this guy out!" Rob Tyrrell used to rely quite heavily on the advice of myself and a few other DJs regarding who should be booked for Ark. So, we booked

Tony and about three or four weeks later, he was playing Ark and this club called The Ritzy; a huge Leeds club that did a one-off bank holiday. I'd had a dodgy curry that night, and I was feeling quite rough as Tony completely smashed it. I was back and forth to the toilets trying to get rid of this cuzza and had to waddle my way back across the dance floor like a gunslinger where there were about 1,900 people packed in like sardines. But Tony was just next-level good. What a DJ.

I remember running back to the loo four or five times during my set. I had to put a long track on and then slip out to the bogs. One of life's valuable lessons there, never ever eat anything out of your comfort zone before a gig. Go for something nice and English and steer clear of the spicy stuff before you play. Because you know what club toilets are like.

## Amadeus Mozart, Tidy Trax, Tidy Boys

*"I hadn't met Rob at this time, but we were probably aware of each other's names, seen them on flyers etc., but we'd never met. I don't think Rob played so many gay clubs. I wanted to play Trade and these really underground gay clubs and followed Tony De Vit's path a little bit more. There was a gay club in Leicester called Streetlife, which Tony played. And there was a night called Goodbye Cruel World, which was a ravey night that was taking over a gay club in Leicester, and I played those sorts of places.*

*So, in the summer of '95, Andy Pickles and I went into the studio and produced a fairly cheesy gay anthem called U Found Out by the Handbaggers, and that was the first release on Tidy Trax, at the end of September 1995.*

*Now, our goal was to have our tracks played by Tony De Vit. We were still a big fan of him. We wanted to be a label that you could go to Trade and hear in gay clubs, played out by Ian M, Steve Thomas, Tony De Vit and those Trade DJs in London who were breaking what was going to be hard house. It was hard, it was fast, it was hot and sweaty. That's where we wanted to be. That's where we wanted our music, and so we based that label purely on getting Tony to play it at Trade. And we got very fortunate, because Tony remixed the Handbaggers' U Found Out. We went from being a fan of Tony to Tony becoming a fan of us really, and he was soon a part of the family."*

Barry Mac and me at Garlands, 2001

Garlands at Kanya, Ibiza, 2002

Chilling at the infamous party villa before Godskitchen, 2001

*Mixmag* tent at Creamfields, 2005

Tidy at Es Paradis, Ibiza, 2004

David Guetta at Kissdafunk, 2007

Judge Jules and me with the entertainers at
Judgement Sundays, Ibiza, 2008

Steve Hill, Technikal and me, 2013

## Great Moments In Dance #2

### Love Decade, Leeds, July 1990

DJ Rob Tissera

**What was it?** Thanks to the success of clubs like Shoom and Hacienda, and illegal raves, the idea of acid house parties spread like a 303 virus. First Hardcore Uproar began in Blackburn, then Love Decade arrived. It was held in a warehouse in Gildersome, near Leeds.

**Who was there?** The promoters, DJ Rob Tissera, about 1,000 ravers and nearly as many coppers.

**What happened?** Lots of people danced to acid house, before the police raided the place and made history by conducting the largest mass arrest in Britain since 1412. 836 ravers were nicked and Rob Tissera was sentenced to three months in prison.

**What do they say now?** Says Rob Tissera: "Looking back on it, I can see why they decided to jail me. Basically, I gave the command for 1,000 people to riot. All I was trying to do was keep the party going." He still vividly remembers receiving his sentence. "I felt physically sick and my eyeballs were shaking. It was like I had a whiteout. Then they said 'Take him down' and shut me in the cells."

**What do we say now?** British society has always had a deep suspicion of young people gathering in large numbers without the supervision of a responsible adult. Tissera and co were hardly scout leaders, after all. The irony of the then government's clampdown is that they were instrumental in creating the institutionalised legal behemoth that is clubbing in 1999. Nice one Tory Party!

*Mixmag* clipping from 2008

Louise Savage Photography - Xstatic Summer Festival, 2015

Steve Hill and me at Frantic, 2015

Shot by Elle Savage - Tidy vs Goodgreef, NYD, 2016

Barry Mac, me, Dave Booth (RIP), Lil Jon Jon Beasant and Leon Knight, Garlands, Dubai, 2017

Me and Anna at Tidy, Sheffield, 2017

Me with Sam Townend at The Warehouse, Leeds, 2017

Lisa Lashes at Tidy at The Opera House, 2018

Tidy Xmas, 2017

Me at The Tony De Vit Memorial, The Mill Digbeth, 2022. Picture By Warren Simmens

Me with the Tidy Boys and Sam Townend from Tidy, at the Tony De Vit Memorial, 2018

The Warehouse, Leeds, 2017

Stu Allan (RIP) and me at Unity In The Sun, 2018

Clockwork Orange with Andy Manston and Danny Gould, London 2019

Me with DJ Vibes & Mark Ratpack. Unity in the Sun, 2021

Clockstock, 2022

Clockwork Orange at Amnesia, Ibiza, 2022

Liberation at Fabric, London, 2022

Me @ The Tony De Vit Memorial, The Mill Digbeth 2022 picture By Rob Farrell

Clockwork Orange 2023: Andy Manston, Alex P, Brandon Block and Jumpin Jack Frost

LHHR, New Zealand, 2023 with Steve Blake, Steve Hill, Technikal, Janelle Kleinhans Matchett, Lucy Fur, Luke Matchett, BK, Donna Birt and April Bordeaux

Dale Castell and me at Amnesia, Ibiza, 2023. Pic by Francis William Johnson

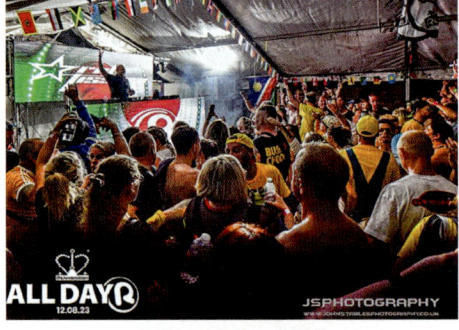

Rejuvenation, 2023

Cream at The Church, Leeds

Dale Castell, Marc Leaf and John Marshall. My fellow Our House residents

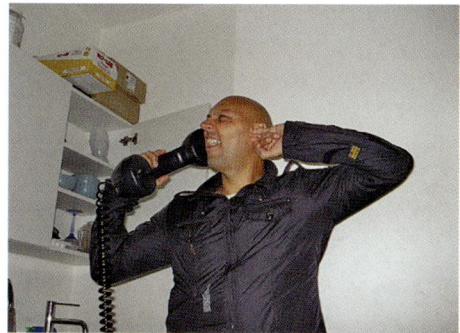

Giant phone

Joe Fossard and Lee Thompson,
sound engineers from Boomtown and the
Blackburn raves

Ian Bland and me clowning around on Zoom

Me at Tidy

Me with Si and Suzanne Frater from
Rejuvenation

Slinky at The Opera House Bournemouth,
2009

Slipmatt and Rachel Hill, Housework, Corfu

Steve Luigi 2nd left with me at
The Warehouse, Leeds

Storm at The Emporium

Tidy Church

London Hard House Reunion, Aukland, New Zealand, 2023 pic by Gary Sly Photography

# CH. 26

## rob Tissera

# The Rhubarb Triangle Of Bad Behaviour

Around the time of the prog house boom, I started a new chapter in my life when my then girlfriend Lis and I moved to Rothwell, a village about eight miles out of the centre of Leeds. It was a detached house in the Yorkshire countryside where I could play music until the cows came home, which they never did. Or maybe they were always at home. I don't know.

Anyway, I assembled my own home studio there, which just was the most enabling, life-changing experience for me. I'd spent years as a kid bashing about out on the bass, playing the same chord riff for hours when there were people in the background probably wincing to the awful din and now I was free to crank it up. Even when I moved to Rochdale, I had to practise mixing in an industrial unit, so to be in a lovely, detached cottage on the outskirts of Leeds, was just a brilliant move for me. As soon as I moved there I got the studio set up.

The cottage was double fronted with two really big double bedrooms that looked out onto the road. It was a big room and perfect for a studio. My dad and his friend Ian came over and helped to build the shelving for the records. And then a mate of mine, Ian Emberton built a really cool glass table that I still use to this day. Ian constructed a big glass table that you could fit three decks on, plus the mixer and tape recorder. I then put a 2K rig in there: 2 x 18" Peavy Black Widow bass bins and some

Martin top speakers for the treble. I now had 2,000 watts of sound at my disposal at all times.

Having a 2K rig at home meant that whenever I went out to DJ anywhere, I was never overawed by the sound. When you go from playing at home on an ordinary stereo to DJing in a club, there's a period of adjustment where you're trying to get used to how loud it all is. But that was no longer an issue for me, which is probably why I'm a bit deaf now. Pardon?!

Around then, Carl Finlow (one third of Circle City) moved from the centre of Leeds into a farmhouse with Ralph Lawson from Back To Basics and another guy called Fraser Brydson. Their farmhouse was just 500 yards down the road from where I now lived. Uh oh! More on that later. When I heard that Craig, Ralph and Fraser had moved to my village, I knew there would be some pretty crazy times ahead.

I was partying a lot at Back To Basics back then. Back To Basics was run by my friends who used to come to Audacity when there were just 30 of us. Dave Beer, Alistair Cook, Huggy and Ralph Lawson had created a monster of a club and I loved partying there once I'd finished my work for the evening. That was the beginning of 18 months of debauchery really from '93 to '94 and represented the pinnacle of my partying.

I went over to Ibiza in '94 with the guys from Back To Basics and stayed in a villa with them. There were us guys and Norman Jay who was as nice as pie, as was Charlie Chester. I met Charlie for the first time out there, even though I'd done a bit of work with him back in the UK. I went to Ku Club (before it was renamed Privilege), which was pretty much the biggest nightclub in the world at that time, with a 10,000 capacity. I was in the VIP bit with Charlie Chester at the top of the club when I nearly fell out of one of the windows. I was sat on a ledge, which had an 80-100ft drop below. I just remember talking to Charlie and laughing so much I laid back and almost fell out of the window. Somebody grabbed me just in time and pulled me back. It was really fucking close.

We all had a great time listening to Jazzy Jeff tapes in the villa and just mucking about. I remember somebody chopping up and snorting a chilli pepper one morning; easily one of the most stupid things I've ever seen in my entire life. In the bravado stakes it was a slam dunk. There'd been plenty of drink flowing and Dave was meant to do it as a £20 bet, but I can't remember who, but somebody jumped in and snorted this finely chopped chilli. Dave simply handed them the £20 and said, "There you go, you win!" Their eyes were just streaming with tears. It was like a scene from a Tom & Jerry cartoon. Ibiza was to be a regular haunt from that summer onwards.

Back in the UK, I was becoming a regular face at Back To Basics, but as a punter. The sound at Back To Basics was a lot deeper than the places I was playing. It was too cool for school in there, and I was definitely classed as being from the rave circuit. But the B2B posse were very accommodating, and we were close friends. We mostly put all that snobby stuff aside and I was quite good at dealing with the bants. You'd take a bit of flak and give a little back and just move on. Some of those guys from that scene could be a little disparaging about the rave sound and Ark and the white gloves and glow sticks, and all that. But that was fine.

The Durham Posse were another bunch of ravers I entertained at the cottage now and again. Pete Noom, Stuart Campbell and their mate Ronnie, plus a whole bunch of other weirdos and reprobates were completely mental. It was like partying with ten Chubby Browns; no topic was taboo. They ended up coming back to my house every single weekend after Back To Basics and because Carl and Ralph and everybody else lived at the farm 500 yards away, little Rothwell became Party Central.

There was a 300-yard dirt track that led up to their farmhouse so once you turned out onto the road, it was only 200 yards from where I lived. There were sometimes maybe 100 people at some of these parties in our houses. People would periodically be leaving one cottage, to go party in the other. Backwards and forwards all through the early hours. Rothwell was right in the epicentre of what's known as the 'rhubarb triangle' which produces the most rhubarb in the whole of Europe. The other guys actually lived in the rhubarb fields and so that meant completely spangled revellers having sword fights with 3ft-long sticks of rhubarb they'd pulled straight out of the ground – as well as other just bizarre wrongness – in those fields.

Dave Beer once went to our local shop in a fur coat, high heels and lipstick at 1pm on a Sunday lunchtime in this little village, which would have sent shockwaves through Rothwell. Because Back To Basics was so popular, and those guys were so connected, you had actors from *Brookside* and *Emmerdale* partying in Rothwell after a night at Back To Basics. These well-known faces would inevitably get the most smashed they'd ever got and would end up coming back to party at our houses. I remember coming back from the shop one time and spotting the neighbours across the road cutting their hedge. They were peering through the leaves to see this character Eddie Banks (Paul Broughton) from *Brookside*, complete with a black eye just jumping up and down on my garden wall. The neighbour mouthed to his wife, "That's Eddie Banks!" I walked past Eddie Banks on the garden wall holding court with all these kids from Back To Basics and said, "Guys, it's 1.30 in the afternoon!" Those guys were like the Shaolin masters of raving. The cream of the crop. 10th dan shit!

I was playing Ark and getting a few gigs at Back To Basics too, but feeling slightly torn between the two because if I wanted to play Back To Basics, I had to play their style; a big compromise for me. So, I ended up playing a techno set at Back To Basics in what was known as The Basement and I loved it. It was brilliant. But I definitely knew that my bread was buttered more heavily on the other side. Out of the back of that, I started getting bookings for Rezerection in Scotland, which was another huge energy-filled rave at The Royal Highlands Centre in Edinburgh. I remember standing in the corner thinking 'Gee, these guys lash it out. I really need to meet fire with fire.' I was watching this guy with gold teeth, who seemed to know Kenny Ken, chatting up my girlfriend. I was asking who he was. "Oh, that's Goldie and he's just done a track that's gonna be pretty BIG!" About a week after I saw him, he was in *Mixmag* and I thought "That's him!" And then I heard *Inner City Life*. Wow, and the rest was history.

***

I did a couple of remixes for Eastern Bloc Records in the summer of '94. I did a track called *Bolivian Angel* for some guys in Northern Ireland called Ubiquity, and that came out on Eastern Bloc Records, which was now being run by my friend Paul Taylor. With the backing of PWL records it also gave me the opportunity to remix a real classic which was *J.J. Tribute* by A.S.H.A. on Disco Magic Records. We did all the production in PWL Studios in Manchester, which was an amazing experience. We bumped into Paul Waterman, Pete Waterman's son, and that led to a firm friendship with some other legends from that area called Rhythm Quest, comprising Mark Hadfield and Stephen 'Woody' Wood. Mark went on to be Lucid and has written for people like Neo and loads of big acts.

Mark Hadfield, Paul Taylor and Paul Waterman became Loveland and were working in PWL Studio 1 in Manchester doing *Let The Music Lift You Up*, whilst Blandy and I were in the studio next-door doing A.S.H.A.'s *J.J. Tribute*; a heck of an honour working with some of the best guys in the best studios. I still viewed these things through the eyes of the 13-year-old me, with my first guitar. It was the stuff of dreams. Whilst we were in the studio, we bumped into this DJ called Anne Savage. Anne had a really bubbly, positive attitude and boy, could she DJ. She was amazing behind the decks and soon became a resident with me at Ark. Anne was an absolute lunatic and really funny.

\*\*\*

My driving has always been a problem. I have always been sober, but have on occasion pushed the gas a little too enthusiastically. I love driving at speed and rushing around from one gig to another does tend to create an impatience to get a move on. Many DJs have drivers, whether it's due to convenience or too many points on their licence, and I have had my share. I got banned for a while back in '95 and I accidentally acquired not only a new driver, but a lifelong nutter of a friend through Adrian and Mark Luvdup. This was my second ban because I was still a bit of a nutjob behind the wheel. My new driver, Wilba, was a proper character from Blackley, Manchester and was as funny as fuck, and we struck up quite a close friendship through our mutual friends. Then, following my ban in January '95, Wilba very kindly offered to drive for me when he wasn't driving Adrian and Mark. I was banned for six months and so Wilba ended up driving for me nearly every weekend and as a result, we became best friends.

I would say you probably have nine or ten people in your life who you would trust with anything, maybe not even that many, but Wilba is one of those, who, when the chips are down, is always there for me. Wilba's in the Diamond Posse. He would give you his last dime if you needed it. We spent so much time in the car, we developed a perfect understanding of each other. Wilba is a joy to be with, he really is.

# From The Club To The Club House

**Nick Halkes, formerly of XL, Positiva and more**

*"The most well-known stories of the UK dance music explosion tend to come from the south of the nation. However, without the pioneering work of Rob Tissera and several other key players based in the north, history would have been quite different and much less exciting. Rob's boundless enthusiasm, work ethic and skills have been a constant for decades and respect is due!"*

I played a lot of golf during the summer of '95. Dad was a very keen golfer who played off an 8-handicap and he taught me to play over the years. Whenever I played techno in Rhyl on the Friday night, I would arrive back in Leeds at 4am, just as the sun was beginning to rise. And it was a beautiful summer. I would go straight from the club to the golf course and play 18 holes. Then go home, get some kip and get ready to do my next gig that evening. I was doing that every week. But I ended up playing way too much golf because it was so addictive. I was happy and settled in my life and having a great time, making more cash than I'd ever made. But my future didn't lie in golf and I really had to rein myself in from too much time on the greens.

I started working for Eastern Bloc Records for a bit late '95/early '96 when things weren't going as well as they had been on the DJing front. The gigs had started to taper off a little bit and not just for myself, but for a few others as well; the winds of change were blowing and musical tastes were changing. I just had this really rubbish summer and this was partly down to the partying and playing too much golf, and all the rest of it. It was now one gig a week rather than say two or three, which wasn't cool. So, I took on this part time role working with Eastern Bloc, firstly in Manchester and then Leeds, when they opened a shop there.

During this period, I did a track called *Kick Up The Volume* with the help of Ian Bland and Nick Worthington who had formed a duo called Dancing Divaz. Dancing Divaz were blowing up and had remixed Baby D's *Let Me Be Your Fantasy* and The Original's *I Luv U Baby*. They did an amazing job on it; like you wouldn't believe. And on the strength of their remix, the track got signed by Nick Halkes at XL Recordings. It was quite different to the mix I'd originally done and on the strength of their remix the track got signed and so I can't lay claim to it all being my idea. Their mix of the track used a huge slice of the disco classic *Relight My Fire* by Dan Hartman and this seemed to really strike a chord with lots of DJs, including Judge Jules, who made it his record of the week on his hugely popular Kiss radio show in London. Jules then invited me to the studio to appear on his *Judge And The Jury* show where I appeared on a panel of other artists to review a bunch of new tracks. This was such a pivotal moment for me as prior to that all happening, I was seriously questioning if I had a future in the game as I had a horrendously poor summer, gig wise with six weeks of cancellations due to lots of promoters struggling during the summer months along with the poor choice of backing the progressive house sound. With the help of Ian Bland, Nick Worthington and the mighty Nick Halkes from XL I managed to get back to winning ways like never before. Nick Worthington also remixed Donna Giles' *I Am Telling You* and that track is pure fire.

All of a sudden, I was getting calls from promoters all over the world. I couldn't believe it and I'm eternally thankful to the three of them for backing me. As a result of their mix, a lot more people got to know my name, my music and everything else. I started to climb the ladder once more. That track was definitely on that massive, epic trip. And of course, those tunes went down really well in Northern Ireland where I was doing loads and loads of gigs. It had this power to it and left people feeling elated. I was very much into that big response to what I was doing, not that there was any kind of marketing strategy or anything. I just went the way the wind was blowing.

Now, this was an enormous up-turn in fortunes to the degree where I was getting phone calls from overseas, places like Germany, Australia and New Zealand. 'Do you want to come over and DJ for us over here?' Carl Cox was playing *Kick Up The Volume* as well. Carl loved the *Latin Love Machine* remix and it just blew up.

There were two charts back then: the pop chart and the dance chart and I was now number one in the dance charts. This was enormous news for me. I suddenly had all this stuff going on and it was great. That track was just this gateway to big international gigs. I owe an enormous amount of gratitude to Blandy, Nick Worthington and Nick Halkes, who would be a huge character and influence in my life over the years; his guidance was absolutely paramount.

### Ian Bland, Dream Frequency and Dancing Divaz

*"Kick Up The Volume was when Rob was struggling at the time and he got a bit of a lift-off in his career from that track. We were flying with Dancing Divaz, and Rob had stalled a bit, so we said, 'We'll help you out with a track.' And that's when we did Kick Up The Volume. Rob was very involved in doing that, and we did a mix as well. Like Rob said, it really put him back on the map. Kick Up the Volume was memorable and it did really well."*

\*\*\*

I got a phone call from these promoters Mal Greene, Rob Milton and Michelle Russell in '96 who ran the Underground Cafe in Sydney, Australia. "Do you want to do a tour for us? We'll bring you out. You can do Sydney, Melbourne and New Zealand." I flew over, knowing this was a monumental moment. My first international gig.

When I arrived, it was around 9.30pm and I was firmly in the 'wide awake club'. They put me up in a lovely apartment overlooking Bondi Beach, and I was thinking, 'Wow!' I just couldn't sleep. I was a young, single bloke and I wanted to find the coolest place to go. I hailed a taxi and just said, "Mate, can you take me to where it's going down in Sydney?" He took me to Kings Cross, which was full of bars and young people. There was a red-light district there too, the whole friggin' lot. It was all going on there. It was about as exciting as it got.

Now, I was literally on the other side of the planet and walking down this road in Kings Cross, coming up towards this big bar. I could hear the muffled sound of music coming out of the bar. And as I got closer, I could now hear the music coming out onto the street to entice punters in. 'Jeezus, that's my track!' I couldn't believe it. Everyone in the bar was going mental to *Kick Up The Volume*! There was a lot of student activity in that area and this bar was full of young people just going mental to this tune. I just stood there for a while thinking 'This is unbelievable!'

I didn't go in for some reason, but carried on a bit further down the road and heard the track again through some outdoor speakers. It was absolutely insane. How could that even happen? It was a remarkable and special moment that will stay with me forever. I'm so grateful to everyone in our team who helped get that over the line.

I'd really been down on my luck and definitely had some dark thoughts that year when the gigs started to dry up. But I think everybody has those thoughts at some point in their lives. But I'm not the sort of person who would ever carry anything out. And so this evening in Sydney was a huge uplift for me.

I played out the following night on the Thursday, and it was absolutely mobbed. I played the track and the response was just phenomenal and so that was a springboard to some pretty fantastic years, which led me to doing super clubs in the UK and more stuff for Club UK and Leisure Lounge as well Bowlers and Ark.

Nick Halkes was keen for me to do a follow up single on XL and he introduced me to a guy called Mick Shiner who ran Strongroom studios in east London. Strongroom was amazing, this beautiful studio with these ornate pictures all over the walls. Strongroom had this flying fader mixing console, which was the latest state-of-the-art technology. Nick also put me in touch with this engineer called Alistair and I brought a musician friend of mine called Chris Rushby to help put this track together. Now, there were loads of other acts recording stuff in the other studios; indeed Mark Morrison was doing *Return Of The Mack* in one room. And we were having lunch in the communal area when Mick Shiner introduced us to these girls who were playing pool. "Do you fancy a game?"

– "Yeah! Go on."

And so we had a game of pool with these girls. And Mick said, "Watch out for them, they're going to be massive." I took this with a pinch of salt. And then a few weeks later, I was sat watching *Top of the Pops* and I saw those girls again: it was Mel B and Mel C of Spice Girls.

This track we were recording turned out shit and it failed to get signed basically, but it wasn't the end of the world. My DJing was getting busy again and although I would have liked to have had a follow up on XL, there wasn't much I could do about it. But it was an amazing experience.

# CH. 28

rob
tissera

# Take A Chance On Trance

Back in January of '96, Adrian Luvdup put my name forward to a few promoters in Sheffield, including Jason Herd who ran Rise. Jason gave me the last set at Rise on a frequent basis, playing the tracks that would lead to trance. Trance had been bubbling away for a while and then we heard the music from Reactivate and those labels, and music being made by Blu Peter, Sister Bliss and Tony De Vit. Things were moving away from handbag and hardbag a little, towards this trance sound. And the Rise gigs were absolutely on point for that sound, which was fantastic.

I was still doing lots of gigs in Northern Ireland, such as Kelly's in Portrush and Kilwaughter House in Larne, run by this lovely bloke Mark Dobbin. The hotel was run by his mum and dad and it had a small nightclub out the back, which would get mobbed. Tall Paul, Tony De Vit and all those guys played Kilwaughter House which probably held about 5-600 people, tops. When you stood in the DJ box, which was not massive, you'd have a lighting jock to your left-hand side. And then if you stepped back there was a hatch. If you opened the hatch, it led down into a snug, located under the stage. The snug was more of a green room, where you could get maybe 10 people in along with a set of decks. That's where all the main faces would go after the show. The other DJs would also sit in there while you were playing.

I can remember Mark Dobbin introducing his little brother to Tony De Vit one night. "Tony, this is Robert and he wants to be a DJ…" Tony and Robert got on like a house on fire. Tony was giving this 15-year-old advice on how to become a DJ. And fast forward a few years and you have Fergie. To be there, as that conversation was happening, was incredible. Rob was just taking it all in, as Tony imparted his colossal wisdom. Rob and Mark were so grateful to Tony for that and it's a memory that will stay with me forever.

***

Anne Savage and I started playing for Cream in 1996, when it was at Liverpool's Wolstenholme Square. Then Ark formed an alliance with Cream that same year with Ark Versus Cream nights in Leeds and a few other places. We did quite a few Cream gigs and I played alongside Carl Cox, Rocky & Diesel, Paul Bleasdale and many more. The first night going over there was a big moment for us. I just remember riding over to Liverpool with Anne who was super, super nervous, although she'd been doing a lot of stuff at Angels in Burnley and for Ark before Cream came along. We stopped at a service station for a quick motivational talk: "You're a tiger!" and all the rest of it, which always makes me laugh because whenever Anne goes on stage, she absolutely smashes it every single time. But she does get very nervous. And then, when it was her turn to play, boom! It was great.

And then that club became what it became, so it was nice to be there right from the very beginning of Cream. And this new alliance between Ark and Cream was a great continuation of that for me, and I bonded with people like Tall Paul through that collaboration. I was also still playing for Strawberry Sundays and Sunnyside Up in London.

***

1996, I get a phone call one afternoon from a guy called Simon Raine. "I'm starting a new night in Sheffield and I want you to be a resident."
- "Oh, cool, what is it?"
- "Gatecrasher."

Gatecrasher had started in Birmingham in the early '90s, but the crowded club scene there had the promoters Simon Raine and Scott Bond looking to put nights on elsewhere, namely Sheffield. It certainly sounded interesting, but I didn't give it another thought. Within a few days I got a message from Jason Herd, who ran Rise saying he was joining forces with Gatecrasher. I thought to myself 'OK, these guys sound like they might be movers and shakers.' I was invited down to do the opening night of Gatecrasher at the Arches in Sheffield; they'd successfully played the Leadmill prior to that. I was playing upstairs with Adrian Luvdup, while Jeremy Healy and Boy George played downstairs.

I was halfway through my set, and the place was bouncing, when this really angry looking bloke came right up in my face. "Oi, I'm Simon Raine and I run Gatecrasher, what the fuck are you doing?!"

– "I'm playing music."

– "I've just paid two grand to have Jeremy Healy and Boy George downstairs, and there's no one down there. So, you better fucking do something about that. Start playing shit music!"

– "What?!"

– "Play the B-sides or I'll kick you off." I was fuming and so was he.

– "I can go one better than that," I told him and took the needle off the record. I put the record back in my box and said, "Ere you fucking go, mate. That's it."

– "What are you doing? Where are you going? Put the record back on!"

– "Fuck off!" I looked him straight in the eyes and told him to do one.

And there began a very fractious relationship with those guys. In fact, Simon contacted me a while later, saying he wanted me to be a resident at Gatecrasher when they eventually moved to their permanent home at The Republic. "It's gonna be amazing, this thing. You are exactly what I'm after." He was fairly brazen about it. "Because we've got the best gig coming in Sheffield and we're going to wipe everybody else out. And I want you to be my resident."

Because of his absolutely stinking attitude, I just thought, 'No way, pal.' He was so ungracious. Most people know me as somebody who's always smiling and always polite, The Smiler! But if you cross me, I will bite back. I wasn't going to be spoken to like that, by a bloke like that. He was so incredibly rude.

Gatecrasher was an aggressive brand – hence the name – and it created a 30-35-mile exclusion zone for their DJs which prevented them from playing at any local rivals. So, any DJs playing Gatecrasher couldn't play for Ark anymore. In fact, Gatecrasher killed off Ark.

I'll hold my hands up and probably say I regret that in some respects because Gatecrasher was right on my doorstep, within 30 miles of where I lived. It would have been far better for me to be doing that on a regular basis. I probably should have managed it an awful lot better. But I turned him down. There's no telling how things will pan out, but it would have meant being in bed with Simon Raine, although I really liked his business partner Scott Bond. A lot of DJs have negative stories about their times with Gatecrasher so in some respects I'm glad I stood my ground. But it was a little costly. Ha ha.

# CH. 29

rob
Tissera

# The Perfect Kiss

1997, I received a call from Tim Sheridan at Kiss FM, who was also a member of Dope Smugglaz. I'd been doing a few things with Kiss through the *Kick Up The Volume* track and done a couple of guest mixes when they decided to open up a station in Leeds, following a recent launch in Manchester. They called me, Graeme Park, Tony Walker and Utah Saints to do shows. I was never ever going to say no to that. I was given my own radio show on Kiss FM doing Saturday nights 9-11pm, which went out across Manchester and Leeds. That primetime-on-a-Saturday-night slot was fantastic news because there weren't really any others. Pete Tong and Judge Jules' shows were on a Friday, so there wasn't much competition on a Saturday. This show gave me an amazing opportunity to ply my trade and it opened a multitude of doors. I started getting lots more work in more commercial clubs as well, which did me no harm whatsoever.

I was receiving maybe 40 or 50 promos a week at that time and I now had thousands of records in my home studio, almost to the degree where the walls were closing in on me. I had records in every room of the house. Some good and some not so good because you got sent some real bullets, and some proper rubbish too. I was being sent loads of test pressings and had people arriving on motorbikes with acetates that they wanted me to play on a Saturday night on primetime radio.

My DJ studio had these great big shelves, just like being in a record shop that went from the floor to the ceiling. The records were face-on with enough headroom in each of these shelves, for me to be able to turn the records on their side so that I could actually see what I was looking for. I used to stand on an elephant's foot to get to the top shelf.

I was starting to get acetates of this newly-forming scene called UK garage around '97; tracks like *Double 99* by Ripgroove. There was a club in Sheffield called Niche that was playing garage at that time and I was playing at a club in Leeds called Casa Loco, run by Phil Easy, that was to become a legendary bassline club. Marc Leaf and I were the residents there right at the beginning with these test pressings of brand-new tracks by Armand van Helden, Tuff Jam and all the stuff on Ice Cream Records, which got a lot of over-the-shoulder action from rival DJs. It was quite a moment. I only played that stuff for maybe a year and a half, but it was bang on trend and as I've said on many occasions, my heroes are people like David Bowie and Madonna because I loved how they could just morph into doing new styles. And so, I wouldn't say reluctantly, but I inadvertently fell into the bassline world for a while. There were some other progressions coming along too, plus the trance thing was beginning to build.

Ark had started to draw to a close at the back end of '96, although we carried on for a couple more months because the demand was so strong, and that was all credit to Rob Tyrell and Tom Edge. However, Gatecrasher was making life difficult for Ark. It was a real shame. But as one door closes, so another opens.

The final ever Ark was Feb '97. It was packed with 2,200 ravers at the Refectory in Leeds University. There wasn't a dry eye in the building as I played the final three tracks, which were Energy 52's *Cafe Del Mar*, Ultracynic's *Nothing Is Forever* with the killer encore of *Unfinished Sympathy* by Massive Attack. I couldn't stop crying. It was truly humbling to be a part of a movement as glorious as Ark. It's still one of the pinnacles of my 30 odd years in the business.

Majestyk was a brand-new club in Leeds located in this amazing old Grade II-listed Victorian building down by City Square. The venue was a huge old cinema or bingo hall in days gone by and it was there that I played alongside Fatboy Slim for the first time, which was quite an experience. It was absolutely rammed with about 2,000 revellers. You really do feel like you're living your best life on those nights. It was fantastic. And then out of the back of playing there, I was gaining more and more contacts.

I started doing gigs further afield especially in the south west. I played for some guys down in Plymouth and Newquay. I played Lizzy

Pentire once a month during the summertime which was Cornwall's answer to Ark for a friend of mine, Adam Sims – it was the best thing down that way. My reputation was spreading out down there and I was now being invited to places like Bournemouth while still doing lots of stuff in London at Leisure Lounge and Club UK as well as gigs in the Midlands for Charlie Chester.

***

I had been DJing on Kiss for about 18 months when Galaxy suddenly took it over. I was invited to carry on doing the Saturday night slot at 9-11pm, which was an absolutely brilliant primetime slot across the Galaxy network. So, I had no complaints even though it felt a bit of a shame to change the name from Kiss to Galaxy. That said, it was still a huge station that had all the same infrastructure and pretty much the same staff as Kiss. Big thanks to Tim Sheridan for getting me that Kiss gig in '96 because that gave me the opportunity to meet Graeme Park, who was also on the network. I actually told Graeme that he was the reason I'd moved to the north. He was very, very humble. "Don't be daft. I'm not the reason you moved up here."
  – "Yes, you are. You and Mike Pickering actually changed my life."
  – "No we didn't."
It was incredible playing alongside those legends. Graeme Park is one of the nicest blokes you'll ever meet.

***

I remember getting sent a curious track while at Galaxy. It was an acetate with very little information on it. It was a funky, but proggy track; and I played it quite a bit. The PR blurb that came with it had a mobile number on it and so I rang it. I ended up talking to this guy and he seemed really friendly and he even suggested we hook up at his London studio sometime to make some music. Not long after, I arranged to meet this bloke and we got down to putting a tune together. We got to a certain point in the record and he was going on about the middle eight section of this track. I was saying, "Look, with the greatest respect, I don't think it needs to be that musical there. Instead, we could pop in a chorus to make it more popular in the clubs." He seemed a little bemused by my comments and said, "Come with me." He led me out of the basement of this beautiful studio and up some stairs. I remember thinking 'Wow!' This building was incredible and in this really posh part of London. We entered this dressing room and there hanging on the door was a white wig that looked like a jellyfish and some gold discs on the wall. This guy was Nick Beggs, the bassist of '80s popsters Kajagoogoo. "So, I do know a little about making popular tracks," he said, smiling.

   – "Ah, OK. Gotcha!" One large slice of humble pie for me.

***

Gerard Franklin ran a promotions agency called VF1 Publicity and he came a-calling off the back of my Galaxy shows. Gerard ended up doing my PR and got me into lad mags as well as on front cover CDs for *Fast Car* magazine. He also sealed two articles for *DJ Magazine* and *Mixmag* and so he was quite an influential character for me back then because he could certainly pull a few strings. His PR agency also dealt with Dave Pearce, Tall Paul, Seb Fontaine and several others. I also got some Ibiza gigs in '97 which included doing my Galaxy radio show live from Cafe Mambo, which was a hell of a moment for me. Gerard was putting me into situations where I was meeting the right people at the right time. And sometimes you need that little bit of help.

# CH. 30

rob
Tissera

# Uropa,
# Madders And It's
# All Gone Tong

Dance music was in a constant evolution. We'd almost gone from the house era into the handbag and Trade-style music and now there were labels like Noom Records, a great German outfit that was putting out the harder, more dramatic, trancey sound. I was in love with all that trance stuff and so were the audiences. I was definitely getting sucked into that world.

The second time the Birmingham night Sundissential came to Leeds I got a call from the legendary Paul 'Madders' Madan who had made the night such a success in Brum. Madders was looking for a second home in the north; Leeds in particular. He had come to me because of my connections with Galaxy and had seen me playing these more commercial clubs including Uropa in Leeds, previously known as Mr Craigs, which was attached to The Gallery. This club was a First Leisure venue; a real Sharon and Tracy night and Leafy was doing the Friday night and I was playing there regularly too, at least a couple of times a month. I got to know the promoter, John and he told me that Uropa had unfortunately gone from being massively popular in the '80s, even the early '90s, but had nosedived recently. Saturday nights were OK, but the Friday nights were totally dead, even though we were doing the Galaxy stuff there. It just wasn't working for him. And John said to me, "Believe me, Rob, this is a brilliant venue."

– "John, it *is* a brilliant club, I love the way it looks and everything else. It's a great club. But I don't know *why* it's not working."

– "Look, if you ever hear of anybody who's interested in doing stuff in here, give me the nod."

And lo and behold, a few weeks later, Madders called up and said, "I'm looking for a venue in Leeds." I instantly thought of Uropa, which had huge potential and was much in need of a new lease of life and a new crowd.

Anne Savage and I met Madders at the Marriott Hotel right in the centre of Leeds, one Thursday afternoon. Madders was really sweating one out; he had a reputation that preceded him – ha ha. Madders was a real livewire; probably the biggest livewire I've ever met. He was such a loose cannon. "I'm looking for a venue, man. What can you sort us out with?"

– "Well, I'll tell you what, why don't we go and have a look at this place called Uropa?"

We went up to see it and he was like, "Woah, this is it!" The DJ was positioned at the far end of this two-level room that held 1,500 people. There was a 6ft drop from the DJ booth to the main dance floor and podiums with raised areas along both sides. If you looked up from the booth you could see the floor above, plus you had about 150 people standing behind you. It was this amazing amphitheatre of a venue; you could look in any direction and see people dancing. Galaxy were only getting 200 people into this place that held 1,500 and so people were rattling around in it. But I'd been to Mr Craigs when it was full and so I knew what it could be like. I knew it could be so good. And so we set about doing Sundissential North.

I went down to Birmingham to do some market research at Sundissential. I didn't ask to be put on the guestlist or anything. I just thought I'm gonna go down as a punter and see what works. I already knew that the guys played a bit tougher and harder down there with a definite nod to trance. I drove down to Birmingham on a Saturday night, paid my money to get in and just looked around. These were the days of silver cyber gear and all that, and Sundissential was a young crowd. 'It's Ark on steroids!' The music was slightly different to Ark in that it was much harder house. It was similar to what Tony De Vit had been playing, but also interspersed with the harder end of trance. I just stood there and thought, 'OK, I'm gonna need to go next level at Sundissential North and make it really, really good.'

I was invited to play down in Birmingham a few weeks later and it went really well. And as a result of that, when it came to making Sundissential work in Leeds, I knew exactly what the level needed to be. The two main residents at Sundissential in Leeds were me and Anne Savage, plus we had Fergie, Ian M (a big Midlands legend) and Andy Farley, Tall Paul, Judge Jules, Pete Tong, Jon Pleased Wimmin, Sonique and Jeremy Healy and all those guys were also booked, plus they had great residents in Nick Rafferty and Paul Kershaw.

It was quite a big deal to bring something as good as Sundissential to Leeds and it took off like a rocket; people absolutely loved it because it was slightly harder than the Gatecrasher sound. Plus, my USP was to switch between playing the really hard stuff and a bit of trance before returning to the hard stuff using the most powerful weapon in music: contrast. I loved sliding in and out of those two styles and people loved it. I used to play bootleg mixes of *Sweet Dreams (Are Made of This)* which just exploded. There was a remix called *Sweet Dreams 99* by Tact 2 (Colin Butts who wrote *Is Harry on the Boat?*) and I played it everywhere. 'Woah, *Sweet Dreams*!' We got to a point where they'd have to bury me in a box with *Sweet Dreams* in it, because I played it at every single Sundissential until the crowd started to demand it. My involvement in setting Sundissential up in Leeds was such a boost to my career.

I was still working with Ian Bland and making music at this point too. We were beginning to pursue our love for the trance stuff and we got offered some work doing a remix of this track by Ann Nesby called *Can I Get A Witness?* This track was a Ministry Of Sound style track; a bit garage and a little Todd Edwards and we did this trance remix of it. We took it to Simon Dunmore at AM:PM and I remember sitting down with him and playing him that tune. However, he turned it down. The track was eventually released on DMC Records through Guy Ornadel.

We did a couple of versions of *Can I Get A Witness?* and as a result there were some other parts hanging around on the cutting room floor that we decided were a bit too trancey. So, we took those parts and worked them up into something else, which is what a lot of producers do once they've established an identity; basically using old songs as templates. So, we took the template of that track and created this trance track. It took us a few weeks, but we eventually got all the music together with the Ann Nesby vocal, in order to give us something that had the power from which we could write the chords, bass and pads around. Then we took that vocal off and we set about writing some lyrics for a completely fresh vocal track. We were sat in the studio one day and Ian said, "What about this line?" and he sang, "The day will come." And I thought wow that's a brilliant line.

I've written a bit of poetry over the years; even at school. I was always quite good at English and so I suggested another line and between us, over the next week or two, either in person or on the telephone, we built this song called *The Day Will Come*, which was to be a full-on trance tune.

And then we set about looking for a vocalist. We got to know these guys from Development Corporation, namely Johnny Ekubia and Lee Monteverde who produced the track *The Key: The Secret* for Urban Cookie Collective. Lee had also worked with A Guy Called Gerald and Lucid and introduced us to this vocalist called Doreen who sang under the stage name Marcia Rae who had done backing vocals for Simply Red. Johnny from the Development Corporation told us, "This girl is brilliant. Use her!" So, we arranged to record her at the studio in Preston where Cornershop recorded *Brimful Of Asha*, which was run by a mate of Blandy's.

We met Doreen (Marcia) at the train station and picked her up. She was this beautiful, mid-40s woman. She had the look of a larger, diva-type singer, but had not a single air nor grace about her; just this lovely, bubbly woman. So, we set off to the studio from the train station and she said, "Right, before we do anything, I need a bottle of brandy. So, we stopped at the offie to get her a half a bottle of brandy which she well and truly tucked into.

We'd sent Doreen the music and the lyrics and Blandy had given her a guide vocal of where the melody needed to go. She said, "Right guys, before we get started, we need a group cuddle." So, we did that, which was a real ice breaker and then I went to make her a cup of tea.

Once we were ready to record, I left the booth and watched from the kitchen. I could see her behind the glass of this proper 24-track desk. She put her headphones on, the song came on and she started. And she sang it. Boy did she sing it. I ended up having to lie on the floor because she was so good. It was the best thing I'd heard in my entire life and it was all of our own making. But Doreen put the cherry on top and even to this day it gives me tingles down my spine. Her vocal chords just blew us away. She was totally awesome and completely nailed it.

In order to get some feedback, I decided to go to Music House on the Holloway Road, London to get the track cut into an acetate I could play out. I went to Pure Groove first, to buy some vinyl and then onto

Music House; a legendary place in the jungle/DNB, hardcore breakbeat scene.

You would queue up in the back streets of Holloway Road in this housing estate in inner city London, which was definitely not for the faint hearted. I was sat in the queue at Music House with Grooverider, Kenny Ken, Fabio and all those guys waiting to get their dubplates cut. Because jungle was a *big* thing now. They knew me from the early breakbeat scene up north in the early 90s and I remember warning them, because you could all hear what was going on in the studio: "It's not jungle!" It took about an hour to get one cut and so all these dnb legends were sat there listening to this trance track. It was quite a stressy situation to be honest. And then when I'd finished, they were all quite complimentary. Kenny Ken told me, "Boss, I'm not normally into that kind of stuff, but that's a tune!" So, even though it was not their thing, they still liked it, which was great.

Roger Faversham used to run a pub in Leeds round the back of the University; a student pub basically. It was a really great pub that had two floors and a room big enough to get 300 people in, complete with DJ booth. We did the Ark after-parties at the legendary Faversham or 'Fav' that hosted Paul Oakenfold, Frank De Wulf, Smoking Jo and all that lot. The resident DJ was Phil Faversham who went from being Roger Faversham's mate to being the resident DJ at these after-parties. He then got himself a job as a runner for London Records and FFRR Records. And before you knew it, he was second in command to Pete Tong scouting for London Records and FFRR in particular.

Phil went to various clubs every weekend looking for new talent and because we were good mates he phoned me up one time to see what I was up to. I'd started playing for Sundissential in Leeds and Phil said he was going to come up and see me play. I'd got that acetate of *The Day Will Come* and played it second to last track in my set. Sundissential was busy and the place just exploded. There were about 1,500 sweat-drenched people in there and they were going mad. The venue was a multifaceted place and the DJ was centrally positioned, providing a great vantage point. So, I could see the damage on the dance floor. It ripped the roof off. I didn't warn Phil that I was going to play this record, because I didn't want to build it up only to see it fail to reach his expectations. I just played it, and straight after he wanted to know what it was. "Wow. That's amazing!"

– "Yeah, it's something Blandy and I have done."

I was sat in a cafe called Opporto in Leeds on a Wednesday afternoon having a coffee when I received a private call from a landline. These calls were usually from Blandy as he had a private number. Bearing in mind that Blandy was a keen practical joker and even had a box of props in the studio with wigs and glasses in it, plus he could do a million different accents, I was pretty sure it would be him. "Hi, is that Rob?"

– "Yeah."

– "It's Pete Tong. I want to talk to you about that Quake track Phil Faversham just played to me. I want to sign it."

– "Fuck off Blandy, I know it's you!"

– "No, it's me, Pete Tong. I'm sorry, but I haven't got my radio voice on. I'm just calling you because that track is absolute fire and I love it. Come down to London and we'll do a deal."

The penny finally dropped; it *was* Pete Tong. I stepped out of the bar and made a profuse apology. "Yes, Pete, sorry, I thought it was a wind-up."

Blandy and I went down to Warner Records HQ not far from Charing Cross and went up in this glass lift to see Pete Tong. We signed a pretty healthy deal for this track. Unfortunately, it didn't do as well as we'd hoped. FFRR had also signed a track by Lucid, which was scheduled to come out on the very same day as ours. I guess it was a simple case of radio pluggers needing to focus on certain songs to push and we lost out and Lucid won. I'm happy to admit that Lucid was a bigger record than ours. So that one did better for FFRR, but we still went to 38 in the national charts, which was an amazing achievement and it did me no end of favours in terms of club bookings because trance was just beginning to break through. I think if it hadn't been for that Lucid track, it would have gone a bit higher in the chart, but no regrets because it was a huge success for all of us in terms of the way it was received in the clubs, and what it did for me as a DJ. That track gave me another lease of life.

The FFRR release, plus the work Gerard Franklin was doing in getting me press had really turned things around for me. Every now and again you need to get your fingers into the rock face to pull yourself up to another level. From that moment on, I would always get somebody coming up to the DJ booth asking me to play *The Day Will Come* and it appeared on lots of compilations from Cream, Ministry Of Sound and Godskitchen. It was also a big track at Gatecrasher and Slinky and so a big landmark moment in my career.

# The Cottage, A Hog Roast Fire And The Little Black Clouds

1998 and I was living around the corner from Ralph Lawson and Carl Finlow and all those guys at the little cottage. My landlady's husband recently passed away and she wanted to consolidate some of her properties so she sold me this place. I'd been living there for the past four years and it was not without its faults. It was a craggy old cottage built in 1898 and it had been the village bakery at some point. Much later, my landlady and her husband, a farmer, bought the house and did it up. They put this disgusting render all over the walls, but instead of it being smooth, they'd done it in big swirls on the outside of the cottage; it looked really bad. However, it was nice inside with my stuff in it, even if it was a tatty old place.

I bought the cottage for £57,000, which was OK for a double fronted gaff; it was essentially two little cottages joined together with a huge double living room. I was just a young spunky 30-something bloke who didn't really listen to people when you really *should* pay attention. I did a survey on the house, but not the full-on structural one to find out exactly what needed to be done. Bad move, because there were a couple of torrential downpours a couple of years into my owning it.

The cottage flooded twice, once where the water went right up to your knees downstairs, which meant it all needed to be renovated on the inside again, after I'd done shitloads of work to it. It was disastrous and all down to the fact that it didn't get picked up in the survey. Had I paid only a few quid more, the survey would have shown a history of flooding. That was one of the biggest disasters of my entire life to be honest and it ended up costing me dearly later on down the line.

At this point I was doing better than ever in what felt like the pinnacle of my career with the Quake remixes and all the trance stuff happening. I was out DJing at least three to five times a week and so I could afford to rescue this cottage. I found this builder through a mate who took the cottage on during his time off from his day job. He worked a lot at the weekends when I was out playing, which was perfect. It would have been very handy to have a management schedule as to how long this renovation would take and how much it would cost, but I wasn't thinking. And then kerching! This builder completely fleeced me like you wouldn't believe. I think my reputation preceded me because he knew what I did. 'Here comes the cash cow!'

So, every weekend for the next two years, he was in my house. In the meantime, I bought every single interiors magazine such as *Living Etc.*, to get ideas on how to make this place pukka. I was always in and out of airports and on trains and so I would pick up all these magazines for inspiration.

I wanted to knock the two living rooms into one big space with a fireplace in the centre that you could run around if you scored a goal on *Pro Evo*. I got somebody to design this fireplace, which was to have a fire bowl in the middle of it. The builder felt I was getting a bit carried away, but I got an architect to design the room and the fireplace. And then all the builder had to do was knock out the central fireplaces at the centre of the room with a J-Beam to support the ceiling to make this an all-singing, all-dancing huge fucking fire pit that you could roast a pig in. It would be cracking. At least 3ft across and at least 2ft wide, this was to be a living gas-fired furnace. Turn the dial and you'd have this huge bloody flame within seconds. 'I'm gonna need to take my shirt off, I'm boiling!'

The builder agreed to knock the old fireplaces out. "It will be done by the time you get back," he told me. I went away to Majorca with BCM doing some stuff with Gordon Phillips and DJ Jason Fubar and a couple of others and got back to the UK on the Monday evening. I walked in the door and every single inch of the room was covered in black soot, where he'd knocked the chimneys through. This cottage was black with dust. And then it hit me. The records! I'd forgotten to ask the builder to move my 2,000 records from one of the living rooms into the spare room before the fireplaces came down.

I opened the sleeve of A.S.H.A.'s *JJ Tribute*, this amazing Italian house track from 1989, which I bought at Manchester Underground. It held such memories for me. The first time I played it out was at Zone in Blackpool all those years ago. I opened the sleeve, just praying that it was OK. 'Please don't be fucked. Please don't be fucked…' Cough. Splutter. It was fucked. There was black dust from both sides of the vinyl that puffed up into a cloud of smoke, almost in slow motion. A piece of history completely ruined.

I tried to rub the soot from the vinyl, but it had gripped onto the surface, so if you blew it, it just attracted your spit. The only way to remove the grit would have been to wet the vinyl with a cloth that was not going to put fibres onto the record. I tried that for a good half a day, but the records were screwed. There was a skip outside and I know this sounds terrible, but I dumped the whole 2,000 records into it. This was a scene that woke me up at nights in a cold sweat, but that's what I did. I dumped the lot. God almighty that was an awful experience. The recovery process went on for at least two years and it must have cost me thousands to replace the ones I *could* replace.

The bathroom was a 70s nightmare. From the moment I first walked in, it had this porn shoot shagpile vibe, with dogshit brown carpet going up the steps into an avocado bath. It was disgusting. For years I vowed that, should the occasion present itself, I would turn this shithole of a bathroom into a sparkly gem of a palace. And that's exactly what I did. I spent £10,000 turning the bathroom into a really cool wet room, even though it took the builder forever and cost me a lot of dough.

The builder did a fantastic job, even if it did go over budget and timescale. Now, all the walls were totally symmetrical and looked fantastic, as did the living room and the hog-roast gas fire. It was a great place and I will always be so proud to have done all that stuff in the house, but it wasn't without cost, that's for sure. And it wasn't without tears. 2,000 records! Poof! Gone. I managed to replace a lot of the stuff, but it wasn't my brightest moment, that's for sure. Although the builder should have known better, the root of all my troubles can definitely be traced back to good old me.

***

Living in that house on my own for four years between '94 and '98 meant I needed somebody to clean the place and take care of my washing etc. I advertised in the local paper for a cleaner and appointed Margaret O'Sullivan as my personal assistant; she would do all my cleaning, washing and ironing, plus she would do the odd bit of driving or a visit to the bank. It sounds absolutely mental now, looking back on it, but that's how busy I was. I had so much stuff going on I actually had to employ somebody to help me manage my 'life', because there was so much to be done.

Back in those days, you couldn't just send a music file to somebody digitally. You had to physically go and take that disc to the post office and post it. Margaret was now doing all that stuff for me. And she was an absolute angel; a gift from the gods. She was also a very interesting person and great company when we both happened to be in the house at the same time. I just could not manage all the domestic stuff with the amount of travelling I was doing. I was definitely clocking up 'sales rep' miles going from Cardiff to Newcastle, then Newcastle to Stoke, then Stoke down to Bournemouth, all in the space of say Thursday, Friday, Saturday. Playing Room At The Top in Bathgate, Scotland and all these sorts of places and having people drive me there. Adam Falkingham was driving me for a bit, as was Chris Duff and my good mate Ian Emberton. You really need that help to be able to prop yourself up so you can get up and go play your records.

I have always been fastidious in practising for sets. I practise a lot. I will prep for two or three days before a big gig in order to deliver a good hour somewhere. I like to have a strong framework and different routes to go down; remember there was no technology to help you mix in-key or whatever. Playing bass as a teenager had given me that ear for what sounded right, so I could play off-the-cuff as well. But there were always some sets where you needed those scripted moves. I loved to blind people with science and to get people listening to me knowing they're watching and moving around to my tunes. You need to be able to pull off some real bobby dazzlers and I spent a lot of time preparing those sets. And in the background, a lot of my friends were helping me win in so many other aspects of my life and career. And so I've always tried to look after them as well as they have always looked after me.

# CH. 32

# RIP

If there's a spiritual home of dance music, certainly for us Europeans, it has to be Ibiza. Chicago, New York and Detroit may have taken that European electronic sound and made it danceable, but it was the culmination of that music, the Balearic vibes and the drugs that established the acid house phenomenon that swept through the UK and beyond. Even Americans growing up in Chicago were reading the NME and other British music magazines to see what was happening in the crazy world of acid house in Madchester and London; a scene that their hometown had unwittingly created. But Ibiza seemed the spiritual playground for the dance community.

I'd been to Ibiza a couple of times as a punter and loved it. That place has a very special vibe dating back to the hippy trail of the 60s. It's hard to think of anywhere else on earth that has a dance community quite on the scale of Ibiza. It's the Las Vegas of dance music.

Off the back of the Quake material, my publicist Gerard managed to get me some gigs with Tony De Vit appearing on line-ups that included Tony, Carl Cox and Sasha. I remember us all playing Warehouse in Plymouth where Tony would go on after Carl Cox. They were such gentlemen and great examples of how to handle success. Every single time I was with Tony, he would be inundated with people wanting to talk to him. There'd be a queue of people waiting to get autographs and all the rest of it, and he would speak to every single person. What a gentleman. And as a result of that, I learned to embrace being humble, something I learned from those guys without a shadow of a doubt.

Tony and I were both playing in Ibiza during the summer of '98; staying at the same villa. The weird thing was that Tony just wouldn't come out of his room during that stint. He came out and did his gigs just fine, but the rest of his time was spent in his room except for one point where we were all in the pool together. I talked to him for quite a while and really valued any time I got with him. The thing was, I didn't have any inkling as to how seriously ill he was.

Tony had HIV and died of bronchial and bone marrow failure on 2nd July, 1998. I was devastated, as were many in the dance community. Tony was such a beautiful man and the influence he had on me is still alive today.

I got to know Tony's dad, Ray De Vit too and he was a beautiful and charming man. I played at a couple of memorials for Tony and his dad came over to me at one of these nights to give me a signed picture of Tony, which I put pride of place on the big shelf unit behind my turntables. Whatever I was doing, I knew Tony was watching over me. I can remember working out sets while staring at his face. "Is it good enough, Tony? Is it good enough?" He was awesome and it didn't matter where he played he would always take it through the roof at the end. It would always be unquestionably good. Tony and Carl Cox have been probably the most positive influences on me, along with Graeme Park, from the early days. DJs who set the bar pretty high.

## Amadeus Mozart, Tidy Trax

*"Unfortunately, Tony did his last track with us. We did The Dawn, but he died before it came out. We were in the studio when he told us he was HIV positive and that was a terribly sad moment. Tony De Vit passed away, but he left a legacy and we have carried his legacy on."*

In 1998, I was doing some gigs at Es Paradis for a chap called Terry Gosling. He was running parties there for the Ministry Of Sound with his girlfriend Kerry Anne and lots of other nights at Es Paradis, as well as running the bar next door called The Blue Lounge. Terry is in the top two street hustlers I've ever met. Along with Andy Matthews from Plastik, these guys literally round up anyone hanging around near their bars and get them in and drinking for hours by using their charm. Watching them work the strip is a thing of beauty. It's an art form and these guys are the absolute best in the business. They are able to talk to you with one eye firmly fixed on their next target. I don't mean that in a bad way. They are just the kings at selling their respective wares to potential customers. They are very much part of the fabric of the island. Generous to a tee, always looking after me with a zillion shots of Hierbas. Proper gents from way back.

I've met so many charming characters over the years and another person who falls squarely into that category is Dermot Condon. I first met him in 1998 when he became resident at Cafe Mambo with another couple of wonderful characters Pete Gooding and Danny Whitehead. I totally knew that all three of them would go on to forge solid careers out there. So, always be kind to everyone, as the folks you meet along the way will invariably ending up running the show. That's my point with Dermot Condon. A very softly spoken Irish demon of a DJ. He started at Mambo and then later went on to run Plastik which I would say is one of the most influential bars on the island. He also runs operations at Eden and now manages Claptone and Masquerade at Pacha. The funny thing is that for the first 6-7 years I thought his name was Declan, and you know what it's like: 'Yes Declan, of course Declan, thanks Declan, see you next year Declan...' It was only years later that he took me to one side and broke the bad news. I was mortified. We still chuckle about it now, but Jesus. That was a bit awkward to say the least.

I'd also like to mention some of the utterly blinding resident DJs I've met over there: Jonathan Ulysses, Rob Marmot, Vicky Devine, Alex Elenger, Jason Bye, Juanito Chanclas and Ryan McDermot to name but a few. All of them are masters of their craft and able to warm up and then smash it out at the end of any night. True heroes whom I admire greatly.

*** 

I was booked to play for Dave Pearce's Dance Anthems at Eden, Ibiza for the first time in 1999 through my association with Gerard Franklin from VF1. The venue had been there for years, but had recently rebranded as Eden: Ibiza's new super club. I was resident on the Saturday night, which as you can imagine, was brilliant. I played 4-6am this Friday night in the UK and then went straight to Leeds Airport. Bearing in mind I'd done a gig and practised all night on the Thursday and Friday, I was knackered. I decided I might as well just go to the airport and sleep by the departure gate. I went through security and took a seat in the departure lounge. I set my alarm to go off in an hour and promptly fell asleep.

I woke up like Homer Simpson with dribble plopping all down my black t-shirt and checked my watch. 'What the fuck?!' I looked all around me and everyone due to take my flight had gone. And so had the plane. For some bizarre reason I'd set the alarm for 6pm. I'd missed the flight by at least an hour. I phoned Margaret and she put me on another flight going from Manchester to Barcelona. That's how things seemed to be back then; I was just burning the candle at both ends. Of course, there was a baggage handlers' strike at Barcelona Airport and so no one was doing the luggage. It was a flash strike and this meant there was a delay on all flights. I was feeling like crap by this stage and even worse when they announced the nine-hour delay. I eventually landed in Ibiza and met the driver Eden had sent to pick me up. They took me around the back of the club where I'd never been before.

We entered the club through the fire escape, which led into a VIP room. I got changed out of my rancid travel clothes I'd DJed in; soaked in sweat and dribble from frantically trying to get to the most important job I'd done thus far. A residency in Ibiza. There was a lot of swearing going on, me having a pop at myself. 'You're such a dickhead! What did you do?!' I had five minutes to spare, I couldn't believe it.

Dave played his last track while I was putting fresh clothes on inside the DJ booth, my sweaty gear screwed away in a placcy bag. I went on and played and it was amazing. I think I channelled all of the day's frustrations into an energy that completely spilled out onto the dance floor. For me personally, it was a monumental session. Then when I finished playing, I really wanted to go back to the villa to finally get some sleep. "Oh no, Rob, you're coming to the Garden of Evil."

The bar next door to Eden was the Garden of Eden, nicknamed the Garden of Evil. I was barely alive I was so knackered. They served up these sambuca shots and this local delicacy Hierbas, an aniseed-flavoured liqueur. And then came the tequila shots, followed by pint glasses of Jack Daniels. I was with these guys until 10am on the Monday morning – we ended up at Pacha. I then got a cab over to the apartment where I was supposed to have gone the day before. I spilled into the apartment and just crashed.

My flight was 6pm on the Monday and I really needed to get my shit together. I had a couple of hours of sleep and did the travel check: sunglasses, records, phone, passport… 'Oh my god, where's my fucking passport?!' I turned the entire Sundissential apartment upside down looking for my passport and then the penny dropped. It was in that plastic bag that I'd left in the DJ booth at Eden with my sweaty clothes. I was so furious with myself. 'You idiot! You fucking idiot!'

I'd been to Spain quite a few times by then, but I'd never really been there as a resident and I wasn't really switched on to the ins and outs of Spanish culture. It was 2pm and I needed to get to Eden. I phoned a guy from the club who said, "Forget it. There won't be anyone there from 4-6pm. It's siesta." For fuck's sake. No work gets done during that 'posh wank break' including being able to get a cab over from Playa d'en Bossa to Eden in San Antonio.

I eventually managed to get a cab over to San Antonio and one of the cleaners let me into Eden. I grabbed that plastic bag containing my stinky clothes and passport. I then got the cab to screech over to the airport as quickly as it could. I didn't care about the costs of all this idiocy, I just needed to get home. Got to the airport and hit check-in, a sweaty mess. I handed over the passport and boarding card and the woman laughed. "You're not flying until tomorrow!" Cue, going straight back out on the lash, cracking on well into the next morning when I nearly missed my flight *again*.

That was how things were back then. I was loving life, but I was living in a blur of clubs, cabs and planes. It was a very full-on stressful time. No wonder I've got no hair.

That entire summer was full-on with hard house exploding and the emergence of trance. I was playing hard house with vocals at Sundissential and mixed some trance within it to provide that essential light and shade. Out of the darkness and into the light; the biggest weapon for me is contrast. That stood me in great stead with the Sundissential crowd because a lot of them came from the trance world and were now craving something a little tougher. And that was my forte from the days of Ark as The Closer. I did closing parties for Cream and Slinky and would play the most euphoric music I could on Galaxy, along with some stuff that would make you go 'Woah, where the fuck did that come from?'

\*\*\*

I was doing a lot of stuff with Peach down in London for Graham Gold at Camden Palace around this time too. I was also doing Frantic, which was a new kid on the block and also at Camden Palace. Those were phenomenal gigs. Peach and Frantic represented a split between the trance and hard house, which was running like a steam train at this point. I was also doing trance for Godskitchen, the occasional Gatecrasher gig and Slinky and so all of that was going great, but there was also a layer of hard house to those sets as well.

Blandy and I were beginning to pick up a lot of remixes following *The Day Will Come* track. Matt Waterhouse from Hyperactive got us a couple of interesting hook-ups including a remix for a track called *Daze Like That* by Fierce. Then we started picking up more remixes for people like Erasure and were asked to do a mix for Subterranean Records of this track *The Awakening* by York. York were a German trance duo founded in 1997 by brothers Torsten and Jörg Stenzel.

We were sent the track as a cassette. Now, mostly the tracks arrived as a samples disc or as a DAT, but this guy sent us a cassette tape of this tiny little twangy Balearic guitar part by Jörg and that was it. 20 seconds of guitar and nothing else. We listened to it, and considered it a good riff, but that was it. So, we sampled from the cassette, and set about doing something with it. We took some parts from *The Day Will Come* plus some acid riffs and a few bits and pieces from the arrangement and put them to this riff by York. On reflection we decided it needed a little vocal sample and I made a suggestion, "I think it needs to say 'the awakening!'"

–  "Yeah, I think that would work."

We had one of those Speak & Spell toys to help kids read and write and keyed 'the awakening' into it and chose the 'whisper' style of computer-generated voice. The Speak & Spell repeated those two words in a hushed voice and we thought it was brilliant. We stuck the vocal into the track and sent it off to Subterranean Records.

Subterranean Records absolutely loved it and then out of nowhere, Judge Jules started playing it and because he was involved with Manifesto Records who were sniffing around in the hope of signing it from Subterranean, we did a deal for the track. We got paid a remix fee of £2,500, plus, we could have points on the track if it got signed on, or should the track do well. The track then blew up ridiculously and Jules was playing it every single week on Radio 1. Manifesto then duly signed it and gave the guy who did the guitar track a £50,000 advance;

the track went on to appear on 125 compilations, including Ministry's *Annual*, which was shifting 500,000 copies around then. Jules ended up playing the York track 52 weeks in a row on Radio 1, which was pretty phenomenal and off the back of that the Quake name got well and truly established. We were now getting calls from all over the place with all sorts of artists wanting us to remix their tracks.

For the next 18 months, we were doing a minimum of one, if not two, remixes a week. We had a complete and utter golden period where things got pretty crazy. My role in it all was primarily managing the situation with the help of Nick Halkes from Positiva, while Ian concentrated on the music side. I would also come up with ideas, but Ian was very much the hands-on engineer of it all, while I was taking on more of a producer's role. Ian was plugging wires in and creating sounds, I was fielding calls from various promoters and record companies.

I got a call from a well-known promotions company one morning: "We want you to remix a new Irish boy band. We will send you a CD." The CD arrived the following day and it was shocking. Absolutely horrendous. We honestly couldn't work out how Quake could remix that. I took the disc out of the CD player and chucked it across the room; it ended up behind the couch. "No chance, that's absolutely shit!" And then about six months later, Ian had a tidy up of his studio and he said, "Mate I've just found that CD you threw behind the sofa. The band was Westlife and we didn't even call them back!" Shit!

We also got a call from this scouse guy, one time. "Hi Rob. It's Holly Johnson from Frankie Goes to Hollywood here…" Now, when I was a teenage boy FGTH were massive and I loved them and to think that Holly Johnson was calling me… now that was quite a moment. Holly sent me this track and it was also rubbish; there was absolutely nothing I could have done with it. So we ended up blanking Holly Johnson as well. It was one of those moments in your life you couldn't quite fathom. I stored his number and was getting a barrage of calls from him, but I didn't have the heart to tell him what I thought. I just didn't want to say no to Holly Johnson, but he eventually got the message. It was quite a strange period really.

## Ian Bland, Dream Frequency and Dancing Divaz

*"Quake were doing quite well when Holly Johnson phoned up with a track he wanted mixing. It was a track about dead disco stars and we were doing trance at the time. Not a great fit. He was also one of Rob's heroes, and so we just couldn't phone him back to say no. It was just one of them. And so we did a backdoor boogie on that one, I'm afraid. Blanking Holly Johnson was just mad. Still hard to believe that it actually happened. But we just didn't know what to say to him. Ha ha. But they were great times working in the studio together. We had such a fun and creative time."*

# Human Traffic

Nick Halkes was managing Blandy and me in the late 90s and through him we were getting all these remixes. I was busy back and forth to Blandy's house in Leyland three days a week on top of doing all the gigs. Our reputation was definitely growing and Nick managed to get our remix fee up to £6,000 per job, which was pretty sweet. It was as golden as it comes. And out of the back of that was the relationship with FFRR, Pete Tong and Phil Faversham.

I got a call from Phil one day in 1998 regarding a film soundtrack. Pete Tong had been asked to put the music together for a film about the UK rave scene and wanted Quake to score some original music. "Are you up for it?" Too right we were. "Tell us more!"

– "There's going to be this new cult film that's going to be a smash hit at the box office and it's aimed at our generation. It's called *Human Traffic*."

– "Sounds great. What do we need to do?"

We needed to supply three pieces of music for this film based around three different scenes. They sent a video copy of the film on VHS that had no music in it whatsoever; just dialogue. They also sent us a copy that had guide music in each frame, with our scenes marked up at certain points.

One of the scenes was when Jip (John Simm) and the girls first get into the club and they're just really excited to be there; Jip eventually gets in via Carl Cox's character. The scene where they first appear on the landing in the club, they're dancing to a big piano tune called *Push It* that Blandy and I made. The guide track for that was *Bells Of NY* by Slo Moshun. The next scene was where Jip is getting paranoid in the back room worrying that his girlfriend's getting chatted up; he's in a real dark place. They wanted us to do this rough hardcore tune – the guide track was a really dark tune by Hardfloor called *Aceperience 1* – and so we made this moody techno track *Dark Air*. The third scene is where the politician is dancing in the club and he's saying, "The homies get the pukka Es and they supply them to the punters." And then when he reaches for the lasers he says "safe as fuck"; well the tune in the background is *Mantra* by Quake.

Those three tracks came out as Quake on an EP a year down the line after the film's release, but what a thing to be involved in; such an iconic project that had to go down as one of the landmark moments in my life. We felt this movie was going to strike a note with everybody, but of course you don't quite know how legendary this may or may not be. *Human Traffic* was a really unifying moment for us.

Once we were happy with these three tracks, Blandy decided to play practical joker again. We recorded a fourth track, a trance number, that built up in the middle, like something you could play at Cream or Gatecrasher and then right in the middle of this trancey riff, Ian played like a really dodgy piano bit, just like the comedian Les Dawson, with all the notes in the wrong places. We sent a note saying, "Check out the fourth track and see if you can use this somewhere" and sent off the files. We got a call back a few days later saying could we 'can the humour and cut to the chase', so that went down like a plate of shit sarnies. I don't know what possessed us to do something so stupid with somebody as massive as Pete Tong, but it was really good fun. In fact, one of the *Human Traffic* tracks ended up as the theme tune for Channel 4's coverage of the World Rally Championships.


## Ian Bland, Dream Frequency and Dancing Divaz

*"What an honour it was to work on such an important film in the dance scene. It was incredible to hear our music in a film. And yes, we probably shouldn't have sent that joke track to Tongy. But that's how we rolled back then. Ha ha. Sorry Tongy!*

*Honest to God, I'm surprised we got anything done. You call it cabin fever when you're in the studio for hours. I'm terrible. If I'm not at the helm doing something on the computer, my mind just wanders off, a bit like Homer Simpson, so it doesn't take much for me to think, 'What can*

*I do for a gag?' We had a dress-up costume box, and it could contain anything from a jaunty pumpkin hat, a vest with a penis on it that Rob got from a gay club in Australia or a didgeridoo, feather boa, or something like that. That was part and parcel of making music and having a laugh. It was just brilliant. And I'm glad there was no social media then.*

*I remember Phil Faversham signing an Armand van Helden track at the time, and it sampled Cars by Gary Numan. I was a massive Gary Numan fan. Rob and I were like, 'What the fucking hell is this?'*

*And so Rob goes, 'Here, watch this.' He got one of my Tubeway Army records, Are 'Friends' Electric? and started sampling it. After, he rang Phil and when the answer machine started recording, he said 'I've got a new track for you, mate.' He started playing Are 'Friends' Electric? and promptly started scratching over it. It was awful! 'Let me know what you think, Phil.' I think we burned our friendship with Phil after that, although Sugababes actually did sample Are 'Friends' Electric?, so maybe they missed a trick there.*

*We had this running gag at gigs where Rob would find the dodgiest wig. I'd go into the venue first and say to the crew, 'Listen, Rob's had a bit of a hair transplant. Whatever you do, don't look at it, don't comment on it.' Rob would then come in wearing the shittest wig ever. 'All right, lads? How's it going? Happy times!"'*

Trance fully exploded in '99, but it was already beginning to go that way from about '97 when *Cafe Del Mar* first came out on Black Hole records; that was the breakthrough moment, along with *Quench*; the quintessential forerunners to trance. It became more commercialised from '98 onwards when it became a headlining genre. I would definitely find a way of playing Quench's *Dreams* and I loved the big hairy riffs and tracks on Noom Records such as *Are Am Eye* by Commander Tom and tracks by Armin van Buuren. I loved the stuff I heard being played by Sasha at Renaissance that had elements of trance and tracks like Hardfloor's *Acperience 1* and the stuff coming out on Reactivate in the mid 90s when I played Kelly's in Port Rush with people like Tall Paul, Carl Cox and Blu Peter. Blu Peter was a big artist back in the day on Reactive Records.

We did a lot of remixes during that time, including Ralph Fridge's *Angel,* which was a big track in the trance scene. All this work just came one after another and in part down to our ongoing association with Nick Halkes. We were put in contact with this new guy on the trance scene called Armin van Buuren and remixed his single *Communication*. That particular track was already really strong. It was one of those remixes where we couldn't do an awful lot more to it, other than just supersize what was already there because Armin was a very efficient producer. He sent us loads of stuff that you wouldn't normally get from all the other remixes where we weren't getting any MIDI parts or anything other than a cassette tape with a guitar part on it or some terrible out-of-tune vocals.

Armin's stuff was perfectly organised, and he had that Dutch efficiency about him. He sent over a comprehensive package of MIDI files and DAT dumps. But that mix did us no end of favours and as a result of that I was playing a lot more at Godskitchen and going over to Ibiza and doing the residency for Dave Pearce. We even did some Quake PAs in Ibiza for Amnesia where we hired a villa for the week and made a proper party of it. I was enjoying some of the best times of my life. More interviews with *Mixmag* and *DJ Magazine* followed and I was doing more stuff with Slinky. Quake were also remixing artists like New Atlantic. It was amazing.

In the summer of '99, Sundissential decided, completely out of the blue to do a residency at Pacha in Ibiza. And so I was going back and forth to Ibiza with Dan Prince from *Mixmag*, Lisa Lashes, Nick Rafferty and Rob Farrell, a *Mixmag* photographer who became a great friend of mine. Rob was a giant of a man who to this day has the best physique I've ever seen. Girls and blokes alike would swoon over him and he's also one of the coolest and nicest people I've ever met. And Dan Prince's infectious personality could open a thousand doors. I'm so grateful to him for taking me under his wing and introducing me to some of the most influential people who ran that island, including the owners of Pacha and Clare and Mike from the mighty Manumission and Pepe who owned Cafe Mambo and so many other venues. Dan was at the top of his game and walking into anywhere with him and Rob Farrell guaranteed me instant acceptance.

Sundissential at Pacha meant playing hard house in Ibiza on Sunday nights for the summer of '99 and that led to meeting Charlie Chester, DJ John Mancini and legendary Scottish promoter Ricky McGowan who ran Colours. I was spending Monday mornings, after the Sunday nights, at a place called the Mezzanine Bar, on the corner of a road near the port. Every Monday morning they would bring out a big box of fancy dress and jokey wigs and everybody would have a crazy time. We did not have a care in the world.

Through playing for Dave Pearce at Eden, I became great friends with the guys who ran The Garden Of Evil (Eden) next door. You'd go in there after your set and they'd shout "Shots!" They would bring out trays of sambuca and tequila and every time you finished one, you had to go out to the front of the place and smash the glass against the wall. I have a very fond place in my heart when it comes to the debauchery and hedonistic times I had in The Garden Of Evil and big props to Richie and the guys who ran that place.

***

The remixes were still coming in and one of the oddest requests Blandy and I received was a commission to do the TV theme for the 1999 Cricket World Cup. They wanted a Quake-style track with a trancey build up that went into the cricket theme. That's right, the steel drums. We did this track and it was pretty much the equivalent of that joke tune we'd sent to FFRR. It was an absolute abomination; the things you do for money. I wouldn't put that one down as a passion project, that's for sure.

We were caning it on the remix front at that time however, so much so we had to finish this one track on Christmas Day. We sent a track to the label a couple of days before Christmas and they didn't like it and wanted a redo. So we ended up having to remix it on Christmas morning. Ian had two kids and we were working through the night until 6am, only stopping so Ian could put the kids' presents by their beds.

Remixing had begun to lose the element of fun. It was becoming a factory line. Ian was having some huge successes with his other projects such as Dancing Divaz and I was busy with what I was doing. And at the same time we were both going to the gym loads and playing 5-a-side football on a Wednesday with some of Blandy's mates in Leyland.

I was a bit of a fitness freak in those days and we were both on the powdered protein shakes, some of which contained creatine, which made the red mist descend in the blink of an eye. Sometimes the red mist would just descend for no reason and we would get really narky with each other. We were in Ian's house one day and he got the hump and just stood up and kicked the door in. The door fell off its hinges and he just stormed out of his own house and left me sitting in his studio. And yeah, we had a bit of a fallout to be honest. We were exhausted.

* * *

Some friends of mine ran a night in Leeds called Base, a hard house night with funky house in the back room at Space and they also ran another night called Union. They were booking Sasha, John Digweed, Markus Schulz, Timo Maas and people like that. As with all the other stuff I'd done in the past, I would get an ear for something and started to reconfigure my sets. I definitely went a bit more progressive because that was what was now required. And then these guys at Union made me a resident there. I was playing early doors, and then you'd have Sasha and all those guys playing later on. I was having to compromise hugely, and I was really playing within myself, but that was OK, as I was playing for Sundissential where I was thrapping the knackers off that. During the summer of 2000, I was also doing the Friday night at Space and so many other gigs on a Saturday around the country and Ibiza.

Progressive house was essentially slowed down trance with a bongo in it and it didn't really suit Blandy and me. When people go on about minimal, I've always thought we were more maximal. And as a result of that, the rise of prog house coincided with our sabbatical. It was just one of those things where he was busy doing other stuff, and I wanted to push on with DJing in particular; sometimes five gigs in a weekend, sometimes three in one day. It was a full-on period of crazy times and doing the music in the midst of it all was definitely causing me a few issues. So, we put making music together to one side. We were still great friends and having a good time.

* * *

Hard house didn't just fall out of the sky. It definitely evolved from handbag and happy hardcore with those incessant hi-hats, hoover sounds and four-to-the-floor beats. My first experiences of hard house would have been tracks like the House Pimps' *Zulu-Nation* in '93. You can hear hard house evolving through Tony De Vit and some of the early stuff he did. His music was hard house, but it also had an affinity with rave. Tony's *Are You All Ready?* had that *Mentasm* stab and bits from *Dominator*. A big slice of rave set to a 4:4 beat. It had been a constant evolution to get to the point in '99/2000 when hard house became a really big thing.

I'd been listening to that sound growing and growing and some trance records were getting a little tougher as well, such as *Time To Burn* by Storm. I would play XVX's *Illuminati*, which had some proper nasty noises in it. It would go alongside *Dreams* by Quench. I loved the light and shade of those tracks. I remember going to Pulse in Birmingham to listen to people playing hard house for the first time listening to Andy Farley, Paul Kershaw and Nick Rafferty. What really ignited all that for me was listening to Ian M playing, because he definitely loved the rave sounds from Sound Corp and Dream Finder and samples from Sour Mash tracks from around '94. There were some huge influences coming from the Dutch music too, such as Olav Basoski and Sharp Boys.

I loved it when I played something hard and people growled in appreciation, just like that *Dominator* roar. Plus, it was also nice to lay down a soft pillow for them to put their head on before you hit them with a sledgehammer. Give them an ice pack for that before applying scalding hot water. I like that style.

It really was an evolution of the music more than just a complete switch off from the trance. But things were changing and the music wasn't quite as euphoric as new waves started up.

I was touring a lot more at this point in time and that included working with a guy called Dave Lee who was involved with Slinky, which was the Gatecrasher of the south west, I guess. Slinky was definitely on the same level as Gatecrasher and Cream and I started doing a monthly residency down there in Bournemouth for them. Out of that, I met some phenomenal people who have stuck with me ever since.

Nights like Sundissential, Tidy and Slinky are like families and for the most part you remain tight for life. Dave Lee, Garry White and Tim Lyall were all part of the Slinky fabric and they all became great friends. And there was Claire Hoare who was also involved in Slinky and she was such a funny person. So much fun.

The Opera House in Bournemouth has to be one of my favourite venues of all time. There's no doubt about it. It's just one of those old theatres that are just something else. They really are. And that one is particularly cool because it's on a couple of levels; it's just the most gorgeous structure. What a pleasure to play at a venue like that. Playing out in a box at the front, looking at one level of the dance floor, ever so slightly down below you, but still close enough for you to be able to reach down and shake their hands. But when you look up you've got this other level above you all looking down into the main dance floor of this old Victorian opera house. Stunning.

It wasn't long after becoming resident at Slinky that they asked me to do a Canadian tour for them. I did Toronto, Vancouver and Montreal, which was an unbelievable experience. Some Slinky gigs in the Philippines and Kuala Lumpur followed. I was going all over the world doing tours for Slinky and had the greatest time. I went to Miami as well. I felt truly blessed. Ian Bland and I did a couple of Quake gigs over in Ibiza for Godskitchen around this time too.

I did a festival in Finland for Slinky in 2001 and many of the big names of the trance scene were playing. We were all staying at this big Radisson hotel and there was this impromptu afternoon meet-and-greet with people like Ferry Corsten, Armin van Buuren and tonnes of big trance artists. It was quite interesting because we'd done remixes for many of these people. We remixed Torsten Stenzel from York; our mix of *The Awakening* went mad, but he never namechecked or called us to say thank you or reached out in any way, which was always hugely disappointing. And the thing that struck me at this particular meeting in Finland was that Armin van Buuren was there and he was as nice as pie and so thankful for what we'd done on the *Communication* single, because it went to number 11 in the national charts. I think a lot of people in the UK really picked up on the mix we did for him. It was really nice having that talk with him and his then girlfriend. We got better props from Armin than we ever did from Torsten Stenzel. I know Torsten bought a couple of Ferraris out of the proceeds of that. We got £3,250 for the *Awakening* remix of York, but we were also supposed to get points on the record, which was 2% of anything that was made including any signings to other labels, and this track got signed to Manifesto Records. But Manifesto wouldn't honour the deal they had with us, which meant we lost out on 2% of the tender, which was really annoying.

***

Our mates Ian E and Adam Falkingham plus 10 of our best friends hired a villa in Ibiza that summer. We hired this villa off a contact of the Ibiza legend Shaggy (Martin Makepeace). I met Shaggy's mate, Paul the year before and he said, "Anytime you want to come over, we've got some villas." I think we paid for 10 people, but there might have been 11 or 12 staying there.

Ian E was involved in motorcycle racing and tuned racing bikes for rich kids who had aspirations to be the next Valentino Rossi, and he had a Volkswagen LT 35 van with the side that opened up. Ian came around to my house, just before I flew over, to collect my 2K sound system. We dismantled it, put it in the back of his van and loaded up about 25 crates of our favourite records with a few lights we borrowed off a mate of mine. We now had all the gear to ensure we could really party in that villa. They got the ferry to Andorra, picked up a load of duty free and then went down to Barcelona. They parked the van at the Nou Camp and watched Leeds play Barcelona. Leeds got tonked 4-0 and then they got the overnight ferry to Ibiza. I flew over a few days later and met them all at the airport.

I remember us jumping off the roof of the villa into the pool like rock stars as soon as I arrived. Me, Adam Falkingham and Ian E going straight in. There was not one single ounce of arrogance about our actions. We were just a bunch of lads from various council estates who were living the dream. I'd like to think that anyone in a similar position would do the exact same things as us.

Once we got the sound system set up, we had a week-long party in that villa. There was definitely one night where I reckon I must have played for 16 hours straight. They would bring me pizza and drinks and I would just keep going. 16 hours can fly by when you're having that much fun and it was about as hedonistic as it could get in some respects. *Wink wink.*

They were crazy times and memories I'll take to the grave, plus plenty of stuff I can't remember. I had a few marathon sessions like that at the Yorkshire cottage because I just loved playing music. If you're there with another couple of DJs you think nothing of playing all the way through the night.

Day four, I remember this bloke turning up to clean the pool. There was this trail of devastation everywhere and he kept looking around in a curious manner. We found out about four or five years after that he owned the villa, and he'd come to see what was going on. He never said anything at the time, but he was just there to spy basically and see what nonsense we were getting up to.

Ian E was like a stuntman; one of those people that goes to a party and goes completely crazy. Ian would deliberately fall down the stairs for example. He was involved in the motorcycle world and because he used to race bikes he'd broken pretty much every bone in his body. Ian was just one of those people who would do the most stupid things. We definitely lived the life that summer. I don't want any of this to come across in a boastful way, because I am really humble and grateful for everything I've got or had. I'll never forget where that comes from and who gave it to me. Never get to the point where you start thinking your shit doesn't stink. I'm just a bloke from a council estate in Milton Keynes, who got the opportunity to live that life.

When we hired a car, we would pay an extra fee for the damage waiver and I can't remember exactly how much it was back in those days, but let's say £30 extra, so if anything happened to the car you were covered. Now I know that this is bad and I'd never condone this now, but Ian would go and wreck the car on the last day. He would take the car down dirt tracks and handbrake it before smashing into a big boulder. He would then return the car with pretty much every panel smashed. Shocking behaviour and we're all expecting to take the bullet train to hell when we leave this earth.

I got to travel all over the world and stay at Philippe Starck hotels and all the rest of it. And it was such an honour, we would be jumping on the beds with joy. It felt like we were winning! Some people I've worked with over the years will complain about everything. "The temperature of the water is a bit too hot for me." I'm not one of those people.

*rob
Tissera*

# Slinky, Firewater And The Bungee Rockets

During 2000, I got some more gigs for Slinky, in Ayia Napa, Cyprus. I made the grave error of drinking too much of this local delicacy called Zivania, a pomace brandy known by the locals as 'firewater' whilst DJing. I allowed them to pour me these big old drinks of Zivania. Way too many of them and anything else on offer. I played until 6am, and then remember waking up in the morning. It was bright sunlight. I'd made the mistake of not closing the big metal shutter on the bedroom window. I opened my eyes and had to hide under the bed sheets from this blinding sunlight. I had a mouth that tasted like a pair of Hulk Hogan's flip flops. I couldn't remember getting home or where I'd been.

I was desperate for a drink, but because I couldn't find my clothes, I decided to make a dash to the bathroom – in just my undies – to get a glass of water from the floor below, while everyone else in the villa was still asleep. There was nobody around so I ran across the hall and slipped on this rug covering the marble floor. I thought 'That's not too clever!' and promptly fell all the way down this marble staircase on my back, in just my pants. I lay on the floor in absolute agony. I needed to get back in bed before anyone saw me, but it was about ten steps, which was more than enough when you were doubled up in excruciating pain.

I'd been out the day before with some mates at a bungee place. Because as I've mentioned before I thought I was bulletproof and I could 'run off' any injury. I went to this adventure playground the day before the accident that had several death-defying rides and a bungee jump. I went on this bungee rocket that shot you straight into the sky. Now, at this point I was in pretty decent physical condition and still quite young. I was still going to the gym a lot so I was in fairly decent nick, but I had an adrenaline day on the bungee rocket and this other thing that dropped you about 90 feet. I was talking to the person operating the machinery and they said, "It's gonna go on 1… 2… 3…" Woah! It was a bungee jump into the sea from 160 feet or something, a fair old jump. I decided I might as well dive forward all the way into the sea. Jesus Christ, what a rush. But that exertion, twinned with the lethal local brandy had totally fucked me over. I managed to crawl back into bed and thought 'Shit. I'm in a bad state here.'

I got home to the UK and thought I was OK. However, I returned home after playing Union on the Friday night and slipped again. I landed on the floor where the pig-roasting fire was. My back felt very dodgy indeed. I went to A&E on the Saturday morning and got an X-ray. "You've broken a bit of your spine off."

– "What?!"

I'd broken my back at T8, which is in between your shoulder blades, but a little further up. I then considered the fact that I'd been playing Ayia Napa with a broken spine. It was like the Man City goalkeeper Bert Trautmann who carried on playing with a broken neck in the 1956 FA Cup Final. I was told to stop working and to take it easy. "But I don't have time for a broken back!" However, I was experiencing huge amounts of agony standing up or just moving around. It was really aggravating and I was like that for a couple of weeks and so *had* to take time off work

It was the summer of 2000 and Radio 1 had organised a Love Parade in Leeds; the equivalent of the Berlin festival. I was playing Slinky during the day and Sundissential in the evening and there was no way on god's green earth I was going to miss that simply because my back was playing up. 250,000 people descended on Roundhay Park in Leeds and being a resident of the city, I didn't think for a minute that I'd have problems getting into that event.

Leeds was gridlocked. The only way we could get me onto the site in time, and I had a reputation for being a bit late, was to take a 'backy' on Ian E's 650 Kawasaki. And so clutching my record box, we sped through the traffic. I was playing on one of the carnival floats and I could just about bear the back pain as I started playing out. I don't know how they found drivers who could keep those floats at like one mile an hour for hours around this circuit that ran all the way around the park. There were people everywhere, and they were getting all these different types of music piped out to them as the floats went past. Sometimes, because the floats were so slow, you'd get a couple of records from one set of people and a couple from the next.

I played for an hour and a half as we did a whole circuit of the park. However, there was this one tiny bit on the site where you could see the main part of the park through this opening and there must have been 150,000 people there. And I got to play Quake's *The Day Will Come* to 150,000 ravers. What a standout moment in my career. It doesn't really get much better than playing your own record at the Leeds Love Parade to that amount of people. It made me well up with tears.

After my set, we were straight on the motorbike again and off into the city to do the after-party at NATO. I shouldn't really have done those gigs, but I wouldn't have missed them either. But I had to pay the piper. I had to take two weeks off after that for the back problem that was to cause me grief for years after.

I met a chiropractor from Roundhay called Doug Olson and he went straight onto my speed dial. Because even to this day, if I sit in one position for an awfully long time, that part of my back seizes up.

**rob Tissera**

# The Tidy Boys

I walked into Sundissential one night and stopped to see these two guys playing. I'd never seen them before. They put on quite a show with a great set. They had a proper element of performance to their set too and one of them stood up on the top surface where the decks were and started dancing. Everybody was going mad. I said to Madders, "Who are these guys?"

–   "They're the Tidy Boys and they're going to be huge!"

And I thought 'Wow, yeah, they're really good.' In fact, they already had a record label. It was the first time I'd seen the Tidy Boys play. Andy Pickles from Doncaster (and a member of Jive Bunny) and Amadeus Mozart from Kettering totally tore it a new one. They were just awesome to watch. They are two of the kindest people in the business with more drive than a fleet of locomotives. They have gone on to give me an absolute tonne of opportunities over the past 20 years and helped to cement my name and reputation by always backing me to the hilt. I really can't thank them enough for all they've done for me.

All of a sudden, Sundissential had joint nights with them called Tidyssential and I loved playing those. Not long after that they started doing the legendary Tidy Weekenders. The Tidy Boys would become a really positive presence in my life.

**Amadeus Mozart, Tidy Trax, Tidy Boys**

*"Our goal was to make hard house the biggest thing ever. And from '95 onwards we became the biggest hard house record label in the world.*

*In 1999 and 2001, we were the biggest independent vinyl selling record label in Europe, with 10 years of success. And that's the point where Rob Tissera and Tidy hooked up.*

*We were literally locked in the studio up until that point working, making music under different pseudonyms and it wasn't until we surfaced and went clubbing, that we realised that Tidy was a cult. We went out and saw people wearing homemade Tidy Trax T-shirts. We thought, hold on a minute, there's been a big scene building here while we've been locked away in the studio, making music.*

*It took us five years to put our first event on in 2000. We had Tidy Trax's fifth birthday party in Wolverhampton at The Mezzanine. We sold 2,000 tickets in about a month. September 26th, 2000, boom! We were now an events company. We couldn't believe it. We had a very small line-up. I think it was the Tidy Boys, Ian M and Lisa Lashes, and we had massive success with that and the rest is history. And so we thought, hold on a minute, let's do more events. There's just as much money in this, if you get it right, as there is in actually putting out records. And so 2000, Rob Tissera got involved with Tidy.*

*Whereas Trade was serious and credible, Sundissential had this, 'don't give a fuck' vibe where you could dress up as whatever you wanted. It was madcap. Andy and I were so busy in the mid 90s we weren't clubbing quite so much, but we would go to Sundissential in Birmingham or Leeds. And a good reason to go there was if Tony De Vit was playing. Now, Tony De Vit took the underground, hard house, gay sound from Trade and brought it to the straight masses at Sundissential, which was more of a straight clubbing environment. And a lot of the DJs like Andy Farley and Lisa Lashes aspired to what Tony was playing. So, Tony shaped Sundissential into becoming a hard house night. And, by the way, the term hard house had never been used before. Tidy Trax used it first. There was hard house and hard dance. But nobody had used the term hard house until January 1996, when we went to the MIDEM music convention in the South of France. We had to come up with a description for Tidy Trax on a form and so we came up with 'For the finest UK hard house, Tidy Trax.' And then we put it on our albums.*

*Anyway, so Sundissential was now playing hard house and we loved what Sundissential were doing so much. It really influenced Tidy Trax and our events and everything. The Tidy Boys came about through clubbing there. 'Fuck it, let's get back to DJing. Let's just make some money, have a laugh together, and play some of our own records, and promote Tidy Trax while we're doing it.'*

*Our first gig was '99, in Jersey, and our second gig was at Sundissential. We got the records in the boot and Madders came up to us in Leeds at Uropa: 'You've got 45 minutes. There are 2,000 people here, so get on the decks and fucking prove yourselves!'*

*Andy and I had a moment's reflection and thought 'Shit, this is our big chance to show what we can do!' So, we went on for 45 minutes, and made a real meal of it. We went down a storm.*

*Back in the day, DJs occasionally waved their arms and clapped around, but we just jumped around like nutters. I mean, Andy stood on the speakers and I pulled his trousers down and played his arse like a set of bongos in front of everybody. And people had never seen anything like it. These two lads just having a laugh. 'They look like they're off their faces!' The thing is we don't actually take drugs. We were just loving it. And we literally became the Tidy Boys that night. And Rob Tissera was on that line-up.*

*Now, we were based in Rotherham, and had quite a few people here that went clubbing in Leeds and so there was a bond between Rob Tissera and Tidy that came through people like Lee Haslam, who worked for Tidy, and the other guys who were more aware of Rob. But our paths crossed at Sundissential, and it would have been in the back room. There was a huge dollop of mutual respect for eachother's careers. 'Fucking hell, Rob. Good to see you. Heard a lot about you. You're on all the flyers.'*

*We started following each other around the country at this point. Because Rob had started to move his sound to that Sundissential scene, which Tony had created; this harder, faster, uplifting gay sound of Trade had infiltrated Sundissential. Rob saw what Lisa Lashes and Andy Farley were doing and I think he adapted to that. Because Rob had such a broad sound in the 90s, whether it was Chicago house, through to the rave and disco. Rob is a chameleon who can turn himself into any DJ you want him to be. And that's what I love about Rob. Many DJs don't have that skill.*

*Rob can adapt to the crowd and read the crowd. He might drop the first two tracks and think 'Right, they want to go this way and I want to go this way with them.' Rob has got that skillset and I have the same skillset, because we've both played weddings, we've played shit gigs and we can work and nurture the crowd. If you said, 'Rob, tomorrow night we're doing a night, and it's going to be bpms of about 125, 130*

*– we don't want to go any faster', Rob would say, 'I'm your man!' He's a fighter, he's a grafter. He loves music of all kinds, and it shows. So, he's not disingenuously playing the music at 125 or 126. He loves it. He loves it at whatever bpm. He loves it fast, hard, melodic, groovy, techno. You can see it on his face. And as many people would say, it's very difficult to stop Rob Tissera smiling. It's the hardest thing in the world. It's such a great smile and the crowd feeds off that. And the Tidy Boys were influenced by it too.*

*There were too many DJs of that era who became head down, too serious, too pretentious, and it reflects on the crowd. I've seen it. I've seen DJs playing underground stuff, with their heads down, moody, and then all of a sudden the front row becomes moody. And I think, Rob's got the right attitude. Rob was playing Tidy Trax releases at the time and became a fan of our label.*

*In 1998, we took hard house to the left, and we released Signum, What You Got for Me, and Tony De Vit did The Dawn, which was based on Signum. We decided to put the melody of trance to a harder beat, and came up with the term hard trance, because trance was a bit floaty. Trance was the sort of thing your mum and dad quite liked when you had a white female singer singing about castles in the sky. It was great in the car, but just boring in a club. We wanted to put the bollocks into trance.*

*And so we did a tour with Signum and merged hard house with trance, and became a hard trance label. And I think that's what got Rob excited, because Rob loves a melody. And I think Rob loved Signum and The Dawn and so we started the Tidy Two label. I think Rob really fell in love with the Tidy sound and we'd hit the back of the net with that production in 2000/2001 when Rob started making music for Tidy. Or, at least, sending us stuff.*

*I've done all the A&R for Tidy for the past 28 years and I can't remember turning much of Rob Tissera's stuff down. I think most of it we've probably had. He had some great releases on Tidy Trax, but he's certainly not had all his tracks on Tidy Trax."*

I walked into Sundissential one night and stopped to see these two guys playing. I'd never seen them before. They put on quite a show with a great set. They had a proper element of performance to their set too and one of them stood up on the top surface where the decks were and started dancing. Everybody was going mad. I said to Madders, "Who are these guys?"

– "They're the Tidy Boys and they're going to be huge!"

And I thought 'Wow, yeah, they're really good.' In fact, they already had a record label. It was the first time I'd seen the Tidy Boys play. Andy Pickles from Corby (once known as Jive Bunny) and Amadeus Mozart from Rotherham totally tore it a new one. They were just awesome to watch. They are two of the kindest people in the business with more drive than a fleet of locomotives. They have gone on to give me an absolute ton of opportunities over the past 20 years and helped to cement my name and reputation by always backing me to the hilt. I really can't thank them enough for all they've done for me.

All of a sudden, Sundissential had joint nights with them called Tidyssential and I loved playing those. Not long after that they started doing the legendary Tidy Weekenders. The Tidy Boys would become a really positive presence in my life.

Sundissential was taking off like a rocket during the early noughties, appearing once a month at Uropa. It was just a rollercoaster ride of full-on joy and it did me no end of good turns really. I would classify Madders and the guys that ran Sundissential as loveable rogues, who weren't always the most reliable when it came to paying everybody, but they really looked after me. Madders wasn't shy to get on the microphone to say some wonderful things about not just me, but loads of the other DJs too. People used to hang on his every word. And as a result of some of the stuff he said, the work and credibility I got through that association was absolutely amazing. I'm eternally grateful for everything they did. I was playing Sundissential in Leeds as well as Birmingham when a tour was announced. Sundissential was going to Australia and New Zealand; golden times.

I had become great mates with all the people at Slinky too including Claire Hoare who took over the bookings down there. Claire sorted my monthly residency at Slinky, doing the closing set to 2,000 people every single time. Some gigs are so monumental they're like cup finals. Playing to that many people who loved how I mixed the trance into the harder stuff was very special. DJing with Lisa Lashes, Tidy Boys, Tim Lyall and Garry 'Gaz' White and all the other residents down there was incredible. We had such a good time. Dave Lee, who was also a Slinky resident became Head Of Operations, taking over from the then boss Richard Carr. Dave really ran with the ball and did lots of world tours.

I was booked to play Slinky in the Philippines at the start of May 2001. I arrived at the capital, Manila at about 11am. I was absolutely shattered. I got to the hotel – part of a chain Slinky always used on world tours – and was treated like a king, just as I always was. Slinky were classy. I'd have to count on one hand, the amount of times where I've thought, 'Oh, God, this hotel isn't very nice.' Everything else has been a dream.

I was in this big hotel right in the centre of Manila. The hotel was a twin tower affair and absolutely beautiful. I checked in, went up into my hotel room, closed the curtains and had a bit of a rest.

I had trouble sleeping and so I turned on the TV. I was watching a bit of the news when I suddenly remembered it was my mum's birthday. I called my mum, which cost a fortune, to sing *Happy Birthday* down the line, which was a custom of mine. £60! I was having a nice chat with her, while flicking through the TV channels.

Sky News was showing these violent scenes in a foreign country somewhere. It was a bit rough to say the least. There were tanks in the street and soldiers and civilians running around with guns; protestors and smoke everywhere. It was a dreadful situation. Suddenly a headline appeared on the screen. Jesus. It was a revolution taking place. In the Philippines. In Manila!

I opened the curtains and looked down in the street to be greeted by a people's revolution. The army was in the streets as the people set about showing their opposition to the current President, Estrada, who was being charged with corruption. It was insane! "Mum, I'm gonna have to go. I'm in the middle of a revolution."

I was confined to the hotel all day. I phoned down to reception so I could speak to the promoters assuming it was 'abandon ship' time. If the gig was cancelled I wanted to get the hell out of there as soon as. I finally got a call at about 8pm. "Hey, Rob. Everything's calmed down. It's all good. The people have won. Do you still want to come and play at the party?"

– "Damn right. Try and stop me!"

I set off into town with my record box and proceeded to play at this party. There were a couple of other DJs on before me and then I was on at midnight. The atmosphere was incredible. I had a really scratchy, five-year-old acetate full of speeches and acapellas. It was close to being unplayable. I found the Martin Luther King 'Free at last' speech and played it into Massive Attack to open my set with the rich smell of revolution hanging in the air. It felt like a million dollars to be part of something so meaningful and historical. That revolution sparked two to three days of parties all over the weekend. I will never, ever forget it.

***

Two of the only hobbies I had outside of music were golf and *Pro Evolution Soccer*, which Leafy and I played for *years*. We played *Pro Evo* from early afternoon into late evening sessions where we'd have 'the best of 37' tournaments. We played *Pro Evo* right up until about 2009 when *FIFA* started to steal its thunder, causing us to switch. I even played in their Seasons League, against gamers from around the world and got into the first division, which was quite impressive, although that meant getting tonked by everyone, because it was a completely different standard altogether. So those are still my hobbies today, other than making music.

I was going over to Australia quite a lot in the noughties, where there were a lot of Chinese and Japanese game stores. Later on, I would buy *Winning 11*, which was the Japanese name for *FIFA*, which always came out before the English edition, so we could try to work out how to play the game as quickly as possible. We were totally hooked.

My mate Marc Leaf was a definite right turn on the motorway of life. But every now and again you take a wrong turn. You end up rolling with some people you really wish you'd never met. I was DJing one night alongside Seb Fontaine and Gordon Kaye at Hanover Grand in London when this Chinese guy called Eddie came over and spoke to me. Eddie was Gordon's driver and he was getting me drinks and seemed very nice. And for want of a better word, Eddie groomed me really.

Eddie was saying he lived in Leeds and if I ever needed a driver, to give him a shout. And at the time, I *was* in need of a driver, plus you could always do with more people who were up for coming out, bearing in mind casualties of war who just stopped clubbing as they got older and had kids and high-pressure jobs etc. I was always looking for new people who were up for a good time and this guy Eddie was always up for going out. Eddie was a very colourful character, and through driving me around for a while everybody I knew became friends with him too.

Eddie had some weird mental ability to be able to predict who was going to win at the horses. He would point at the newspaper and say "That horse is going to win, that horse is going to win and that horse is going to win." And then you'd watch these races and they would win. So then you'd think to yourself, 'Jesus Christ, tell us some more, Eddie!' Eventually, we ended up putting some money on the horses and winning. It was amazing. We had no idea how he was doing this. We assumed some insider knowledge of some description, but who cared? He had boasted that he had some connection to the Triad gangs in Manchester and we thought this could've given him some of this info via betting syndicates. I guess that made it plausible in some way.

I got a call from Eddie one day saying, "I've got this tip and it's going to win and you should lump big on this horse. It's definitely going to win." Eddie collected a load of money from me and my friends, some of whom he met while driving me all over the country. Whilst I was DJing, Eddie was getting to know these faces, namely the main players in the UK club scene. Eddie got a load of people to give him money for this one sure-fire bet, and… fucked off. With the lot. I know he collected at least £4,000 off some of my mates. He became friendly with a mate of mine down in Bournemouth and this guy called me one day. "Your mate Eddie, is he alright?"

–    "Well, first things first, he's not strictly my mate. And please, no matter what he's saying, take it with a pinch of salt."

–    "Well, he wants to borrow some money off me."

–    "How much?"

–    "10 grand."

–    "Do not, under any circumstance, lend that man any money!"

Whilst I was talking to him my phone was going off. It was Eddie on the other line trying to circumvent the conversation, to try to speak to me before that other guy could. "It's too late. I've already given him the money." And to this day we've never seen anything of Eddie since. He just disappeared with everybody's cash. So yeah, along the way you do meet some people you just wished you'd never laid eyes on, because I was getting lots and lots of other angry people contacting me saying your mate Eddie is a very, very bad man. "He's not my mate!" Not cool, Eddie, not cool.

# CH. 36

rob
fissera

# Middle Aged Boy Racer And The Tidy Weekenders

I've already confessed to being a bit of a boy racer. I've been banned four times. Just speeding and totting up. I've also got off with a couple of bans as well where I've had to pay £500 to a solicitor to go plead special hardship and all the rest of it. But I would never speed through a housing estate or anything like that. However, the motorway is a different story and I've done some pretty unscrupulous things in order to get to gigs on time. Because sometimes the timings you're given by either an agent, or through your own stupidity, mean you really need to cut some corners, like going on the hard shoulder for instance. I know, I know.

2002, and we were going to a party. We'd left it late. There was torrential rain on the way to this Gatecrasher festival and we were racing through the downpour in the fast lane just so I could stand behind some turntables. There'd been a big crash on the motorway and we were soon caught up in a huge tailback, which meant that all of a sudden, we were in a situation where I might not make it to one of the most important gigs in my career thus far. My mate Adam Falkingham was driving and we got to this point in Warwick near to where the festival was, where this dual carriageway led to a roundabout – and both lanes were bumper to bumper. I was starting to get quite jumpy because I knew time was running out. I looked at all the cars and thought 'We need to be in front of all of those! How are we going to do that?' Adam suddenly bolted upright and said, "Hold on!" Adam pulled a right turn and went down the empty lanes going the other way. "Shiiiiiiiiiiiiiiiiiit!"

We were now bombing down the wrong way on a dual carriageway, doing our best to avoid any cars coming towards us. I felt my stomach rising up my throat. "Please god, I don't want to die!" We drove down the other side of the dual carriageway and beat the traffic on the left-hand side without crashing into anyone. People were pointing at us as we sped towards the roundabout and down the other side of a single track where there was another huge line of traffic heading towards the car park. Once again, we took the outside lane and somehow managed to get all the way down to the entrance until another car came along, which just wouldn't budge. "We're not letting you through, you dickhead! What are you doing?! What are you even fucking doing?!"

Luckily, we managed to get the cars to park to let us go into a space in the line of traffic whilst everyone was just staring, open mouthed. Phil Arrowsmith, this 6ft 4" giant was with us, and we bolted out of the car carrying two boxes of vinyl through a corn field, bumping into Russell Pate and Matt Chester from Gatecrasher during the dash. Matt was on a walkie talkie and he let us through a gap in the fence. I got behind the decks with about a minute to spare. Adam was still way back parking the car. It was one of those days where I must admit we'd been really bloody stupid, but I just can't stand letting people down.

I had a good friend called Jack around then. Jack Daniels. And there weren't many times when I wasn't in possession of a bottle of JD. Because I couldn't drive while banned, and I was pretty much always banned, I would drown my sorrows with some whisky and that got me into many more scrapes. There was always one, or 10, for the road.

***

I had become good friends with the people involved with Tidy Trax: Amadeus Mozart, Andy Pickles and Lee Haslam. They'd built up such a brand by this time. Tidy was a phenomenon with the record label Tidy Trax doing very well for itself. They then started putting events on just at that point where hard house was beginning to get to the pinnacle. It wasn't quite at the pinnacle yet, but it was getting there. Tidy were a driving force behind hard house along with Sundissential and Insomniac, and a couple of other nights. But Tidy entirely superseded them all really because what I loved about the Tidy team was that they treated everything they did just like a proper business, with a true passion for music. Everything they did, they did really, really well. I guess that was partly down to Amadeus and Andy being involved in Music Factory, the home of Jive Bunny among many other things. The guys ran a brilliant operation, which meant that their marketing and PR was so on point.

Tidy became the biggest name in hard house really. I was very fortunate to be up there with Anne Savage, Lisa Lashes, Paul Glazby and BK doing the main slot. I think because my sets had a slight tinge of trance along with the hard house, they thought 'We'll put him on at the end.' I loved playing for those guys and the Tidy story is truly inspiring..

## Amadeus Mozart, Tidy Boys

*"I started, like most DJs, as a mobile DJ in 1982, playing at weddings with my own little disco setup. And if you can play at a wedding and you can play at an 18th birthday party, you can play anywhere. The DJing in clubs that we do is very easy once you've got a wedding crowd dancing.*

*So, back in '83, I became a member of Disco Mix Club and Mastermix. They were the only two brands in the UK to have a licence to remix and megamix any record. They had a blanket PPL licence. You paid £25 a month and you would get exclusive remixes, megamixes and mashups that nobody else could buy in the shops. So, a subscription service for DJs essentially.*

*I was always interested in playing something alternative or those songs you couldn't get in the shops. So, like all DJs, I would hunt out Italian imports and special records just trying to be different from the crowd. But what got frustrating, as a mobile DJ, was they just wanted you to play the obvious chart stuff. So, you had this battle during the 80s where you were a DJ wanting to break new ground and play different things, and yet you were being asked to play the obvious stuff.*

*By 1986, I wanted to be a club DJ, moving from the mobile circuit into being a credible nightclub DJ. I'm from Kettering, Northamptonshire, born and bred and there are not many clubs there. It's a small town,* so it's very difficult to have a credible club there. Most of the clubs in Kettering were what we call cheesy clubs, where people would turn up after they got kicked out of the pubs. They'd turn up and get drunk, dance, ask for obvious requests and try to cop off during the erection section at the end of the night, where they'd play a ballad. But by '85, '86, I was playing hi-NRG from the gay clubs. Now, I must stress that I was brought up as a clubber, by going into gay clubs in '84. Because the gay scene was where you went to hear music that wasn't in the charts. You didn't have to be gay to go to a gay club. I actually went with my girlfriend at the time and we would literally go because it was a safe haven. You weren't going to get beaten up or have a pint poured over you. And you weren't going to hear Come On Eileen and all the chart rubbish. You were going to hear underground imports from Europe and America. After all, the gay scene is what broke house music in Chicago. It was the underground clubs of the gay scene, which really inspired me as a straight man. And that's why I became a fan of Tony De Vit and I became a fan of the clubs. And it was the disco in me as well. But this was faster, it was harder, it was underground, and there was no cheesy talking from the DJs. It was a great place to be in '84/'85. And that was before house came along.

And then when Chicago House came out in 1986, I was one of the first to get the imports from Chicago and New York and this garage music that was coming through, and I played it to an uneducated audience. And you'd get looked at, and you'd lose the dance floor, but the belief was that dance music in '86 was going to be the next big thing. DJs were about to fight back in a way. We were starting to rebel. We didn't want to play what the audience thought they wanted. We didn't want to play chart music. So, like Carl Cox and Tony De Vit, I decided I was going to play this music from Chicago and New York and you're going to like it. I don't care what you think. And it was that attitude that broke dance music. We wanted to break the mould.

I was there at the birth of house music and I watched the transition from the gay clubs playing hi-NRG songs and Euro beats. I remember listening to Tony De Vit in Birmingham at The Dome at a night called Bolts, which was a Monday night gay club in '85. And I remember hearing this, 'Jack–Jack, Jack your body.' And I loved it. These tracks coming through were minimal. These were not what we traditionally thought of as songs. New cheaper technology had given younger producers the chance to create fresh and exciting new sounds.

And I remember DJs in the gay clubs getting caught between still playing the old hi-NRG and this minimal sound from Chicago. And for about two years, we had a really weird situation going off in the underground clubs, where you didn't know what you were going to get. It was a great time.

As a member of DMC and Mastermix, the DJ subscription service, I loved playing megamixes and remixes, so much so that my next step was wanting to be able to do it myself. 1989 I went to Barclays for a loan and they turned me down. The Yorkshire Bank turned me down, too. 'Why do you want to buy studio equipment? It's just a fad.' The Barclays bank manager kicked me out, although Jive Bunny was in the charts. I said, 'Well, look, Jive Bunny have just had three number one records, and they're just mash-ups of old records. I want to do that.' And he laughed me out the room.

So, anyway, my wife went and got a loan from the Yorkshire Bank, for £7,000 by pretending that we needed a new kitchen, and I bought studio equipment with that. I bought a small studio and you needed a lot of money back in those days, because it wasn't all done on a laptop. And I started making mixes.

Now, I wanted my music on Mastermix, which was owned by Music Factory: Andy Pickles and his dad, John. They had this DJ-only service called Mastermix and in 1990 I got my first remixing track on that label. And I'll never forget seeing my name on a piece of vinyl. Nobody ever forgets that feeling. It was a four-track megamix of Westbam on Issue 50 of Mastermix. And if that had been my final act, I would have died happy, I was so proud of that.

I was 100% self-taught. There was no YouTube then and so I had to read Japanese manuals on how to work keyboards and stuff. It was hard work back in the day. I was still DJing too. So, through my lucky break I was in at Mastermix and met Andy and John Pickles who had a compilation album in 1990 called Megabass, which was a commercially released album, which had upfront mash-ups, which got to number one. But for the first time ever, these tracks were cut up, mashed up and remixed. This was a TV-advertised album and I fell in love with it and got to know Martin Smith, who worked for Music Factory and said, 'I really want to do this.' And he said, 'Well, you've got to get yourself a computer. Get rid of the sequencer and get a computer.' Which I did.

Martin took a shine to me and we hit it off as friends. And the next thing I know, it's 1991 and he rings me up and says, 'Right, your stuff's so good, we're going to put a new album out called *Hit The Decks*, which is going to be a battle of the DJs. And we're going to do this under the name *Two Little Boys*,' believe it or not. We were called Two Little Boys because we'd done a rave track called *Stylophonia*, which was a minor hit. We actually went to Rolf Harris' house to re-record the vocals. He charged us £3,000 to go to his place for an hour, sit there and get him to re-record the vocals. And we got him to do loads of different things, such as singing 'It's time for house!' He didn't know what he was saying. Anyway, my DJ partner, Guy Garrett and I became Two Little Boys. It all sounds a bit sinister now, looking back.

Martin Smith said, 'We're going to have an album out called *Hit The Decks*, TV advertised and it's going to sell 300,000 copies. Do you want to do Side B? We'll mix Side A, you do Side B.' I thought, 'Shit, this is it!' So, on February 7th, 1991 at 1pm, I got my wife to ring up where I was working, Booker Cash & Carry, to tell them I was never fucking coming back. It's a shit job and I'm going to be a producer and a DJ for life.

So, the album came out and we had a big success. Sold 300,000 copies. Hit The Decks broke new ground. We were the first to break The Prodigy, because XL rang us and said, 'We've got this new act called Prodigy and they've got a track called *Charly Says* and they're desperate to get this to chart. Can we get it on this album?' So we said, 'Yes, let's do it.'

It was a really strange position to be in, because we had this really underground music, being advertised during the commercial breaks in *Coronation Street*; this obscure European/Italian/German techno and rave music at 140 bpm. And yet, it was a TV-advertised album. A lot of people come up to me today and say that those albums got them into music. Quite proud of that.

We had Hit The Decks, Volume 1, 2, and Volume 3 was *Battle Of The DJs* with Carl Cox mixing one side, Slipmatt and Lime doing the other.

By now I was part of the furniture at Music Factory and was best mates with Andy Pickles, who'd had three number one records at the age of 19 with Jive Bunny. Andy and John Pickles were based in Rotherham, in south Yorkshire and they'd invested all the Jive Bunny money – they'd sold 15 million records – into this backstreet studio and it was a great place to be at that time in the early 90s, doing this underground music with Martin Smith and the guys.

So, I'd had the success with the mix albums, but the only thing missing was producing my own tracks and so 1994, Andy Pickles and I went into the studio and came out with what was to be a big hit with a track called *Only Me* by Hyperlogic, which got signed to London Records – Pete Tong loved it. And it was also going to come out on Systematic Records, an offshoot of London Records, which released the Whigfield tracks.

We put 1,000 copies out on red vinyl to try and build up the hype. And then, in the background, London Records said, 'We'll put another 1,000 copies out on Red Jerry's Hooj Choons, and make it look like it's come from that label, rather than going straight out of London Records.' So, we had it released on Hooj Choons, which was a great privilege, because we were fans of that record label. And then it came out on London Records and got to number 35 in the charts, and ended up on *Now 31*. We were up and running.

Now Andy and I started to get a bit frustrated with the major record labels and John Pickles, Andy's dad said, 'Well, why don't you just have your own record label? Fuck the majors, they take too long for it to come out; it's just a nightmare. Why don't we set up our own underground dance label?'

Andy, Martin Smith and I were sat on a train one day and I was looking at the back of a can of Tango and saw the 'Keep Britain Tidy' logo and a light bulb flashed. I worked for Keep Kettering Tidy in 1986, and I remembered that the logo was public domain so anybody could use it. You were allowed to put it on anything. So, if you owned a drinks or crisps company, you were allowed to have the Keep Britain Tidy logo on the back, without permission. So, I thought we could do something with that.

So, we got a pen and paper out and Martin redrew the bin man, but turned the bin upside down, and put a record deck on top of the base of the bin. And we said, 'Right, let's give it a name'. And we came up with Tidy Tunes, but that wasn't quite right. And by the time we got to the end of the train journey, we had Tidy Trax.

Fast forward to 1998, and we took hard house to the left, and we released Signum, *What You Got for Me*, and Tony De Vit did *The Dawn*, which was based on Signum. We decided to put the melody of trance to a harder beat, and came up with the term hard trance, because trance was a bit floaty. Trance was the sort of thing your mum and dad quite liked when you had a white female singer singing about castles in the sky. It was great in the car, but just boring in a club. We wanted to put the bollocks into trance.

*And so we did a tour with Signum and merged hard house with trance, and became a hard trance label. And I think that's what got Rob excited, because he loves a melody. And I think Rob loved Signum and The Dawn and so we started the Tidy Two label. I think Rob really fell in love with the Tidy sound and we'd hit the back of the net with that production in 2000/2001 when Rob started making music for Tidy. Or, at least, sending us stuff.*

*I've done all the A&R for Tidy for the past 28 years and I can't remember turning much of Rob Tissera's stuff down. I think most of it we've probably had. He had some great releases on Tidy Trax, but he's certainly not had all his tracks on Tidy Trax."*

There was now an annual Tidy Weekender at Pontin's in Prestatyn and it was debauchery on steroids. I've never seen anything like that in my entire life. 3,500 ravers there all weekend, staying in chalets, and there were more shenanigans than you could ever imagine. Often I'd be fortunate enough to play the closing set at some of those gigs.

I remember the very first time I was to play Tidy Weekender. I'd been playing down south somewhere and rather than staying in a hotel I went up to Prestatyn to stay in my chalet so I could get some much-needed kip. And then in the afternoon I was to play in the Tidy football tournament. Bearing in mind that I'd played semi pro at Chippenham Town and Bracknell Town, great things were expected of me.

I arrived on camp at 6am and just remembered the sun coming up. It was like something out of *The Walking Dead*. The place was overrun by zombies, like nothing I'd ever seen before. It was bright sunshine and the whole camp was alive. I'd just driven through the quiet Welsh countryside to be hit by this shock to the senses. 'What the hell has been going on here?!' Mental.

Following a few hours' kip, I played football in the afternoon. And I missed a penalty. There were about 4-500 people watching this game and that penalty miss still haunts me to this day. The grass was a bit long, so why did I put it along the floor? I can't imagine what it must be like for those guys who missed penalties for England. I never really got over that penalty miss. Even now I'm cringing because of the laughter that followed that pathetic drive straight into the arms of the keeper. It was a desperate new low.

I played out on the Saturday night and bearing in mind that Jack was definitely my friend at this period, I got completely obliterated. I remember finishing my set on the Sunday morning, and then went to visit all these chalets with Adam, Ian E and a few others to play some tunes. Jez and Charlie were residents at Sundissential and they introduced me to a whole bunch of other degenerates who were quite a lot younger than us, by maybe 15-16 years. And we went on a rampage for a few days. It was crazy. Tidy Weekender was definitely a place where, if I had any hair, I would be letting it down. They were great times.

## Amadeus Mozart, Tidy Boys

*"Rob has played all of our Tidy Weekenders; three days and three nights in Prestatyn at the Pontins holiday camp. We started those in 2002, and so Rob has done 22 years of Tidy Weekenders because he's a guaranteed crowd pleaser. Simple as that. Rob is a safe bet. He's a safe pair of hands. So, he has to be on our line-ups. He's a huge part of our heritage.*

*Tidy Weekenders are the spiritual home of hard house. There's a party in every chalet. People bring their own decks and so it's hard work to get them out of the chalets. One guy turned his whole room into a club. He brought lasers and a smoke machine. They're obsessed. I mean Tidy's a bit of a cult.*

*Tidy Weekenders would see Rob arrive on a Friday, play on a Friday, and he'd still be there on a Monday morning. He'd play the Kissdafunk set and a house set in the pub on a Sunday. So we'd always have to try and find him on the Sunday. And I remember Andy and I found him asleep in a bush once at Tidy Weekender 3. To this day, I still don't know why, on a Sunday morning, he was in these bushes. But if anybody was going to get into a tangle at a Weekender, it was Rob Tissera, the King Of The Tangles. Because Rob is a clubber at heart. He's a kid in the sweet shop at Tidy Weekenders, because he's got 2,500-3,000 clubbers there and he's got the music and all his hard house DJ mates, onsite for three days and three nights. And I think that's why clubbers like Rob Tissera so much. Because he's one of them. He's not the sort of guy that puts himself in the green room and drinks champagne. He's out on the dance floor, he's chatting to people, he's hugging people. Too many DJs lose the plot, and they have to be in the back room, with a big bottle of Moët, and they don't want to speak to their audience. Whereas Rob's a man of the people.*

*Tidy in Ibiza would be a 16-week season and Rob would always be part of the tours; he has travelled the globe with us whenever we've done anything anywhere in the world."*

# Harry Tee, Eddie H And A Massive Foghorn

Back in 2000, I got a call from these guys who were starting a new night in Manchester. Totally Mashed was run by these two cousins called Ben Spier and Barry Almond and they wanted me to play the opening night of a new project. They sold me the dream if you like in terms of what they were up to with their latest brand Goodgreef. It was to be me and Judge Jules on that night along with their residents Alex Kidd and Eddie Halliwell. So I said, "Yeah, no problem. I'm up for that."

The venue was at this place called Phillips Park Hall in Prestwich, right near where I worked at the Porsche garage, when I first moved north at the back end of '88/'89. I drove past where I used to work and then into a housing estate. "Wow, this is quirky!" We eventually arrived at some park gates and went down a track to see Phillips Park Hall; a country manor. A real pile of a place. It looked like the kind of stately home that would host banquets, with roasting hogs on a spit and all that caper.

As I parked up, I got that tingly feeling I used to get when playing underground raves. A little like driving my Golf through Northern Ireland. Edgy. But this place was tingly in a positive way. There was something special about Phillips Park Hall as it was definitely off the beaten track.

We entered through the main entrance and woah! The buzz was incredible. The music was firing. Amazing. What a sight! It was 3D crackers in there. I loved it from the moment I stepped inside the door. The guys playing in there were pretty tasty too. I only had 20 minutes to kill before I went on and so I disappeared into the toilet to psyche myself up with the 'I'm a tiger' speech. I was feeling quite nervous because I really wanted to nail this set. I gave myself a few soft punches to the stomach. "Come on sunshine, you've got this!"

This club had got something right from the get-go. It was like making 700 new best friends. That club had an instant crowd and a genuine sense of community. It was amazing and I loved playing that first set and it must have showed, because I was invited back on a number of occasions. Barry and Ben knew what they were doing and went on to do a number of highly successful enterprises after Goodgreef. In fact, they would go on to appear on the front cover of *Mixmag* in 2003, having been voted Club Of The Year by the journos and photographers who used to drop by.

Ben and Barry were proper go-getters and their Uncle Steve, who must have been 20 years older than me, was such a rum character. Uncle Steve was a law unto himself and just a superb bloke. Knocking around with those guys and doing loads of parties for them was a pleasure.

2001, Miranda Cook from *Mixmag* was running a night in Sheffield called Bed – a night orchestrated by the people behind Gatecrasher – and she invited me to play the Friday night. Sheffield was only 30 miles from my house and so I thought I would just go over, play, and take it easy. Maybe stay for 15 minutes and then go home because I had a busy weekend coming up.

I finished my set and Miranda suggested I stick around. "Eddie's playing after you."

– "OK, cool."

I'd first met Eddie Halliwell very briefly at that Goodgreef party the year before, but hadn't seen his set. Anyway, Eddie appeared in the booth and… my god. He went on and just ripped it a new one. I can honestly say that in all the times I've been DJing the only person to have ever given me that kind of feeling was watching Carl Cox for the first time at the Phoenix Club back in Leeds. Eddie could scratch so good he must have suffered with scabies as a kid. I just couldn't believe it. He was able to scratch over music at 150 bpm – nearly twice the speed of hip hop – flawlessly, for ages and ages all the way up to the breakdown of a track. Scratch, scratch, scratch, scratch into a huge breakdown and then he'd mix something else into it. He had his amazing energy, and his performance level was like nothing I'd ever seen before. He was jumping up and down all over the booth.

Before I knew it, it was two hours later, and the night was finishing. I was actually dancing on the speaker stack next to the dance floor, looking down into the DJ box. I was astounded by Eddie Halliwell and his marvellous talents. He was flawless.

I spoke to the guys at Sundissential. "Have you seen this guy, Eddie Halliwell? If not, you should. Trust me. This guy is going places. You need him on the team. He's something else."

– "OK, we'll have a look at him."

– "Tell you what, I've got a gig next month in Leeds, so why don't we let him play back-to-back with me and we'll see how it goes?"

I am certainly not in any way suggesting that I made Eddie Halliwell, by the way, because many people were probably saying the exact same thing as they were also seeing something they'd never seen before. We could all see that spark of creative genius. Plus, Eddie was a joy to work with. I did quite a few back-to-backs with him, including a couple of big ones for Sundissential at The Works in Birmingham to over a thousand people.

There was a massive foghorn at The Works that made an enormous noise not dissimilar to one of those horns you hear on the American railroads that you could sound by pulling on a chain. I said to the guy who was doing the lights, "Can I let the foghorn off?" He just shrugged. I remember Eddie dropped this banger and used both hands to pull this chain like a drunken bell-ringer. HHHuuuuuuhhhhh!!! The crowd loved it. I was soon like a dog with a bone. Every now and again I pulled on the chain. HHHuuuuuuhhhhh!!! It was ace. And then the crowd started chanting: "Pull the chain!" Every now and again I would give them a comedy pause before letting that horn off again.

\*\*\*

2001 was such a great year. England beat Germany 5-1, which I remember watching in an Ibiza hotel bar in the blazing sunshine. What a day that was. I think even Heskey scored! I adopted a border collie in 2001 too.

One of my mates, Carl Smales started dating a woman who needed to find a home for her dog, Harry Tee. She had a young child and was finding it hard looking after both and so introduced me to this seven-year-old border collie. He was a bit smelly, but such a lovely dog. I was sat there talking with my friend and when I looked down, Harry Tee just stared up and fixed his gaze on me. I just thought 'He's awesome!' My then partner, Katy said she was OK with it, and so Harry Tee and I embarked on the best friendship. It was untouchable.

Harry Tee was literally the best friend I ever had and I doted on him. He was such a bundle of joy and so well trained already. He was no problem whatsoever. I spent pretty much every free moment with Harry Tee and he kept me so grounded, because I now had that responsibility of needing to get home at a decent hour to take care of him. I would often get back from whatever club I was playing to take Harry out for a quick stroll at five or six in the morning. I used to love watching Harry Tee sauntering around the garden sniffing the flowers and plants. It used to fill me with so much love. The amount of times I would be playing tracks and Harry would be sat by my feet. The track *Birds* by Question Mark on Tidy Trax has a middle eight that featured bird song, funnily enough. It's this pumping hard house track and every time it broke down into this bird sample in the middle, with all this tweeting, Harry would come barking up the stairs. Sometimes I would put it on just to get him up the stairs at night.

I remember trying to nail this mix CD one time, which were tricky things to do on vinyl. Getting those mixes completely smooth was a struggle sometimes and I just remember finishing that CD that summer with Harry Tee sat on my feet as we listened to Cassius' *Sound Of Violence*. That track will always be mine and Harry Tee's. I don't think those memories can ever be beaten. They're just the most innocent and beautiful feelings, they really are.

\*\*\*

Sundissential North moved out of Uropa around this time. Sundissential was the only successful night at this place and it just wasn't sustainable and so Uropa shut down their operations. Now, Sundissential was snowballing and had such a reputation for being so good, we were getting people coming from outside Leeds to party there. And so, the brand was very much a hot ticket.

We became quite good friends with the guys from *Mixmag* who were loving the hard house thing and so we were definitely flavour of the month, as well as nights like Insomniac, which was going very well. We eventually moved Sundissential to Evolution. I'd been doing a bit of work with Jim Albentosa from an organisation called Taking Liberties who were very involved in big student gigs at the University. I knew Jim from back in the Ark days and he was another example of the importance of getting out there and meeting people. Over the years, I'd met all these ambitious people who left an impression on me. These people will probably end up doing stuff with you for years. And Jim was one of those guys I knew from the student days with Ark.

Jim had been running some very successful student events with his company Taking Liberties, including this club Evolution, which was at an out-of-town retail park in Kirkstall, two or three miles outside the city centre of Leeds. There was a McDonald's there and a few other bits and pieces. Anyway, Jim said to me, "If you can think of anything that's going to fill this place, you should give us a shout." And then pretty much in the same period, John from Uropa was saying "We're gonna have to shut Uropa down."

I got Madders and Danny Kirk from Sundissential up to check out this new venue and everybody loved it. This place was big and had enough space to get 2,500 people on the dancefloor. It had three rooms: one main room on two levels, a little like The Works in Birmingham. It was very 80s and you had people on the same level as the podiums. It also had another room, which was circular and had a projector that could fire visuals around. It was very impressive.

Funky house was coming through at the time with some pretty big tracks like Stardust's *Music Sounds Better With You* kickstarting the scene back in 2000. Other tracks from around 2000 would have been lots of stuff on Defected like Junior Jack's *At Nite*, Bob Sinclair's *I Feel For You Baby* and Kurtis Mantronik's *77 Strings*.

I loved the funk-fuelled sound and started buying loads of it from a shop that Marc Leaf was working at called The Record Box. The funk was also becoming very big in Ibiza. And on top of all the other stuff I was doing I still kept dipping my toe into the house world, but not as much as I'd done in previous years. But I was still buying anything that was current and good, including the beginnings of funky house. I was definitely interested in that and had been collecting a few of those records.

Sundissential moved to a venue in Birmingham called DNA in 2001, which was almost like a dirty cousin to The Pulse, but with exactly the same kind of layout. Everything was just a bit grimy, but what a venue that was and Sundissential just became this phenomenon. They moved to Saturday nights in Birmingham, and so I was doing Sundissential in Leeds and then going down to Birmingham for the Saturdays; followed by after-hours stuff in Subway City. Just great times with Danny, Madders and his girlfriend Helen. They were just the hosts with the most and really looked after me. We would spend hours after the parties, just sat around talking absolute rubbish.

The Sundissential guys had also tapped into the funk house scene and had started something in Birmingham called Funkissential in 2002, which was in a separate room to the hard house. This second room was a chill-out place called Rosie's Bar and the residents in there were the Trophy Twins. I met them a couple of times in the back room and they were great. There might only be 100 people out of 2,500 in that second room, but it had a great vibe. And then the next month, there'd be 200 people in there. And then at the next one there were 300 and you could see where it was going. I asked them if I could play some house stuff in there and they said, "Go for it!" I played there and everybody seemed to really enjoy it, which was great. And then I did the next one, and the room just kept growing and growing.

The Sundissential and Tidy crowds were a young crowd from the cyber generation who were quite often students who loved dressing up and having fun. They would turn up with furry boots on, *Monsters Inc*. backpacks and dummies. It was very playful. There was a lot of neon make-up and wigs. These were fun times at Sundissential. Even before I'd play, I might stand for at least 35 to 45 minutes signing *Monster Inc*. backpacks and *Beano* annuals, talking to people who were completely off their chops. Their chi was infectious. As time went on, a lot of those people who'd been there right to the end of my closing hard house sets were now plonking themselves in Rosie's Bar for Funkissential. They had also started to get a bit more dressed up and glued into this funky house. They loved that Junior Jack sound as well as Nomad and Shakedown and all that crowd. There were a lot of mullet haircuts and trilby hats and people just loving the funk and Funkissential just kept on growing.

I said to the boys, "Listen, this thing is so good, how about taking it out of here and making it a standalone night, because I know some people who run a club in Leeds called Mint. It holds 800 people and it might be perfect for Funkissential." We had a couple of conversations about it and they were like, "Yeah, you know what, that sounds absolutely great. Why don't we have a conversation with them?"

# CH. 38

**rob tissera**

# Tolley, Frying Pans And The Funkissential

I was in studentville around the back of Cardigan Road, Leeds, not far from Evolution. It was post Sundissential and everyone was piling into those back-to-back terraces on Cardigan Road for after-parties. A lot of the Sundissential crowd would filter back and forth, house to house having these little parties. I got talking to this guy Glyn Tolley who made a progressive house track back in the 90s called *These Things Happen* under the name All Boxed In. It turned out that Tolley was from Huddersfield and it suddenly dawned on us that he was friends with that guy Tom who ran off with my vinyl while I was in prison. We ended up having an affinity straight off the bat. Tolley was also doing some work with Sundissential and I couldn't believe we'd not met before.

Tolley was a big, big guy. Over 6ft tall and built like a brick shithouse. Tolley was also a cage fighter, as were a lot of the people he knocked around with at Sundissential; all gym nutters and ripped. We were talking about old times and about rave and the KU Club in Huddersfield when a fight broke out in the street.

This guy, known as Stavros, was threatening people because somebody in the party owed him some money. He was shouting the street down. "Go and get the fucking money or there will be trouble!" Somebody ran out of the house and cuffed him around the head and Stavros did a runner. About 15 minutes later, Stavros was back with a bandana around his face and a bloody big bowie knife in his hand. Tolley had seen what was kicking off through a window and strolled into the kitchen. Tolley opened a cupboard door and pulled out a massive frying pan. And with that he was off out into the street by the back entrance of the house.

Tolley strolled down the alleyway to the end of the houses and could see Stavros wielding this great big bowie knife. Tolley suddenly appeared and just blindsided Stavros. THWACK! Tolley creamed Stavros around the head with this frying pan, and like a scene from *Tom & Jerry* nearly knocked him off his feet. That was the end of Stavros for the night as Tolley had well and truly neutralised his threat. I remember thinking 'Jesus Christ! I never want to get on the wrong side of Tolley.' Anyway, we ended up being best of mates.

Tolley was involved in the security game including Sundissential and he had a big love of house music. And so we decided to work together. We spoke to Danny and Madders about taking Funkissential to a Friday night at Mint. Funkissential could remain within Sundissential on those Sundays, but we reckon we could get it going on a Friday too. They gave us the green light. Tolley and I knew the guys from Mint, and they agreed to a party, once a month, every single month for the next two years. We were in business.

The first Funkissential at Mint caused a roadblock. There was a queue that went literally around the block. It just went crazy there and soon became the most important funky night in Leeds, for a long time. And again, that involved me playing final sets after the Trophy Twins and some of the other people we booked. We also started booking people from brands in other cities too such as the guys who ran Garlands in Liverpool. Dave Booth and Hugh Garry would come along and play and they *totally* understood what the vibe was, because Garlands had a young crowd and some of them also liked a spot of hard house as it was the sound of the time. They also liked a bit of a surprise now and again. 'Wow, where did that come from?!' Those guys might be playing a funky house tune, when out of nowhere, they would play Dolly Parton's *9 To 5* or *Billie Jean* or a slightly tougher record. It was such great fun and it truly sparked a new chapter.

Dave and Hugh from Garlands then returned the favour and I got to play there as well. Traditionally, Garlands had always been this fantastic club that entertained everyone in the LGBTQ+ community. It had been around for donkey's years, smack bang in the heart of Liverpool on Eberle

Street. Garlands had always been a funky house anything-goes venue, but as they grew and became more successful, they added another string to their bow by putting on trance and harder music downstairs in the basement, which held about 400 people.

The first time I went over there to play Garlands, I'd done a set somewhere else first. I went over there with four of my closest allies at the time, one of them being Eddie, the driver who ripped off most of my mates. Adam was there, as was my then girlfriend at the time, and some of her friends. And then another carload of people turned up too. We went over mob-handed. I remember going to the front door and speaking to the doorman, and he said, "Yes, it's downstairs in the basement."

Dave Booth was the guy responsible for those eclectic mixtapes I used to hear at Vinyl Exchange in Manchester when I first met Adrian Luvdup. Those tapes were so good and he would mix everything from Inspiral Carpets into Young MC and acid house. Then you'd get a Cure track before going back to house. I always used to think 'Wow, that's how you do it!' I'd never heard anyone do stuff like that before. Dave Booth used to DJ in Manchester during the 80s at Pips, which was a new wave club; the best thing in town for a long time. I'd come across Dave Booth quite a few times in the past, but this was one of the first times I got the pleasure of actually working with him and as a result our relationship became more entwined.

You could give Dave any old box of records, be it anything from techno to rare groove and he would put together a blinding set with it and just blow it out of the park. That's how good he was.

Dave was downstairs playing a full-on trance set with tracks like Mauro Picotto's *Lizard* and all these booming tunes. Garlands had 400 people in the basement getting down to the trance with funky house going on upstairs. It had this great atmosphere and Dave was smashing it out and I remember thinking I had my work cut out for me there.

I had only just started playing when this guy came over to speak to me. He said, "Hello mate. I've been asked to look after you for the night. Is there anything you want?" He went off with my order and came back with a bottle of Jack Daniels. He just stood there all night pouring me these huge measures of Jack and laughing and dancing with us, having a right giggle. He was such a nice bloke I introduced him to all my mates. He said his name was Barry Mac. When the night finished, I asked the posse what they wanted to do now. "Well, we could all go to the hotel we booked for you next door," Barry suggested. And so we had a party at the Adelphi Hotel, which was a bit rundown, but had clearly been a really decent hotel at one point in time.

We were in these presidential suites, which were all done out in that flocky wallpaper featuring colourful orchids everywhere. And so me, Barry, and the *Mixmag* guys, Dave, Tracy and Duncan and a whole bunch of other people became great friends with the Garlands posse too. All of these things helped to cement us in the next few years, and we ended up partying until stupid o'clock. And I said to Barry, "I know you've been asked to look after us, but I still don't know what you do at Garlands."

– "Well, I'm Barry and I run Garlands."

– "What?!"

Barry Mac was such a beautiful soul and so incredibly humble. Barry was also one of the biggest fiends I'd ever met in terms of debauchery and drugs, although he successfully reformed. I've been in some really scary *Scarface*-type scenarios with Barry where things have gotten a little unruly, but on the upside, he was such a genuine soul. He's still one of my best mates to this day and I always stay with him in Ibiza where he lives every summer with his incredibly talented son, Harrison. The two of them now run a hugely successful kids event called El Kiddo. And so I was now back and forth playing for Garlands.

# Kanya Dig It?

If you keep walking around the rocks past Cafe Del Mar and stand facing the sea, you will see a footpath that goes all the way around the coastline. After 500 yards or so, you will arrive at Kanya, which is right next door to Kasbah. If you stand looking at the sunset from the Kasbah terrace, Kanya is just below you on the left-hand side.

Garlands asked me if I wanted to play Kanya in San Antonio, Ibiza, which of course I did. Any excuse to get back to Ibiza and I loved the association with Garlands. Kanya had a DJ booth in the courtyard outside with a giant yellow ship's sail covering the terrace. Kanya ended up being a really pivotal place in my DJ journey.

Kanya could hold 300 people on the terrace, with an indoor restaurant terrace too, and from the DJ booth could you look out at the sunset while playing to a whole bunch of tables below. Kanya wanted to do some parties, which was quite revolutionary for San Antonio at the time. Garlands was starting to become popular with all the workers from the clubs who adopted it as their playground. They would go to Garlands first and then maybe on to Space Carry On.

Garlands was on a Tuesday at Kanya during the day and into the evening. I started doing some parties for them and because they had so much clout with the workers who felt so much love for Garlands, word soon got around the island. It was just where everybody who was playing there went to chill and it really lit the touchpaper for the house stuff that had been lying dormant.

Garlands managed to assemble a whole bunch of crazy people. Such a strong team with 30 dancers all head to foot in gold outfits wearing glitter running through the streets with Garlands banners, accosting people on the streets to administer shots of Garlands punch. God knows what was in that. Never drink the punch. I once spent an hour and a half in the bog after drinking that. I remember someone banging on the door and I suddenly came to. The next ten hours were interesting.

2002, Garlands at Kanya, Ibiza was off the scale. Garlands workers were well known as the happiest and craziest of all the workers on the island really. They had Barry Mac, Dave Booth, Les Calvert and Huey (Hugh Garry) as well as the residents alongside myself. I was honoured to be asked to DJ in such exalted company because those guys were the kings of being eclectic. In terms of the relevance of 'the message is the music', Garlands just got it right every single time and playing alongside those guys was something else. I was playing Garlands one night, with the idea of lining up a suitable record for when the sun went down. A large portion of Kanya looks out into the ocean and I had *just* the record in mind for when the sun finally set. I placed Cassius' *Sounds Of Violence* – my dog Harry Tee's favourite track – to one side and just kept checking to see if I could time it just right; the window of opportunity was not long. Bearing in mind that this was pre smartphones I had to trust my eyesight as to when to drop that record. And then the time came.

There were a thousand people there that night. Many people were dancing on the rocks or on the beach, as well as all those inside the venue. There were people hanging off every conceivable surface. I dropped the needle onto the Cassius track just as the sun dropped into the water and the place exploded. That felt like quite an accomplishment as I've always believed in the message being in the music and I think that's what those guys liked about me. It was in my DNA. It wasn't about an ego or a name, it was about playing the music you loved to the punters who loved you back. All these ravers were coming up to me to say thanks for such a moment in time.

Moments like that really bonded us together and Barry's complete kindness and acceptance of everyone made that place so special. His persona was a huge part of what made that night so magical. They had the best dancers and the best crew of people working for them, who had the biggest smiles on their faces. The PRs hardly had to do anything to get people to come to this event because word of mouth was everything and Garlands had such a good aura from the team that it drew people toward it. Lovely people and lifelong friends.

Later that summer, Garlands did a series of one-off parties and their reputation just kept growing and growing. They did a 'Hat Party' where everybody had to wear crazy headwear culminating in a competition for the best. I remember being there with Daniel Kelly, John Kelly's son and the rest of the family, plus a whole bunch of people I'd met through Barry from Liverpool. It was such great fun and the owners of Garlands were all there at this hat party, with 2,500 punters trying to get into this tiny little venue just down the road from Cafe Mambo. It really was a spectacle. The winner of the hat competition was wearing a hollowed-out melon, with a real trout Sellotaped to it. The trout was smoking a spliff.

Garlands would also hire this Elvis impersonator called Buff who paraglided into the sea. I remember him getting it monumentally wrong one time and dropped unceremoniously into the sea like a sack of spuds. On a more serious note: he actually did himself some damage, so hats off to Buff. He was a brilliant, madcap character and a true Ibiza legend. Ibiza was such a great place to work and play.

Once Garlands had finished on a Tuesday, everybody would go to Space on Tuesday night. Including us, of course. We would go to In Bed With Space with Barbara Tucker and Jon Ulysses. Jon was such a good DJ who could just read the crowd out of nowhere and he deserved everything he got because he is a 100% superstar.

Because Kanya was an outdoor venue, Pepe and Salvador and a few other people who ran it, were having some serious issues with noise complaints to the degree that a few years later, they ended up having to knock down that terrace where everybody partied to make it an all-indoor enclosure to contain the noise. But they still had problems because they built some flats above it and the people continued to complain as the parties went on until all hours.

\*\*\*

I'd been doing so well out of all the trance and hard house stuff, but I hadn't fully dipped my toe into the water with funky house with the exception of Funkissential. The combination of house and funk was a dream come true for me and so I started playing for them in Liverpool in the main room which was quite an honour as hardly anybody was given that opportunity.

# CH. 40

### rob Tissera

# Trance Gets Mothballed

There had been a lot of discussion regarding the state of trance in 2002 and there did seem to be less interest in terms of the headcounts at certain nights. What does a DJ do when these cultural shifts occur? Do you stick with what you know and love? Or do you change gears and follow a new path? Or… maybe you do both. Interestingly enough, a lot of those trance guys stuck with what they knew and loved and what had been very prosperous for them. And credit to them, they managed to march on through a very tough period, many of whom managed to become huge successes once more.

Some of the scene's big players, such as Armin, never went away, but from a club perspective, the sound was definitely mothballed for a while. And all of those factors made my decision an awful lot easier to make. I guess you could say I put trance on the back burner for the time being and made a couple of hard house tracks. I had to keep moving forward to see what was right for me. And it worked wonders.

I was DJing for Judge Jules at Judgement Sundays in Eden back in '99, my association with them going all the way through to when he was supporting us with *Kick Up The Volume*. Those stints at Judgement Sundays were great. But now, the trance craze had started to lessen a little and the music was changing. All of a sudden, Judge Jules wasn't doing Radio 1 on a Friday night anymore, and Seb Fontaine took over and his style was much more progressive house and that had a lot of influence on the music being signed by the major labels. Prog house was just a level down from trance which didn't require those euphoric movements; prog house was essentially trance without the massive riffs.

Funkissential was going crackers however. It started as a standalone event, but was now starting to outgrow the venue. The car park was about 300 yards from the venue and once I'd pop the coins into the machine, I walked across the road and turned the corner to get a first glimpse of the queue. We were so nervous on that first night, as you can imagine, because we'd taken it out of its comfort zone. But the thing is, we could see from the rising popularity of Rosie's Bar that we were witnessing an evolution. It got to a point where it was 'one in, one out' in that room. So, we expected a little support for the Mint night.

I came out of the car park, turned the corner and saw it. Jeezus. There was a queue all the way down the street. It was maybe 100 yards to the corner of the next road, and so that was pretty impressive. I wandered over to see just how far the queue went. What?! It was another 75 yards down the road. People were three deep, and the club could only hold 800. From the moment we opened the doors on the first night, I remember walking around that club thinking, 'We are going to need a bigger boat.' It was just breath-taking to stand in the middle of all that and it brought a lump to my throat. Funkissential gave me a problem I never ever thought I'd encounter: thinking about a bigger venue on the first night. Politically, however, this was a sensitive area and was bound to piss people off if you ended a contract that early.

That same year, a new event started on Wednesday night in Leeds called Base At Space. Space was started by Chris Hanley and a couple of others. It was a hard house night on a Wednesday and it had the same kind of roadblock situation. They had a queue that went out of the alleyway and around the corner and all the way down another street, which then rounded on itself. It was two tequilas for a pound too. There were quite a few nights where I staggered out of there, that I definitely can't recall.

A lot of the people that were into the funky house stuff in Leeds were students who came from all over the country to study because of the quality clubs like Base At Space and Funkissential that were right in the thick of it in studentville. Funkissential and Base At Space were on fire with all the best DJs coming in from all over the country to play. It was carnage actually because Space was a small venue and the punters were right on top of you as you played out. Plus, there was Sundissential and all the other stuff in the city right next to you and so it was a brilliant time to go clubbing in Leeds. I absolutely loved it.

2002 saw Slinky expanding loads too and I was playing for them once a month, going down to Dorset on a Friday night. They then started a night in Leicester, followed by Bristol at the club I used to go to while in the RAF. Formerly known as Papillons, it was where I got down to the jazz funk at this venue now called Creation. It was mad to think back to the teenage me, boogieing away while off the RAF base.

***

I started playing a night called Fever in Northampton, back in 2001, which was originally called Goldiggers in the 80s. Fever was a trance night set up by Andy Owen and Jim Gold. When they paid me my money at the end of the night, we would inevitably start talking about football; well, it's the absolute universal language of the world, isn't it? It's the unifier and the divider. After a brief chat, we realised that we had a bond. Jim and I both supported Luton Town. Jim also owned a Mexican restaurant and a gentleman's club in Luton and he suggested going to see the Hatters when they next played Rushden & Diamonds, which was not too far from Northampton. He was going to get tickets from one of the Luton players who was a mate of his. Sounded like a plan.

A few months later, March 2002, I was duly booked to play Fever on the same weekend as the Rushden & Diamonds game. I played on the Friday night and had quite a lot of tequila with those guys.

We went to the Rushden & Diamonds game the following day with my mate Adam Falkingham. And Luton were shocking that day. Insanely poor. A game so bad the ball was in the air more than it was on the ground. It was one of those horrible games on a windy Saturday afternoon in March and every time the ball went up to our centre forward, it would bounce off his head like a thrupenny bit or it would ping off his shoulder or his knee and go out of play. He just couldn't hold the ball up. I remember thinking I'd had enough of this. I stood up, seconds after another ball ricocheted off this clueless Luton forward and shouted, "You're an imposter!" It went awfully quiet in the away end and the centre forward actually looked over to where I was standing. I sat down next to Jim and said, "Sorry, but he's terrible!"

I was a bit of a fairweather supporter at the time and wasn't taking much interest in the team. "Who the fuck is he?!" I asked Jim.

– "Oh, that's Steve Howard. He got us the tickets."

We were supposed to go and meet Steve Howard afterwards, but I made my excuses and got the hell out of Dodge quick smart. I really didn't want to meet up with the bloke, because I felt so embarrassed. The free tickets dried up for a while after that.

\*\*\*

Summer of 2002, I did a live broadcast for Radio 1. It was an hour long set for Dave Pearce's *Dance Anthems* live on a Sunday night. I was overjoyed at being asked to do that. The venue was The Windmill in San Antonio and this Sunday night was the wrap-up show for Radio 1 Week, which was just a dream come true. To think that all of your endeavours could come together like that. I was looking out over the bay of San Antonio, with this Windmill behind me, and all the Ibiza clubbers live on Radio 1. That truly was an honour and I was very grateful to Dave Pearce for giving me that opportunity to shine.

Shortly after that, I treated myself to a new BMW 323Ci, which had that beautiful rounded shape. A silver coupe with black leather interiors, it was sweet. Adam, Ian E and I used to love tearing about in that thing.

I was playing the Room At The Top on the outskirts of Glasgow and drove up there with my then girlfriend Katy in this new car. I played that night and had a great time before setting off to come back south because Sunday was Sundissential.

I was driving back from Glasgow with not a care in the world when it started raining. I was driving responsibly and keeping to the speed limit as the rain came down. I pulled out into the outside lane to overtake when I hit this huge puddle of water that had collected in a massive dip in the road. I just hit the water and thought 'Woah!' I'd always been used to front-wheel drives and this BMW was a fairly heavy rear-wheel job and I just touched the brakes, stupidly and it spun.

I was now going backwards down the outside carriageway. Heart racing, I was facing the traffic coming towards me when the car spun back round again. A lot of cars were hitting their brakes, thankfully, while I did a proper 360 through the other two lanes. I assumed it was going to stop in a second although I was facing the wrong way.

And then the back wheel caught the edge of the barricades on the side of the road and I mounted it, flipping the car up and over off the motorway and into a ditch. We landed upside down with the airbags inflated. That was a very scary moment. I checked that Katy was OK and phoned the emergency services. I don't know how we survived that, but we had.

I was playing the last set at Sundissential every single month and it was vital to be there even though we'd had that harrowing experience. We got towed to a repair centre just off the next junction and when we got there, they said, "Oh, this happens all the time."

– "I bet it does. It's a death trap!"

I managed to persuade the RAC to allow Katy to take the car back to Leeds on the back of a tow truck to get it repaired – it was a total write-off – while I drove to Sundissential in a hire car. I remember thinking I might collapse when I got to the club, after experiencing all that. I'd been to London, then Scotland, then back down to Leeds, with a car crash thrown in for good measure. That really shook me up. The annoying thing was that the car must have cost me about £28-29,000, but the extensive damage to it was priced £500 lower than it needed to be for a replacement car. And so they had to repair it. And once it had been repaired, it had some niggly shakes and knocks that they just couldn't seem to locate. As soon as you got to about 70mph the back seat would start to vibrate. I was forever singing the 'I fucked it up' song to myself because I had to take it on the chin. I'd fucked it up.

***

Tidy was a on a roll. A successful record label, club nights and festivals, the Tidy brand was a leading force in hard house and they deserved it too. I will always stand by their team ethic and the way they manage everything. Andy Pickles, Amadeus Mozart, Lee Haslam, Johnny Dangerous and Russell Pate and so many more people who worked for them, just had the best infrastructure. I just knew they would go on for years, and their parties got stronger and stronger.

I played this Tidy Weekender that coincided with the 2003 Rugby World Cup Final. And my brain was fried while watching that cup final with Jasmine, DJs Jez and Charlie and all the guys from Sundissential and

Tidy in a pub called the Queen Vic, Prestatyn. There were 600 people in the pub when Jonny Wilkinson made that game-winning kick. What a moment!

I was asked to do a Sundissential tour of Australia and New Zealand that same year. It was me, Eddie Halliwell, Ilogik, Danny, Helen, Tolley and Andy Farley. The first gig was in Auckland, and whenever I went to a city like that I loved to embrace the local culture. Eddie and I went up the Sky Tower, standing at 328 metres high. I've always been a bit of an adrenaline junkie. We abseiled down the outside of that tower, which was quite an afternoon. And then we did the gig in the evening. I was standing there watching people's responses to seeing Eddie Halliwell for the first time. He was just a whirlwind. I'd done a few back-to-back sets with him and he really made you pull your socks up; you had to come up with new tricks and ideas to keep you super fresh. This was something I'd always done anyway, but Eddie definitely kept me on my toes. The response to Eddie was crazy.

We also played Sydney as part of that same tour, and I got completely smashed whilst not feeling very well; I had jet lag too. I remember waking up the next day at about two in the afternoon, my body clock all over the place. I called Eddie, which cost me £30, to make a UK call when in Australia, and he said, "We're not far from the hotel actually." He had also been out partying all night. They gave me the address for this place in Kings Cross; a real den of iniquity: peepshows, dirty book stores and all the rest going on. I found this location which looked like a sex shop and walked into this private suite. There were the crew all sat in a Jacuzzi, fully clothed. They were wasted! I politely declined the offer of a Jacuzzi with them and left them to it. I'm not sure what had been going on there.

That same year, I did a track under my own name with two guys called Vinylgroover & The Red Hed. I went down to Portsmouth to work with them and took along some vocals from Marcia Rae, who did the Quake stuff with us back in the late 90s. I had a few of her vocals that never saw the light of day, based around some lyrics I'd converted from a poem I'd written for this track *Stay*.

While spending Saturday with the guys it came to light that Jim Sullivan (The Red Hed) wasn't only in Vinylgroover & The Red Hed, but was also one of the Wideboys. They were really talented and fantastic company who would go on to do some great stuff over the years. Jim had real skills. I played him the vocals of the track and Jim got to work, as Scott Attrill (Vinylgroover) and myself took on the executive producer roles. We decided on a bassline direction and then added a great trancey synth to it. Now, Blandy is an absolute genius, The One Fingered Riffmeister, the king of making the most catchy melodies, but Jim had some serious tricks up his sleeve too. Jim was a full-on player. He could *play*. He must have been classically trained.

Jim listened to the vocal and said, "OK, the track's in E minor." He played the vocals into Logic and had the vocal circling around this 16-bar piece and just played this ridiculously good riff underneath it all. His left hand played the octaves while his right did the lead line over the top. I've seen some guys in action, but Jesus Christ, this guy really took the biscuit. I couldn't believe it. I don't want to put down what Ian does because he's also a total genius, but this was next level impressive. This riff was incredible and through that we turned this acorn of an idea into a track within about five or six hours. And it was one of the best things I've ever been involved with. That's certainly not how all of them have gone over the years, but that one was just a joy to do.

Around 2003, I devised my own system of working out the keys of songs just as Jim had. I went through my entire record collection and got the keyboard out to work out the key of every tune I played. Then I made 13" header boards just a little bit taller than the records; each one stating the key. All the tracks were also in categories. Then lo and behold, two or three years later, Mixed In Key came out, which was pretty much what I'd spent all that time doing.

I remember we finished off that track and I drove up to Brixton Fridge for Frantic and did a superb gig. I'm definitely putting that one down as one of the best musical days of my life. The track got signed up by Tidy Trax and did very, very well for us all; further cementing my relationship with Tidy. Everyone's a winner!

There were a lot of great Frantic parties on around then and I loved working for Will Paterson who also started up the Hard House Academy at Brixton Academy. A couple of times a year I was getting to play on the main stage at that legendary venue alongside Lisa Lashes, Paul Glazby and all the biggest fish in the hard house scene in front of 5,000 people going mad on a Saturday night. It was breath-taking stuff. A fantastic production and an awesome atmosphere in there.

\*\*\*

There were some great nights going on in London around 2003. There were a lot of Kiwis, South Africans and Aussies who were on those temporary work visas at the time where you could stay in the UK for at least two, if not four years. Damo (Damian Gelle) started running a night called Heat at Brixton Fridge, as well as at other places in London and they were great parties. He also set up the really big SW4 festival on Clapham Common, which he did with his business partner Anton Marmot. Damo became a great friend of mine and when he moved back over to Australia to continue what he was doing in London, we kept in touch. Working with Damo was a real pleasure.

These were peak years for me thus far running around with three to five gigs every single weekend. Sometimes, it was three in one night, which shouldn't even be possible; driving like complete maniacs in order to get to these places.

I was DJing at Global Gathering at a time when there was really only that, Gatecrasher and Creamfields in terms of the big festivals. Ian was driving and I had a BMW X5 at the time, which was a lovely machine. I got rid of the silver Beamer after all the trouble it caused me when I rolled it in Scotland. We were driving to this gig at Global Gathering, after I'd been playing somewhere down south and I had my laptop plugged into the Harman Kardon sound system, via a mini jack. It sounded great and it also meant I could create my own edits and work on stuff in Logic while we made our way to Global Gathering.

I created this new intro to my set using the speech from *The Warriors* movie when the leader of the Gramercy Riffs asks the crowd "Can you dig it?", which we added a drumbeat to. I was playing after Lab 4 who played at a million miles an hour. Playing after those guys was hard; you had to hit them with something really special. I got the strongest beats together and made it boom down into the 'Can you dig it?' speech from the Riffs gang leader Cyrus: "20,000 hardcore members!" When it goes, "Can you dig it?" I was gonna play *Dreams* by Quench; a newer version by Miss Shiva remixed by Paul Glazby, which was a *proper* tune.

I was mixing this riff from *Dreams* into the speech and I looked down to see this guy on the dancefloor who was 6ft 6". Or even taller. He looked like a prop forward rugby player he was that big. He had a Sundissential T-shirt on and across the front it said: "It's Tissera Time!" What the fuck?! Somebody had gone out of their way to actually have that embroidered on a T-shirt. It was mental! I saw it just before I went on, after standing there watching Lab 4 tearing it a new one and I just knew that this set was going to be a good one. I got up after Lab 4 and I went down a storm. And then I looked down and saw the huge guy with the Tissera Time T-shirt on. He seemed like such a nice bloke and he stayed there through my entire set. Moments like that give you this incredible confidence. 'I'm gonna smash this! I'm gonna give it my all!'

I made a point of going down and speaking to this guy after and shaking his hand. We got chatting and he was such a nice bloke and really funny. And I said, "If you ever want to come out partying, you're welcome anytime you like." And that's precisely what he did. Wayne used to come out with us all the time and did all the circuits. Because clubbing was my job, I always needed people to party with, to replace those who'd got married or had kids etc. There were always casualties of war, and many friends would come out for a few years, only to get to a point where their age/job/marriage couldn't handle it anymore. I had a purpose for going out every single weekend, but not everybody could do it. And so you always needed good friends who could join you on the road. Wayne travelled the length and the breadth of the country with us and we'd have such huge belly laughs; an unbelievably funny man. And not only that, but he introduced me to a lot of really lovely people who also became my friends.

***

It was 2003 and my birthday week. I was 37 and playing Sundissential at The Sanctuary in Birmingham. I was almost doing a little bit too much at that period, but the opportunity was too good to turn down. The company was now pretty much run by Danny and his girlfriend Helen, because Madders was no longer around. The party lifestyle had really caught up with Madders and he needed to take a step back. Everybody enjoyed the crazy aspects of his personality, but he was in a bad place and so he fell by the wayside for the time being. This meant that those other guys had to pick up the pieces, which was a massive shame because I've got nothing but love for Madders and it was always sad to see somebody fall on their sword.

Danny and Helen were good friends of mine and we spent a lot of time together whilst doing all the Sundissential and Funkissential parties. This particular party at the enormous Sanctuary was one that got the juices flowing. I went in through the back doors of the Sanctuary and the team came over to see me. There was a room out the back where everybody used to chill out and I was backstage for quite a bit. In fact, it felt a bit odd, because people were in and out of that room all the time. Anyway, the time came to get on stage.

It was the busiest I'd seen it in ages, and the place was bouncing. I then looked up and saw the huge Happy Birthday banners dripping from every balcony. Wow! There was so much love in that building and I will be eternally grateful for that experience. It was fantastic to play at your own birthday party with thousands of your closest friends. They let me play for as long as I wanted too. What a night!

Unfortunately, not long after that, things went a bit sour between me and Danny because of certain others who were involved in the background. For some bizarre reason, despite its success, things didn't seem to be going too well for them. Sometimes, clubs peak and then you get a natural drop off and things were starting to look a little worrying. There was something in the air.

However, Funkissential was going great guns. The parties were so strong and the timing was just right for that kind of night. Friday nights we would always go back to Tolley's house to count the money, and this particular night we emptied the bin bags, piled the money into stacks and did a double take. "There's something a bit off here." You could tell by sight how much money you'd made, roughly speaking, and because you could only get a certain amount of people into our events it didn't vary that much, even if it was 'one in one out'. But if that was the case, there would be even more money. But on this occasion, when we put the money into piles on his coffee table, we knew something wasn't right. "That's well short and we were rammed tonight!" The takings were definitely down, but how?

On this particular occasion Danny and the Birmingham crew had not come up to Funkissential as they normally did. In fact, they'd been to every single one prior to this. Instead, they sent up these two guys to run the door for us. The thing is, I'm a very trusting person until that trust is broken. These guys were people that ran their door down in Birmingham and so they were not just random people or anything. I'd met these guys quite a few times before, but things were not looking good.

We contacted Val, a lovely woman who ran the Mint club in Leeds and asked to look at the CCTV footage. She gave us the DVD and we went back to Tolley's place to watch it. We watched at least three hours

Kissdafunk crowd shot at Mission, Leeds, 2016

Kissdafunk crowd shot, 2007

Kissdafunk crowd shot at Gatecrasher, Leeds, 2011 (Afrojack gig)

Kissdafunk crowd shot. Afrojack, 2011. Picture by Leo Dyson (RIP)

Carly Hammond-Millard (Head of Entertainment)

Carly's Angels

Carly's Angels, Kissdafunk with the Shapeshifters

Kissdafunk 2 flyer

More of our Kissdafunk entertainers (Costumes Designed and made By Carly Hammond-Millard)

Kissdafunk L.E.D.

Kissdafunk awesome crowd shot

Kissdafunk crowd and decor

Me, Gyn Tolley, Carly Hammond-Millard, Carly and Alex Smith

Me, Tolley and comedian Ben Random

The Trophy Twins at Kissdafunk

Me and my best friend Danny James

Adam Falkingham and Nev Scott, 2009

All my friends from We Love Hard House

Dad and Mum in France, 2016

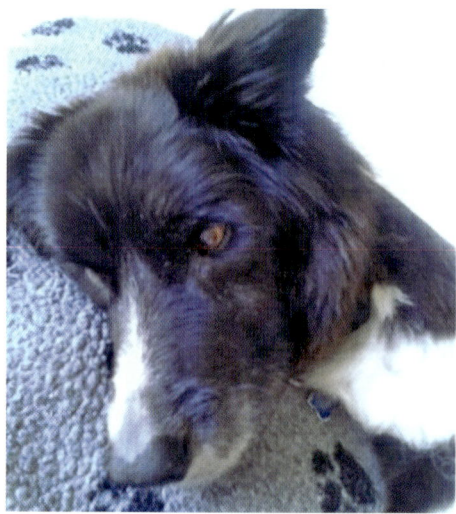

My first dog Harry Tee

My beautiful wife Anna

Our Wedding Day. 8/1/2017

Our wedding. Maggie O'Sullivan on far right

My Brother-in-law Magnus Gledhill with Me,
Anna and Anna's Mum & Dad

Our son Sweep

BK and me, Melkweg, Amsterdam, 2018

Anna and me

Me and Alex P at Centreforce, 2019

My Beautiful Mum

My sister Diane and my nephew Matthew

Anna and me Clockwork Orange, Ibiza, 2019

Our wedding

My stunning wife Anna

Our son Sweep

The amazing Nikkie Hainsworth

Clockwork Orange at The Printworks, 2021

of footage of these guys running the door. They were pretty much taking three tenners for themselves to every tenner they put into the bin bag. 'Three for us, one for them (us)'; £30 into the giant pockets of their parka coats and just £10 into the till. We were down £3,500.

We had two viable options. Either we could confront these guys about it, which would end up in massive acrimony or let it go, bearing in mind, I was pretty much a stalwart of everything Sundissential was doing in the north. We decided on the latter, but also let them know that Funkissential wasn't happening again.

Now, things were beginning to come to a close for Sundissential and Madders' removal from the business had been messy and it was such a shame because we'd been such good friends over the years, but this was a real game changer. And so, rightly or wrongly as a result of that incident, Tolley and I decided that Funkissential was no more. We didn't want to be a part of that and so we killed it off in Leeds. We would go our separate ways and do our own thing. 'The king is dead, long live the king!' We didn't actually make it public, we were very dignified in that regard, but the next gig would be the final Funkissential. Tolley and I told the guys in Birmingham that under no circumstances were they to come up that weekend and we used that night's takings to recoup what we'd lost – and to start a new brand!

# Funk, Beetles And Get Guetta

The timing was right to branch out on our own with a new brand and so Kissdafunk was born. It was getting to a point where we were making a lot of decisions around Funkissential anyway, because those guys seemed to be pulling away a little bit and we knew there was a market for the funky house. I honestly think they (Sundissential) were just acting out of desperation with the takings issue. I've not spoken to Danny since, but I'm not one for holding grudges and I don't know who made the decision to skim the door. I think sometimes when things go pear shaped, people make decisions they're not particularly proud of and this was one of those occasions. Anyway, we were going to use it as a bit of a springboard to something better. Something we owned.

I am certainly not one to do anything by halves. If you're going to do something, do it right. We had all the know-how, all the whys and wherefores as to what was needed to make something fly. I contacted my friends from *Mixmag*, Assistant Editor, Gavin Herlihy, Paul and Tracy and a few of the others and invited them all to come up for a soft launch. I invited Gav to DJ on the opening night. Because it was a soft launch we didn't invite anybody huge to come up and play or anything. We treated it as more of a rehearsal.

I'd met Carly Hammond whilst I'd been doing all this stuff in Leeds, with Sundissential and Base and she was just this charismatic, brilliant individual who wanted to be Head Of Entertainment for Kissdafunk. Had we ever expanded Funkissential we would have had Carly as Head

Of Entertainment there too because she was the queen of the party. Everybody knew her and loved her. She was so bright and good at directing the party.

Carly put together this set of five dancers called Carly's Angels who were great at what they did. Carly would make all their outfits for them and embroidered them with different themes depending on the evening. Carly just made it her own. She was a whirlwind and as a result of that, we became big with all the students who loved the funkier side of house, rather than the harder stuff.

I'd met Jim Albentosa years before when we were doing Ark; he ran Taking Liberties that did student promotions. Jim ran Evolution, the nightclub that Sundissential moved to and he took on our student promotions. We had some productive meetings with Carly, Jim and Shaun Wilson, who ran Federation in Leeds. Shaun had started a club called Mission in the Arches in the centre of Leeds not too far from the train station. It could hold 1,150 and Shaun agreed to host the opening night in the last week of January, 2004.

I was walking from the car park, past the Marriott Hotel – where we put the guys from *Mixmag* up – towards the railway arches and right in front of me was Mission and this little 300ft path. I walked down this path and then the view of the club opened up. It was *mobbed*.

Tolley and I wanted to create something that had the feeling we both got standing outside The Haçienda. We decided to stay away from all that nonsense with Sundissential to create something really positive and meaningful. We wanted to make it the best night we possibly could. We wanted anyone who couldn't get in, to be *gutted*. We wanted to create the feeling that this was your family, your community. We drew on all the experiences we'd had before with how popular Back To Basics had been where it was quite dressy and cool and wanted Kissdafunk to harness that vibe. And we certainly managed to create that feeling; the place was packed on what was a great opening night.

Opening night over, we started booking some bigger acts. We scanned through our contacts book and started hitting people up from all over the place. Many we spoke to wanted us to take Kissdafunk to their towns and cities. One of the first gigs we travelled to was the Bug Jam 'Run To The Sun' event down in Cornwall. Bug Jam, the VW enthusiasts' festival hosted loads of great entertainment. My friend Robbie from Virus was running Bug Jam and he asked if we could book some names and bring ourselves down with all the crazy decor we'd created.

Jez and Charlie were residents at Sundissential who lived in some student houses, not far from those parties in the back-to-back terraces, and their friend Jamie Bugler was a really talented graphic designer. I'd met Jamie a few times playing *Pro Evo* at their place. I would sometimes see some of Jamie's artwork, and it was super crisp and so we got him to do all the imagery and everything for Kissdafunk. Our 'look' was very upbeat with lots of colour; loads of flowers and butterflies. We wanted to look really presentable right from the off, and be right up there with the best, in terms of branding and identity, and I was so chuffed that we achieved that.

We created loads of decor for Run To The Sun, all based around the Kissdafunk artwork. We had big inflatable flowers that were 15 feet across. The venue also had a swimming pool area that would host 2,000 of the 5,000 that would attend, although the pool wouldn't be used; it was filled in. And then there was a balcony all the way around the top of it, like a leisure centre really. We would be up above on that level, where that top seating row would be, looking down into the crowd.

We really liked this tune *Little More Love* put out by a fairly unknown DJ and musician called David Guetta. It hadn't charted yet, but we thought, 'Why don't we invite him to play this Bug Jam event.' We got David's number through the guys at *Mixmag* and called him. "Hey, do you want to come over and play for us?"

–   "Yeah, of course. I'd love to, no problem there."

We flew him into Newquay airport and picked him up for a bite to eat before the show. At this point, he'd done one or two gigs in London and that was it. He was around our age and so it wasn't his first rodeo, but he hadn't made it big just yet. He looked pretty dishevelled when we picked him up and he probably would have rather gone to the hotel and had a shower, but he came for a burger with us. After lunch we took him off to his room, which was a rather ropey boarding house and paid him his money. David Guetta's fee was… drum roll… £400!

David Guetta cost us £400. Not sure what you'd get for £400 from Guetta now, maybe a smile? Anyway, he went on and destroyed the place! He was ridiculously good. I will not have a bad word said against that man because he's one of the brightest, most intelligent blokes I've ever come across and so gracious and polite; one of the nicest people I've ever met. Soon after this, his single flew into the charts and went to number one much to our delight as this meant that everyone knew him. You couldn't have made it up really.

I often get asked the question: what's your favourite type of music? But I don't have a personal favourite. I like them all for different reasons. I like house music because it's sexy. I like the hard music because it releases a completely different energy. I like the breakbeats because it reminds me of the early days of rave. I love the old skool stuff too. For me, they all play a part in the science of making people go nuts to music and that's what David was like.

David went on and played one of the most eclectic sets I've ever heard, including Nirvana's *Smells Like Teen Spirit*, which nobody would have also played in a house set at the time, apart from possibly Dave and Huey from Garlands, but I'd never even heard them do something like that. And it just struck a chord with everybody because David had done his homework on the Bug Jam crowd, who wouldn't just be people into sexy house music or a Hed Kandi vibe. There would be all sorts of people there, including some grungy, rocker types. He also played The Prodigy's *Breathe* and some electro tracks going across the board and every single thing he did, made the crowd go nuts. I have very rarely seen a DJ work a crowd like that before. He was ridiculous. And as a result of that, we asked him to come play in Leeds although his reputation was now growing quite quickly. He was now costing us £600! Daylight robbery. Ahem…

We soon became friends with David as he was definitely one of those people you wanted to be around. He was also very curious about genres he wasn't too familiar with. "Tell me more about trance," he asked me once on the way to a party. He just wanted to improve his knowledge of the entire scene. Because he was on the way up, we made sure we picked him up from airports and got him to any other gigs following ours, because it was important that we maintained that reputation for looking after our DJs. By sending a driver for him, we established that first-hand contact. We had many a car journey with David where we would chat about music; he actually made notes on some of the tracks I'd been alerting him to.

I just remember him as someone who never rested on his laurels. OK, so he's gone off and done something completely different now in terms of his commercial success, but he would play for us quite regularly back then.

\*\*\*

2004, right at the beginning of the funky house scene, I was asked to do an *Essential Mix* for Radio 1, which was a great opportunity to showcase my work to a national audience. The *Essential Mix* was the highest accolade any DJ can have really; to get a chance to play on those hallowed turntables. So, I dedicated the first 40 minutes of the show to playing the latest funky house type stuff to showcase what we were doing with Kissdafunk alongside our other resident DJs, the Trophy Twins, to a global audience.

After that, I went through the gears and played a bit of trance. Pete Tong looked quite startled, but was definitely entertained by how hard I went. I can't remember his exact words, but I definitely remember him mouthing 'Jesus Christ, this guy's nailing it' with the tunes I would have played at Sundissential and Tidy. To go across the board was a real pleasure for me. Probably in hindsight, I shouldn't have gone quite so hard because as a result of that, I wasn't invited back. Ha ha. Some people go across the board like Ben Nicky and Ben Hemsley and that younger generation of DJs who do that kind of open format set. But in 2004, I think it startled them to say the least, but hard house was massive in those days. It was the sound of then, so I don't have any real regrets, but I think I could have played it a little cooler.

I don't really want to talk down what was such a great experience, though. It was such an honour and I can remember it taking at least three or four weeks to get the playlist together. Because it was vinyl in those days as well, everything had to be bang on. I wanted to do it all as a two-hour mix too with no editing involved. It was just a two-hour mix on vinyl, going through the gears, which definitely takes a lot of working out.

I remember putting that mix together with Harry Tee sat by my feet listening to the music. I'd often glance back at the signed picture of the mighty Tony De Vit that his dad Ray had given me and ask: "Is it good enough, Tony? Is it good enough?" It was a real blood, sweat and tears job to make sure I delivered on every level. But I'm really glad I got that opportunity to play in another musical World Cup final.

The planets aligned once again soon after when the Trophy Twins were offered a weekly show on Radio 1 which was a real honour for those guys and thoroughly deserved.

# CH. 42

rob
Tissera

# The Prodigy

My mate Steve Hill told me about this musician he'd met called Alf Bamford. Alf had sent Steve some demo tapes in 2005; he was about 16 at the time. Steve did a track with him and I thought it was brilliant. I was doing a mix CD for Tidy called *The Dirty Weekender*, which was probably one of the hardest CDs in terms of how hard, hard house had got at that point. It was like a good old fashioned hoover-fest peppered with some nice, big, hard trancey bits that I was getting fairly well known for. Alf Bamford fitted perfectly into that kind of category and so I had a chat with him over the phone and we agreed to meet up.

Alf lived down in Winchester and so I travelled down there to record a remix of a track called *Madagascar* by Art Of Trance. Alf's studio was in the downstairs of his mum's house in a suburban area of Winchester. I had a cup of tea with him, sat down and played him the track. My first observation was that he only had a laptop and a single Tannoy speaker that worked. No equipment. Everything was done inside the box. I came from a background of working with Blandy and a few other people where it was all done by plugging wires into the patch bay and using hardware and I'd never really worked with anybody who'd done it this way. Alf was using a programme called Fruity Loops, which was absolutely brilliant, but which some didn't consider as 'pro' as using Cubase, Logic or Ableton, which had only just come into existence.

So, we sat down and I played him the track and he said, "Right OK, I don't play, but I can just pick the notes out." I played him the main riff and he said, "Right, OK, no problem. I think it's in B flat minor and that's the first note there." He then put one note on the screen. And then he said, "I think it's a chord." So then he put another four notes above it and then another note above in the harmonising key. And then he paused. "The only problem is that I don't have that much processing power in the machine." We'd already built a few beats; a little bit of bass, but once we'd done that, there wasn't enough processing power in the machine to be able to keep that rolling in order to hear the riff over the top. So he programmed the first couple of notes and said, "Right OK, I think it goes here." And he put some more notes in.

Finally, he said, "I think that's it." He then pressed a key on the keyboard and it played the riff perfectly. It was one of the most uplifting and brilliant moments I've ever had in a studio (bedroom). I had just witnessed a piece of utter wizardry by this 16-year-old kid and we couldn't even hear the whole thing all in one go.

Alf then mixed it all down and sent me a CD through the post after. It was amazing. It was way beyond my wildest dreams. It was complete and utter genius. And as a result of that, I forged a working relationship and friendship with Alf. It turned out that Alf had done the same thing with virtually every single trance track known to man. He worked out all the MIDIs and the notation for everything. Just a genius. A wizard.

I met another young lad around then too: Guyver. It was a real pleasure meeting such a prodigy as Paul Maddox, who was coming through the Tidy ranks at the tender age of 19; the whole world in front of him. He was living with his mum at the time too and spent all his time making music and playing *FIFA,* which was great for me. Guyver went on to take the bull by the horns and not just on the hard house front.

I hadn't really made an awful lot of music over the previous couple of years, but in 2005 I was asked to do a track for BK's album *Klub Kollaborations* due to my connections with Frantic. And we cooked up a little number called *Zulu Nation*, the inspiration coming from digging through the crates. The sample was from a track I used to play in the Ark days by The House Pimps, although, BK actually re-did the vocals in his studio at Nukleuz HQ.

And yeah, it was a bit of a nerve-wracking moment, going down to the Frantic Studios in London, SW4. I went there with my samples and met BK for the very first time. Now, I was very excited, after all, this guy was the king of hard house; the inventor of that Nukleuz sound and the mastermind behind so many great remixes over the years including a mix of OD404's *9 Bar*, Praga Khan's *Injected With A Poison*, Cortina's

*Music Is Moving* and *Kick It* by Beatniqz; seminal tracks in our field. So, what a complete and utter honour it was to make a track with BK.

A little bit of the song we recorded drew inspiration from BK's track *Revolution*; just loads of tribal drums. And then we added the *Zulu Nation* sample. And yeah, it was a proper breeze. And BK was one of the nicest blokes I've ever met and got on with him like a house on fire, and we still make tracks to this day.

I've recently been on tour with BK over to New Zealand and Australia. He's become one of my best friends. And he's such a font of knowledge due to his production skills, which are second to none. So, working with him, and being guided by him at times, was a real joy. Such a monumental moment working with the king of hard house.

***

2005, Tolley and I went to the Miami Music Conference and spent some time over there with Gavin from *Mixmag* who introduced me to this new kid on the block, Steve Angello. "This guy's gonna be BIG," Gav informed me. I got talking to Steve, who was about 28 at the time, but so knowledgeable. He was a very interesting character and so we invited Steve to come over to the UK to play for us. We were deliberately picking these people who were just about to break and I've got to thank all the people from *Mixmag* for helping to facilitate all that by tipping us the wink and saying, 'You need to get this guy!' If *Mixmag* took out a huge feature on someone, then there would usually be a reason behind it.

We were also great friends with Kevin McFarlane from *M8* magazine and the guys from *DJ Magazine* who would give us a heads-up. When Steve came over and played, he loved it. He said to me, "Well, I work with this guy called Sebastian Ingrosso and I bet he would love it here too. Why don't you bring him over?" So, I brought both of them to the UK and they were great. I played back-to-back with them a few times more at Kissdafunk in the early days and we got on great, which was phenomenal, because all our crowd knew who these guys were and acknowledged their importance within the scene.

Just as Funkissential hit a roadblock, so did Kissdafunk. We needed a club with a much bigger capacity. Mission was rammed to the gills every single month to the degree where I tried my best not to go towards the front door very often because you had a load of people outside going "Rob! Rob! Rob!" in the hope that I could get them inside. I remember going up to the cash box in the front office one time, and people were offering us £30 just to spend the last hour in the club. It was getting ridiculous. People were literally begging us to let them in for an hour, but it felt wrong to take their money.

Mission was our home in Leeds and in that first year we were very grateful for the help that Jim Albentosa and Dave from Taking Liberties provided. Their promotion was just a whirlwind because they knew exactly what they were doing and this was pre Facebook-driven advertising and pre-ticket sales. It was a simple case of 'build it strong and they will come'. Taking Liberties did us loads of favours and they were so keen to help us out.

Mission was smack bang in the centre of town and was packed every single time. We were doing VIP sales as well because our clubbers were at the cooler end of the spectrum. It was a golden time. And it didn't matter who played, I always did the closing set after David Guetta, Sebastian Ingrosso, Laidback Luke, Steve Angello and even Erik Morillo. That was a tough number, but somehow, I had the love, trust and respect of our fiercely loyal crowd and it was always packed to the end.

The music was more electro than funky house with a lot of tracks by Chris Lake, Tocadisco and quite a few electro remixes of indie tracks being played too as I guess we had that student crowd who loved the occasional Snow Patrol remix or the Thin White Duke remix of The Killers' *Mr Brightside*. And it was a real pleasure to be involved with Carly and all the crew who took complete control of the entertainment side of things. Brilliant dancers and great entertainment; the crowd doted on them. And we became the winning ticket in town really. An unstoppable force.

The downside to booking the top DJs was dealing with their agents. I mean, I have never encountered such nasty pieces of work and I've been in prison. As soon as a DJ started to do very well, they aligned themselves with the top agents in the country and that presented its own unique set of challenges. Not only that, but the DJs would start to exhibit some pretty lousy behaviour too, although David Guetta seemed to retain his humanity and humility. Some of those boys really let their egos run away with them and that was a great disappointment to me.

When we picked DJs up from the airport in the early days, it was all fist bumps, bear hugs and high fives. Now those very same guys were a lot more distant as their agents became more powerful; I think that's the best way to put it. Some of them were downright horrible, certainly in the way they treated the people who worked for us.

Swedish House Mafia became world class penises. I always picked them up, dropped them off, even if it meant going out of my way in order to get them to play. I would drive them from Leeds down to London to do a gig at Ministry and then to Bristol for my gig, which was not really on the way exactly. I did whatever it took to make sure they were happy.

I remember picking up one of them from the airport before going onto London one time. The first part of the journey was spent talking about my brand new X5 I'd just bought. I went over the details of the car, because he had one too. We stopped at services and when I returned from the loo, he was sat in my car, with his feet up on the seats, smoking a cigarette. In my brand-new car! Bang out of order! There's something's not right if you think that's OK. That was something that disappointed me massively as these people had lost sight of reality. Don't get me wrong, some of these names were worldwide superstars, but their behaviour was deeply uncool. I got stories back from some of the dancers too and there was some number exchanging going on and all the rest of it. Some of these DJs would be hitting on the girls with all the 'Chica, Chica!' crap.

That's what we were up against. Some of these big names were doing a lot of drugs and coughing up blood before carrying on. The money and the coke were turning them sour. I picked one of them up at Manchester Airport one Friday night and he was very low on energy. We were just hitting the motorway and I was talking to him as he got out his laptop bag, plugged these headphones into his Mac, put them on and said, "Just drive!" I was clearly viewed as a servant. All the things I'd done throughout my career, including going to prison for acid house, and that's how they treated me. It was massively disrespectful. They knew my history. And if they didn't, they could have researched me to see what I'd done. But they just became these despicable people.

It just got to a point where every single time I had to deal with any of these people I had to sell another little piece of pride. Their manager was the most hard-nosed I've ever met in the music business. I've never met anybody like her in my entire life. I'd send a nicely worded email, to request whatever DJ and I would give her all the details. And then she would use the cursor to go right into the centre of the page and would just type the word OFFER slap bang in the middle. Not with a question mark. No niceties. Nothing. Just what was I offering in terms of money? I think her influence over her acts was toxic.

That particular serpent was managing lots of artists who were key to our business. It was £600 when we first booked Steve Angello at mates' rates and of course it was soon £35,000. They had us over a barrel really, which was understandable, but it was such a clinical way of doing business with people who had previously been close to her artists. There was an entourage of people looking after them as well. It was a very corrosive situation and often highly toxic. The world was their oyster and it still is, but having worked with people like Carl Cox and Tony De Vit, I really struggled with that kind of ungracious behaviour because it was not cool in any way.

David Guetta was always gracious, kind, thoughtful and way more successful than any of those other artists we're talking about now. It's such a shame because I hate having to bring the mood down, but I think it's important for people to know that for some it's all about the money and the fame and doing far too much nonsense.

***

On the upside we were getting more and more offers to go do Kissdafunk and Garlands together at Kanya in 2006. This led to more crazy times with my old mate Barry Mac, including an all-day session with him and the Garlands crew, where I got more drunk than I'd ever been before. In fact, I remember trying to speak to some mates back in the UK, but I'd managed to lose my voice so the only way I could communicate was by blowing one of those little whistling toy streamers that you get in a Christmas cracker. Don't even ask where I'd found it. Basically, it was one blow for a yes and two blows for a no. The streamer made a tiny noise like a strangled chicken much to the amusement of everyone around me. I'd activated full-clown mode. Jack Daniels 10: Rob 0. Ha ha. After that I had to get a flight back to do a gig in the UK on the Friday night, so they sent me back to the airport still exceedingly drunk.

Still wobbly, I dropped a box of Kissdafunk decor all over the airport. This box split open and all the decor spilled out all over the place. Then I managed to drop my wallet on the floor, and my money fell out. I then stepped forward to pick my money up and my sunglasses fell off. Of course, I then walked over the sunglasses and smashed them. I was sweating profusely as you could imagine, but at least I'm not horrible when I'm drunk. I am just useless! Ha.

We started doing some Ibiza boat parties with Garlands, which was great fun. Eventually, we started doing our own boat parties too. We've always remained really good friends with Garlands and there's never been any acrimony or anything about us doing our business and them doing theirs. We've always remained really good mates because we didn't want it to be that the two things were always completely hand in hand. We had that understanding, which is so important. Because of my association with Issac Hidalgo from Eden and Judge Jules' Judgement Sundays, they used to come to some of our parties. Then a friend of ours called Mo Chaudry, God rest his sweet soul, who ran Cream at Privilege asked us to do the opening night at Kanya on a Monday.

We rented a villa through a mate of ours, Ingo (Tom Ingamells), the really famous hard house producer who now produces house for Hot Since 82, Kryder and a ton of other cool acts. Ingo was out there for the summer, and he rented this villa in Santa Eulalia and so we sublet half the villa off him. The trip from Santa Eulalia to San Antonio could take hours if the roads were busy. I remember thinking I was going to be late for the opening night at Kanya, and I really didn't want to let Mo down as he was a really good friend of mine and a bit of a kindred spirit because he had a tie to Sri Lanka, my dad's birthplace.

I made it on time, at 9pm to set everything up and there was no one there. Of course we got the music going with a couple of the residents, Filthy Rich and the Trophy Twins. Anyway, we had to keep the music going, but there was still nobody around. Mo said, "Listen, don't worry. It will be fine. It might take a little while for this thing to fully blow, but it will work. Don't you worry. It'll all be good." We were just sat there thinking, 'Is this gonna tank?' And then at about 2am, all of a sudden people started appearing and it was just like Garlands had been years before as word of mouth spread. The club workers were pouring into Kanya now their work for the evening had finished. And then it soon got to a point where every time we did it, which was every Sunday night, you could see people running down the road to get in. By this point, Kanya had moved inside with a big indoor area. They put glass all around where the outdoor area used to be, so it became much more enclosed and the sound wasn't as much of a massive issue. Those were great nights.

The Trophy Twins, residents at Kissdafunk were doing Radio 1 every week and that did us loads of favours as well. Everything was feeding everything else; as their popularity boomed, so did the club's. They now had loads of contacts through Radio 1 and I'm very grateful to Mark and Adam who introduced us to a whole new bunch of DJs, club owners and producers, like Micky Slim who was very popular at the time and much easier to deal with than most; all of those factors meant that Ibiza season really was in full effect. It was an awesome summer.

I was still doing gigs in the UK in Harrogate and Ministry and Pacha in London, Emporium in Colville and Tall Trees in Yarm, which was a hugely popular club in the mid-noughties. The offers were coming in thick and fast. On top of that, we started to do some stuff in Marbella and Majorca as well. Annabelle Marner was managing our PR at the time and was speaking to the magazines and all the rest of it because everything was just snowballing. Everybody wanted a bit of Kissdafunk action. The good times really were rolling. There were moments when I put the company card into the ATM and gasped when I saw the balance. Those were some of the best days of my life.

I hooked back up with Wilba who used to drive for me in the early noughties. For whatever reason, some people go in and out of your life, don't they? You just go in different directions and do different things. I didn't see Wilba for like eight or nine years; he was doing other stuff and so was I. There was never any fallout. Around 2006, we decided we'd have to get together. And just like all the best people you've met in your life, we simply picked up from where we'd left off as if we'd last seen each other yesterday. Don't you just love that?

\*\*\*

I bought a standalone tower Mac purely for making music in 2006 to learn how to do everything myself. Working with all these talented people meant you picked up a lot of tips along the way. If you can capture 20-30% from people you work with, you're going to be on a good path. Ableton came to prominence in 2006 and I just got on with that program like a house on fire. I found it much better than Logic, which I sometimes called Illogic because it had so many sub menus in it. Whereas on Ableton, you could treat samples like musical Lego pieces and just make a track out of a whole bunch of them. I loved that program. And, and as a result of that, I really started to gear up towards doing a lot more stuff 'in the box' before working with other producers to finish it off.

Wilba was making music on Ableton too. And from 2006, we'd been in contact every few days to do lots of house stuff together under the name of Bobby Tee & Mark Williams. Wilba and Blandy really helped get all that stuff working for me. Their help was totally invaluable at that time.

***

2006 and we were booked and ready to depart for another season in Ibiza with Garlands and Mo who ran Amnesia and Cream over there. Barry and Huey offered us the use of an apartment of theirs in Ibiza town. Obviously, we had to pay them, but we also got to use their VW Beetle. This Beetle was well known on the island and we got pulled over by the police, back in 2005, for squeezing eight people into this tiny car. We were travelling back from a boat party in San Antonio to DJ at the Space Terrace. These were pinch yourself moments, going from a great boat party straight to Space. There was a load of people wanting to get into the car and Jasper who worked for Garlands was driving. We got stopped by the police and all piled out. There was me, Jasper who helped to run Garlands that season and six dancers in this VW Beetle painted up in the colours of Herbie from the popular kids' films. There was a girl in the boot too, so no wonder we were stopped.

Fast forward to 2006 and we were travelling over to Plastik after doing a Kissdafunk party on the old Space Terrace when the Beetle broke down. It had a bit of a problem with the radiator and decided to spin out and stop working. I couldn't really be late because I'd already had a call from the club to say that the DJ who was currently playing had to go. "So we need you to get over here as quickly as you can!"

So, I got a taxi to Space and asked a mate of mine called Ben who I knew from the Slinky days in Bournemouth if he could get in the cab with me to take my car back to the VW with a tow rope, and then move the Garlands car. I gave him some money for doing it and set off to do my gig. Once I was finished, I looked at my phone and saw ten missed calls. I got hold of Ben and he said, "The car's not here! I've been up and down that road so many times, but that car is not on that road." We went to the police station and they even sent us to the pound. "Your car is not here!" We even went to another car pound and got the same story. And that car has never been seen again to this day. It's still something that gets joked about although it sticks in my craw. I can't quite believe we didn't locate that car and whenever I speak to Barry, it always comes up in a conversation. "Where's my car, Rob?!" Ha. But it was another classic season in Ibiza and it was a real pleasure to stay in that apartment. The Garlands lot were a real family and so much fun.

# CH. 43

*rob
Tissera*

# The Egos Have Landed

Back in the UK, a lot of the big acts we'd been working with were now becoming worldwide superstars who'd had international number ones. Swedish House Mafia and David Guetta were now massive concerns, and it was tricky trying to keep hold of them so they didn't go off and play for other people. It was so important to have exclusivity in the county and some of them had started playing the night before in Manchester or Sheffield, and that was becoming a bit of a problem for us, because we were historically attracting people to Leeds *from* those cities. But now they could go see Guetta in their own city, why would they come to our place? Their management were pulling stunts like putting them on in Sheffield (30 miles down the road) the day after our gig. It was more than a bit of a mickey-take as far as we were concerned.

Mid-June, 2007, I was sat there in my craggy old cottage, which was all nice on the inside, but still looked rather cranky from the street. I was there typing sternly worded emails to these absolute dickhead world-class tosspots of agents we were dealing with who were giving us the worst headaches. It took me about two hours to get what I felt was the right message. And then I did it. I pressed SEND and decided to have a celebratory beer. Managing the agents and the talent was becoming a real ball ache. But I was happy to have fired off some emails in order to try and exert what little control I could when booking these names.

I looked down at the floor. "Jesus, the floor's wet, what's going on?" It was torrential rain outside. The rain was hitting the windows like a toffee hammer. And then I looked outside to see the heavens opening. There was going to be a flash flood!

We were flooded back in 2001, it only reached two feet, but it still wrecked everything downstairs, and I needed new carpets and kitchen units. But this looked like it was going to be biblical; and of course the house sat below the road in a dip. Because the cottage was in a dip, kids would sometimes skateboard on it. It was all downhill from the centre of Rothwell to the cottage and so you could halfpipe around this little bit of pavement outside my house.

This dip now resembled a small swimming pool just below the level of the window and it was rising. Fast! Shit! Anyway, the water started coming in through the top window. It was like the Titanic. Water just started pouring into where my computer sat.

I'd already been moving stuff upstairs, but obviously there was only so much stuff I could move on my own. I got the TV and the computer and everything else upstairs, just before the windows blew in and the place filled up to four feet of water just above the light socket. It was soon up to the top of my chest. It was ridiculous

I called my mate Eppy who came round and helped me to put some of the furniture upstairs, even though it was already water damaged. I then opened the porch window which fully opened out and climbed through with my dog Harry Tee. It was a case of abandon ship. I was flying to Ibiza the following morning. 'I'm totally goosed here.' Because I had to fly to Ibiza, I had to leave the flood situation in the hands of my personal assistant Margaret who contacted the insurance company. It was a complete and utter nightmare. I ended up having to rent another apartment in Rothwell just around the corner from my place because I needed to monitor the work that was going to be done on the house.

It ended up taking them nine and a half months to put that cottage right at a cost of £110,000. And then on the final day, the insurance company called me as I was just about to sign the paperwork, to inform me that there was an anomaly on my insurance. They didn't have my correct occupation written down. They wanted me to pay for all the repairs. "It's your liability." I then had to get hold of a solicitor who gave me some advice on how to tackle it. I took them to task and won, which was absolutely great news, during what was a very, very stressful time.

Keeping Kissdafunk successful was proving to be difficult and it was really taking its toll on my physical and mental health, and this flood wasn't helping. You would always have people trying to bring your brand down who were in direct competition with you and would copy and improve what you were doing in terms of marketing or the talent you were booking. They would go to the people who did our flyers to try and cause waves. There was a lot of sneaky business going on and that, coupled with the flood damage, meant my mental health was taking a battering.

But Kissdafunk was still a strong proposition. Trophy Twins, Mark Knight and Micky Slim represented the funkier side of things and played a lot for us and were all instrumental in making that electronic sound that had a bit of an indie element to it as well with a few remixes of tracks like *By The Way* by Red Hot Chili Peppers and a few Arctic Monkeys tunes. There was a definite marriage between those two styles.

I remember watching David Guetta playing one night and I went to the far edge of where the DJ box was to get vodka and an ice bucket. I was walking back when *Smells Like Teen Spirit* came on and there was this deafening roar from the crowd. I took one step forward and was just planning to take my next when the crowd surged forward. I was actually in the air with both my feet off the ground, carried forward with the ice bucket under my arm for what felt like 35 feet.

I was just so happy to have created that level of happiness. That was the whole point of doing this, so people loved the unique atmosphere. Carly and the dancers were a massive part of that: six of them at the front in the Kissdafunk costumes. Everybody involved was pulling in the same direction, even down to Dave the lighting jock. He was totally in tune with what he was tasked with and knew exactly when the confetti cannons were going to go off and all those other special effects. It was brilliant and a really special time to be alive.

We had adopted the same principles as the best operators in the business. So, just like Tidy, we assembled the finest people to work alongside us. One of whom was our PA Annabel Marner. Without her help we simply wouldn't have been able to cope. She was a total whirlwind of a lady who managed our diary, our public relations and at times our personal lives. I can't stress enough how much effort she put into assisting. Without her we would've been nothing.

2007, just as the summer season kicked off in Ibiza, Mission won Club of the Year in *DJ Magazine*, which was quite an accolade. Kissdafunk was the main night at Mission and so we were very proud of that. We also forged a great relationship with the boys at *M8* magazine in Scotland too.

Kevin McFarlane and Euwen Fox came down to play for us on a regular basis and they put us on the front cover of their magazine.

Kissdafunk took up so much of my time that my personal gigs had taken a real backseat, just as hard house was starting to run its course. It hadn't completely fizzled, but I was not getting the same kind of feeling I was experiencing two or three years earlier. You can wear the crown, but you never own the crown. Sometimes you have that golden period, but it's not forever and hard house was beginning to dip without a shadow of doubt. There was still some good, strong stuff going on with Tidy and Storm at The Emporium in Coalville and Frantic in London. I was still involved with all that side of things, but Kissdafunk was so big I needed to be on point every minute of the day. It was a proper logistics job.

2007, we did a compilation album. We enlisted the help of Jamie Bugler who did all our designs and made our brand look absolutely bang on. We put the CD out and soon after, I got a call from Lohan Presencer at Ministry of Sound: "Do you want to come to the office and have a chat?" Bearing in mind that those guys also ran Hedkandi, it was a little strange to be asked that. "We know you're doing very well and we want to see whether perhaps there's a conversation to be had, where we might be able to help you manage that," they said. "Just like we do with Hedkandi, so we've got more than one option and more than one product."

–  "OK, cool." That sounded like a meeting I definitely wanted to attend.

I had a meeting with Lohan who was second in command at Ministry as well as Jenny Cochrane who ran Hedkandi and Head of Music, Dave Dollimore on a Thursday afternoon in May. I'd met Dave Dollimore about six years prior to this when I did a gig for Ministry in Ibiza. I'd been over there with my mate Ian Emberton, and the people who ran Ministry at the time asked us to look after this intern of theirs. "It's his first time in Ibiza, so could you keep an eye on him for us." So, Ian and I took this guy under our wing, taking him out and showing him the sights. We took him to a few clubs and bars and all the rest. He was a nice guy.

Fast forward six years and this intern was now Head of Music for Ministry. I've always tried to impress on people to make sure you always look after *everybody* in the way you would want to be treated. Because some of the people you meet at the bottom of the ladder could be very important in the future. Dave was certainly grateful for the way we treated him in Ibiza and it was nice to see him in that position. This meeting with

Ministry was like an episode of *Dragons' Den*. All the heads at Ministry, with the exception of James Palumbo, were there for this meeting.

Kissdafunk was properly cooking on gas, but Ministry's Hedkandi was the perfect business model, and they were going from town to town, city to city and country to country. We had this feeling that we might be able to replicate that. Not the same sort of scale, obviously, but a similar operation.

Whilst we were discussing Kissdafunk, Lohan was pulling the cover of the album apart to see how it was manufactured; really testing the quality of the cardboard. "We're very, very interested in getting involved with the brand. Could you make a quick call to your mate Tolley? Could you call your accountant and get them to send your books over?"

– "Well, it's not as simple as that. I'm not so sure I'm going to be able to get a hold of him now to fax our books over."

I was getting the distinct impression that whilst one person was talking to me, I could see somebody sending a text to one of the others who would then reply. Something seemed a bit odd. Then they would look up from their phones and ask me a question. It seemed as if they went from professing an interest in working with us to a more forensic investigation. Were they simply more interested in the threat we represented to Hedkandi? I mean, they were *super keen* to get hold of the books. I just told them I needed to chat to my business partner, who couldn't attend the meeting on account of being seriously ill.

I felt under a lot of pressure in that meeting, but there was no way I was sending them our books or doing any kind of deal there and then. I am pretty convinced that they were pumping us for the secrets of our success, presumably to try and protect their own brand.

That same year, Gatecrasher moved into Leeds and the same kind of meeting we had with Ministry occurred with them where they pumped Back To Basics and loads of other promoters in town to see whether we would move our night to Gatecrasher. They wanted to see our books too and have a good look through all the paperwork and everything. They wanted us to do the last Friday of the month and promised to help pay for some of the acts due to their fat fees. But had we got involved with them they would have owned a huge slice of our business. I didn't really need that kind of arseache bearing in mind previous dealings I'd had with those guys. But in short, the sharks were circling now.

Back in Ibiza, Giles and Isaac from Eden wanted us to move to El Divino for a season; a beautiful club overlooking the port in Ibiza. We were well up for that as you can imagine because that club felt like something special. We booked all the DJs and hired an extremely cool apartment in Playa d'en Bossa for the summer which was above this amazing Tapas place called the Grifferia. The smell of frying garlic and chorizo had me feeling permanently hungry.

Giles took care of the flights and accommodation for the talent, while we got all the artwork and the flyers made in the UK and had it shipped out on big wooden pallets that were stored at the club. It was a military operation to get everything running smoothly. Carly and her Angels moved to Ibiza for the summer and we embarked on a truly exciting and eventful four months.

The opening night at El Divino and we were just about to open the doors and Giles came up to us and said, "Oh guys, before we open, I've got a bit of paperwork for you to sign. Just to wrap up a few of these little details. Could you sign that for us?" It was a contract between the two of us, (me and Tolley) and those two, so it was a quarter split if you like. I sat down at this big table and he gave me a pen and pointed at a big cross where I needed to sign. I mean fair play for trying that. "Er, I'm going to need to read this and run it past my music lawyer."

Our lawyer, Andrew Brabyn had helped to negotiate a load of contracts for us, including the *Kick Up The Volume* track. He was also The Prodigy's lawyer and he was good to have in your corner. "So, I'm not signing anything right now. Let me just have a very quick look." I scanned through the contract and the upshot of it was they wanted a partnership for all our worldwide dealings, which was totally ridiculous. They were completely blindsiding us. So that was the end of that.

Things seemed stressful behind the scenes, but front of house, Kissdafunk was just this phenomenon. A fun-filled joy ride. We had such a great time in Ibiza that summer. Although it would have been nice to have had more than one key fob for the apartment. As a result of that, Tolley and I often had to scale the security fence like Spider-Man – full of Jack Daniels – in order to get into the compound. Luckily, we were both quite fit back then. We did forfeit our £900 damages deposit, though. Having got in from a big night out, and generally mucking about, Tolley was more than a little unsteady on his feet in the living room of this apartment. I didn't get time to warn him, as he started teetering on his heels before going backwards into the glass-topped coffee table which shattered into a million pieces. Luckily, he was OK, but we were picking shards of glass up for the next two months and lost £900 in the process. It didn't occur to us to simply buy another coffee table. Doh!

*** 

2007, we were doing Kissdafunk in London on a Friday night at Pacha while also doing the same night in Leeds at Mission. I would go with a team of people to put the decor up with my right-hand man, deco expert and driver, Chris Duff. Chris would come down in the car with the dancers and then put all the decor up so we would crack on with the show. And then after we would drive back up north and meet up with Tolley and everybody after Kissdafunk finished in Leeds. Then it was on to the afterparty until at least midday the next day. We would sometimes do Saturday gigs too, often in Bristol. And then sometimes we would fly out to Ibiza to do Judgement Sunday or our own parties at El Divino. I would then spend the rest of the week making plans for all the stuff that was going on over the summer and the media coverage and interviews with *DJ Magazine* and *M8*.

It was hard to sleep in those days. And I have to say, although I loved this life, it probably made me the most fiery I'd ever been. I wasn't the smiling nice character everybody knew me for. For that particular period I had to put my 'game face' on because we had quite a few people working for us and the sheer amount of excuses from the Great Book Of Lies you would get from folk for why they couldn't make it or why they were late were innumerate. And you couldn't do everything yourself either. Sometimes it would be very disappointing when elements went wrong, and I became a bit of a firebrand as a result of that, which was a real shame. But there are definitely two sides to the coin. Out the front, you've got the show and all the carnival atmosphere that Kissdafunk generated, but in the background, me, Anna, Annabelle and Tolley were getting very stressed.

The El Divino nights went a bit tits-up to be honest. Even though the club was really busy, the owners were saying they were having to give out free green wristbands as they were finding it hard to sell the party. At the very last minute on a Tuesday evening they would see how many yellow wristbands they'd sold and if they hadn't sold enough they would generate a different colour wristband. They're called pulseras in

Spain, and when we saw the green ones, we knew those people had got in for free. However, we found out later that summer that those green bands were being paid for and the club was pocketing the money. And after that, the relationship got a lot more fractious. In fact, it got very fractious. I had some very, very, angry conversations with the guy who set us up with it all. In general, I'm a really nice smiley guy and all the rest of it, but if you fuck me over I will say my piece, which comes from my fiery mother with her flame red hair and that Celtic streak. Knowing somebody's ripping you off is not a nice feeling.

We went for a meeting with these guys from El Divino in a restaurant and I got straight to the point. "You need to cough up some fucking money!" They'd been withholding thousands from us. And we still had bills and staff to pay and you don't want to keep dipping into your personal account for all that. This was one very angry exchange in a restaurant. People were sitting there with their cameras out.

I was getting fobbed off with the old 'mañana, mañana' routine, and so I stood up from the table and shouted, "Get the fucking money!" I slapped my glass down on the table and it shattered into a million pieces. It created quite a stir and the guy who owed us the money, finally got the message. "OK, Rob, you wait here. I'm gonna go sort this out." The guy lived above the restaurant and so he went upstairs to the safe. He came down not long after with the money. That was just how that side of the business could be sometimes. It was not good for the old heart rate, I can tell you.

They always made out they were doing us a favour with the green wristbands to make the night busy, when in fact, they were just taking the money, which was pretty shocking. The club owner lived in this huge glass-fronted villa nestled into the mountainside with an infinity pool that overlooked the Port of Ibiza. It was an amazing, beautiful place. He had all these female servants who worked in his massage parlours in Ibiza Town. It was hard having dinner with someone who was ripping you off. We carried on with Kissdafunk at El Divino, but on a totally different deal as they realised they'd been rumbled. The parties were still popping though as nobody else saw all the nonsense going on in the background.

I always think of Ibiza as being a bit like the TV show *Lost*, where it's very difficult to ever get anything off that island. *They* tend to win a lot more than you do. And the problem with putting on nights was that I was neglecting my DJ and recording work. I put my recording career on hold and wasn't putting out any music really. After I put out the Tidy records in 2002 to 2003 I might have had one or two more. But then, I didn't do anything for a number of years just because I didn't have the time. Every day was a firefight, just trying to keep it growing, while also trying to keep a lid on everything. It was definitely a fraught period with people coming at you from all sides.

We were probably doing too many gigs in too many locations; it was very easy to take the devil's shilling. Some nights we were down by 300 people at the flagship event at Mission in Leeds, which was really scary after the outlandish successes of the previous few years. The reason? Because those people went to see the other gigs we did in Sheffield or Harrogate and so we were diluting the brand. I guess, looking back through the old Hindsight-O-Scope, we should have resisted the temptation to expand the brand so close to home.

That same summer we also started doing BCM in Majorca as well as a few clubs on the Strip; one of them was Bananas. We played Majorca every Wednesday after a Tuesday in Ibiza. We would then go home for a day or two and then start again. And it was like that all the time throughout that year. I had also been busy mixing the Kissdafunk album too, which was exhausting. I was probably doing fewer hard house gigs as well, because 2007/2008 saw a little bit of a drop off on that front. The hard house garden was not quite so rosy. And that's why I'm so grateful I dipped my toe into different waters because things ebb and flow and I'm very glad I'd chosen this path. They were great times, but exhausting, and dealing with those shitbag agents and their unrealistic demands – clean hand towels, somewhere to tie up their llama and a particular brand of granola you can only buy in Canada and have to mail order six weeks in advance for the gig only for it to be left in the dressing room untouched – does wear one down. These were people who had been our mates right at the beginning, who would now only communicate through their agents.

As a result of the horrible situation with El Divino we were definitely haemorrhaging money in 2007, probably to the tune of 50 grand that summer, which was a bitter pill to swallow after putting in so much effort. The risks we were taking from week to week and from month to month were astronomical. We were sometimes putting our houses on the line in order to pay for some of these stellar line ups, and given my time again, I would have pulled the plug on it all much, much sooner and saved ourselves from this incredible pressure. And I was working like a madman to make up for some of the wrong turns we made along the way. But as Jesus, or someone equally famous said: "You live and learn."

***

2008, I was booked to play Big Weekend in Skegness, which was an Ibiza weekender for all the workers who'd come home to the UK for a big party after the season ended. There would be thousands of people there. The Big Weekend was run by Lee Mileure, John Davis and Chris Brown and I'd known those guys for donkey's years. They used to run Tonic in Ibiza.

We went up to do this gig and the guys met us backstage before we went on and did our stuff with the Kissdafunk dancers. It was a great event and we had a brilliant time there. They were paying me and Tolley £2,800 for the KDF brand fee, but when I went to get paid, I got a horrible surprise. Giles, our Ibiza business partner hadn't paid John Davis' travel company for the flights and the accommodation for all their DJs during the summer of that year. He had scarpered and we couldn't get hold of him. They said, "If you write us a cheque for £11,800, we'll give you one for £2,800. How does that sound?" It's something I encountered a lot with other promoters as well. The one thing you can't account for in this business is 'the blindside'. The amount of times you think you know everything and then out of nowhere you get body slammed. That was definitely one of those moments where it was really hard to go on and play with a smile on my face when I realised we were nine grand in the hole and they were well within their rights to do that. I understand why they did it because they were never going to get it off this guy. But still... ouch!

May 2008, we did a Kissdafunk event at Tall Trees in Yarm up in north Yorkshire, which was a massive club and hugely popular. I used to play for Goodgreef at Tall Trees for a number of years. Paul Taylor ran these impressive retro parties. We did a Kissdafunk up there with Sandy Rivera from Kings Of Tomorrow, who did the track *Finally*. Sandy came and played for us early doors that night.

Tall Trees was a massive club that could get 5,000 people inside, but this was one of the worst Kissdafunks we'd ever done. It was a May bank holiday, which was sometimes a bit of a damp squib. There are a number of bank holidays in a row in May, and sometimes they were flat and this night definitely fell into that category.

We had Sandy Rivera playing to just 500 people rattling around in this cavernous venue that held 5,000 under these 60-ft ceilings. It was dreadful. I also did a Vinyl Sundissential Reunion gig at the old Uropa venue from the halcyon days of hard house and that was rubbish too. But you had to keep moving and looking for the next opportunity.

I played a Sundissential gig that weekend. Sundissential had been taken over by some other operators who bought the brand from Danny Kirk and Madders to keep it going, but it had also been a rubbish gig. They said, "Unfortunately we don't have very much cash to pay you with, however, because our main business is doing parking meters in Telford, we can pay you £600. In 50p pieces." Oh, the glamour! I was then given this huge bag of change I had to lug home with me, plus my canvas bag of vinyl, which was ridiculously heavy.

I then ran into a mate of mine, Damo Pennals; a proper livewire from Leeds, probably 20 years younger than me and a Sundissential and Kissdafunk stalwart. A really funny guy, Damo had a flat above Gatecrasher. "Do you want to come up?" I was absolutely shattered and I had all this vinyl and the bag of 50ps and so I wasn't really feeling it. "How many floors up is it?"

–  "Listen. I'll carry your bag."

With that Damo carried my stuff up the stairs and into the flat. There was this great party going on. The building itself was one of those really nice, ornate old 1900s Victorian buildings with a mezzanine level in it and everything. It was beautiful. Damo had these big lights and KRK Rokit 8 speakers thrashing out the hard house to 150 people in the flat.

At this time, my relationship with my then girlfriend had well and truly hit the rocks. Sometimes things just fizzle out and people pull in different directions. It was a really great party, though, but because I was shattered I went to the mezzanine level and sat on the bed for a bit to chill. I was sat there, in a trance, when out of nowhere this lady appeared with the brightest blue eyes I'd ever seen. She was one of those people who just illuminated the room with their beautiful persona. 'Who's she?!' She was amazing. She introduced herself as Anna and for a second, time seemed to stand still. It was the most beautiful feeling and a moment I will never forget. We just connected and ended up talking for the whole of the party. It was like there was nobody else there. I didn't see her again for 6 or 7 months, but I couldn't stop thinking about Anna.

We started talking with each other on Facebook after a while and got on like a house on fire and we still do to this very day – because she's my wife! Every single day is like the first day and it's an absolutely beautiful thing to meet the person of your dreams. I truly hope that everybody experiences that in their lifetime because it's a game changer.

# CH. 44

**rob Tissera**

# Call The Bailiffs!

2008, I moved the studio out of my house and into a complex not far from Leeds. Mabgate Mills was a creative hub and a great meeting place for musicians and artists and I just wanted to get my creative juices back and make more music as I'd really put that on the back burner for a few years.

I moved all my equipment into my own unit that sat inside this impressive complex with loads of other studios. Utah Saints and Andy Durant from Galaxy Radio and loads of big producers from Leeds, all had their own spaces there. It was a real hub of creativity and a great way of getting out of the house.

I had been there for about four or five months when I turned up to the unit one Thursday morning. On the front door was a big notice saying that the building had been repossessed. It also said all the contents were now the property of whoever the actual owner of the studio was, because the guy we paid was actually subletting it, unbeknown to us. And of course, he hadn't been paying the actual landlords.

This notice said that everything in the studio, including all of my equipment – computer, laptop, decks, torrent files and vinyl, including all the stuff that I was going to be playing that weekend (and I had several gigs on) – was gone. I had four gigs in three different styles that weekend and now I had no equipment. Nothing.

The notice had a telephone number to call for more information and I called it and spoke to a lady who turned out to be the actual owner of the building. She said, "Tell you what I'm gonna do. I'm gonna come with a bailiff on Friday afternoon and meet you all there. You've then got one hour to take what you want from your unit. And then after that, everything's mine." What?! That just didn't sound right whatsoever. How on earth could that be? Maybe she wanted to fire a shot across the bow so this guy would pay all the money he owed.

I went down there on the Friday to get in the queue to get my shit back, especially my 2K rig with 1" PV cabinets and Martin tops, plus all the vinyl. There were probably 12 people waiting for their stuff when I arrived, but you had to wait your turn, which was a strange way of doing it. I nodded to Utah Saints and a few other people milling around this industrial estate in downtown Leeds.

When it came to my turn the landlady said, "Oh, you know what, we've had enough of this. We're stopping now."

- "What?! You're not gonna let me get my shit out of my studio?!"
- "Nope, sorry."
- "But that's *my stuff*! I need it for this weekend."
- "No sorry, no chance."

And then the bailiff put a padlock on the door and started marching off to their car. I wasn't having that. I wasn't having that at all.

It was a really bad thing to do, but I was so angry I ran over to the car and rugby-tackled the bailiff to the floor to get the keys off him. The owner immediately called the police. It was going right off. Somehow, a few of the other tenants got me off him. I then went for a massive rock and started bashing away at the padlock. The police arrived in no time. I was in deep shit.

The policemen were quite young and I just unloaded on them. "I just don't feel this is legally correct. I just don't think they're within their rights to do what they're doing. I've got a load of gigs to do this weekend and all my gear is in there!" This young Asian copper suddenly burst into life. "Gigs?"

- "Yeah, I'm a DJ."
- "No way, who?"
- "Rob Tissera."
- "That's crazy. I used to go and watch you play at Ark!"
- "And that's Jez from Utah Saints."
- "Wow! Hi, Jez!"
- "I'm really sorry about all this, but I do feel that this is not legally correct."
- "Leave it with me."

This copper went over to the owner and brokered a deal with her, that in return for me paying for the damage to the door I would also get an hour to retrieve my stuff. Get in! I should have got done for assault really because I'd knocked this guy to the floor and he could have split his head open or anything. It was an ugly situation, but it ended with a few selfies with the police, plus I got all my stuff back.

# CH. 45

rob
Tissera

# The Scag Zombie

Seven or eight weeks into my house being renovated, following the flood, I met these guys through my now girlfriend, Anna. I would play *FIFA* with Dean Hyden, Malcolm Ladkin and their mate I still only know as Parker, just as I did with Leafy. I met these guys at a great rooftop party on New Year's Day in Leeds; they were 15 years younger than me. Because I was a bit older they asked me if I knew what the controller on the Xbox did. Cheeky! I just played dumb. I'm very fortunate to say that I ended up on top during that *FIFA* tournament, which they couldn't believe at the time. That said, they certainly gave me a shit-load of thrashings on many occasions after that. But they soon became some of my best mates. We would do anything for each other and it was great having people join us on the journey, who just wanted to come out and have some fun. Constant bellylaugh situations at every opportunity.

I had just finished a *FIFA* session with them one night, and I was in a foul mood having got absolutely battered all evening. I got into my Range Rover and drove back like a man possessed. I was living in a new apartment about a mile and a half from my old house, paid for by the insurance company. Halfway home, I decided to retrieve some records from the old house for a gig that following weekend.

The first thing I noticed was that the porch windows were smashed.

I entered the front porch and… shit! The front door was smashed too. What the fuck! The downstairs was all stripped out so none of the lights worked due to the removal of the electrics. I was shining my phone torch into the darkness thinking 'Shit, there's water running everywhere. What's going on?' I went to the stopcock, which was on the dining room wall and looked down to see that all the copper pipes had been cut.

Now, sometimes smack heads broke into houses to steal the copper pipes so they could sell them for scag. And so now my flood-damaged cottage was filling up with water again after all the restoration work that had been done on it. I was beyond fucked off.

I managed to get the water to stop and decided to do a quick check on the studio to make sure there were no problems there. The padlock hadn't been opened, so that was promising. I now had to get a locksmith and glazier out to secure the place.

I went to have a quick wee and on my way to the bathroom I heard a rustling sound from the bedroom. I walked gingerly towards the room. There was something in there!

About 10 feet away from me was this guy. He was busy loading my valuables from the chest of drawers into one of *my* rucksacks. He was twitchy and had that sketchy look about him. He was probably quite young, but gaunt like the undead. I decided to be firm, but fair. "Hey, can you do us a favour? Why don't you just walk away, out of the house and I won't call the police."

－ "Mate. You're not taking this job away from me!"

－ "Job? It's my fucking house! Now do me a favour and fuck off!"

I was genuinely shitting it. I mean, this guy could have been off his nut, and carrying a knife. But it was my house and I needed to get him out. He didn't seem to be too bothered by my presence there and casually sauntered past me as I stood in the doorway.

There was a little staircase that went down into the ground floor with plastic sheeting all over the place, like a scene out of *Dexter*. The sheets were for dust protection; protecting the bits that weren't damaged while they were fixing the downstairs. And so it was pretty slippy with no carpet on the stairs or anything. As he moved past me I realised he had my favourite Franz Beckenbauer Limited Edition Adidas track jacket on. I kinda lost it at that point and slapped him around the back of the head as he strolled past. And with that he came running back up the stairs. And I'm thinking to myself, 'I think he's got a knife.' He must have been packing something as he quite clearly smashed the window with an object in order to gain access.

He swivelled round and came at me full pelt. I think all the years of watching *The A-Team* and Bruce Lee movies as well as doing judo at school to beat off the racist bullies, must have had an effect as I kung-fu kicked him square in the nose as he ran up the stairs. I made contact smack bang in the middle of his boat race and he took off all the way down the stairs, bashing his head at the bottom. I ran down after him. He was lying there unconscious.

I noticed a big flap of skin that had been ripped from the back of his head. He must have hit the bottom step or something and split the back of his head open. There was now a stream of claret forming a puddle that ran right the way across the entire 30ft-long kitchen. I was now panicking that I might have killed him.

I picked him up by the lapels of my favourite tracksuit top and dragged him out into the dip at the front of the house. I thought the fresh air would help although in truth, I didn't want a potentially dead burglar in my kitchen. And that's where he came back to life. Jesus! This smackhead zombie was now trying to get his hand in his pocket. And I'm thinking, 'He's going for his knife or a hammer!'

"Get your fucking hand out of your pocket!" And with that I went for him. I have never used a level of violence like that before or since, but I had to protect myself and my property. What followed was a tussle reminiscent of that Peter and the chicken fight from *Family Guy*. This battle just went on and on for a good 15 minutes. It was ridiculous. I was desperately trying to stop him from getting away. I mean, fair play to the bloke he put up a decent resistance considering the pain he'd suffered. Maybe the heroin had anaesthetised him. I eventually managed to get my foot on his upper chest and called the police. I was thinking there's no way on God's green earth that this bloke is leaving here other than in a police van. I'm not having it. He's getting so nicked.

Two of my neighbours had heard the disturbance – this was one or two in the morning – and so they came to help restrain him. And then the police arrived and they called for an ambulance.

The thief left the scene in a neck brace on a stretcher and even as they were bundling him into the back of the ambulance, he was threatening me. "What's your name? We're gonna fucking come back!"

– "I'll tell you what my name is: I am your fucking nemesis!"
– "Fuck off!"
– "If you ever come back round here, I'll finish you off in the ambulance!"

To my amazement, the police were as nice as pie. They were so helpful, which was great because I was really concerned that he was going to press charges for what I'd done to him. But if anyone deserved it, he did. The police talked me through the whole thing and took a statement. One of them came around the next day to make sure I was

OK. He said he'd listened to the 999 call and I'd apparently said, "You need to get around here because I've got my foot on his fucking face!" I was so angry. Anyway, the young copper chuckled and shook my hand for what I'd done.

This intruder went to court and got done for Aggravated Burglary. He had a claw hammer with him and that was what he was trying to retrieve from his pocket. I was well within my rights to do what I did to him. My spider sense had truly kicked in. He was going to go at me with a claw hammer. It was a nasty situation. The most frightening experience I've had in my entire life. Not cool whatsoever.

That incident made me quite fearful for a while and glad not to be living there because I thought there might be repercussions. If I had taken a beating like that, I would definitely want some retribution.

I was in the corner shop one time, a few months later and there he was! He clocked me and couldn't get into an aisle far enough away. Our eyes met and he shat himself. And that was that. I never saw him again.

# Have Records Will Travel

Kissdafunk was going great guns in 2008. We were now a global concern. We were doing monthly residencies in Singapore, Bali, Jakarta, Los Angeles, Texas, Marbella and Ibiza as well as lots of nights domestically. We did Coloursfest in Scotland, taking care of the funky room there for them. There were so many things going on, it really was hard to keep a lid on it all. There really wasn't that much time for sleeping, although shut-eye had become a rare pleasure for me, going all the way back to the Blackburn days.

I remember doing a Kissdafunk gig for Pacha at Sharm el Sheikh and from there I went to Texas. I just remember waking up in a darkened room thinking 'Where the fuck am I? What part of the world am I in?' I had no idea. I was absolutely shattered. I was living the dream, but having a nightmare at the same time. I don't want to be too dramatic about it because this was what I'd always wanted. To be touring these events worldwide was amazing, but it was just relentless.

Touring China was incredible. I did the Beijing Warehouse and then went on to Shanghai before jetting off to Bahrain and Dubai. It was insane, but I was absolutely loving it. At the same time I was having to call back to the UK to speak to Annabelle and Tolley to try to orchestrate stuff there. There was no Zoom in 2008 of course and I couldn't even get email in some places. Every single week, I would be playing out from Thursday, Friday, Saturday and Sunday somewhere in the world. But a lot of other stuff was taking a backseat in terms of making music or the hard house stuff. I was just about keeping my toe in the water by playing for Frantic, Tidy, Storm and Xstatic. I was also doing a lot of stuff with Pam's House in Norwich and had some great times there with those guys. I'd been fortunate enough to be given the honour of doing the closing set at a lot of those places, hence my nickname 'The Closer'.

That same year, I did some live PAs of the Quake material complete with a vocalist, bringing all those tracks up to date, and that inspired me to work on some new material. I did the Tidy Weekender and Creamfields, which were amazing. I did a live set with my friend and lighting guy from the Blackburn raves Nathan D'amour who electrocuted himself all those years ago. He came in and helped us out with some live keyboards. We ended up writing a brand-new track especially for the occasion called *Bring The Lights Down* that my amazing friend and mentor Steve Hill Released on his Y2K label.

I made another track with Alf Bamford called *Freefalling,* which got signed to Tidy Records and that set us on another path to getting lots more worldwide gigs, including some stuff in Australia with him. The hard trance track *Freefalling* was a big moment for us. Never underestimate the power of a good single.

I did a remix of *We Come One* by Faithless in 2008 with Jason Herd who did the track *Just Can't Get Enough* (Herd & Fitz) that was a massive hit on Subliminal Records. I'd known Jason for years; he used to run a club called Holy City Zoo in Manchester where I used to play funky house. Jason is a brilliant producer and this mix was a bit more electro than funk really. We did the mix under the name Bobby Tee and Juan Kid and it eventually got featured on Carl Cox's *Space* album; as a result of that, quite a few people bought it on Beatport. And then I got a message to say that Tiesto had been playing it loads at some massive shows. I looked it up on YouTube and there it was being blasted out by Tiesto at Sensation White, a massive party in Holland. People were now wanting to book Bobby Tee; my pseudonym for the funky house stuff resulting in Kissdafunk tours of China, Bali, Singapore, Dubai and Bahrain.

I was sat in a restaurant in the centre of Singapore having some food with the promoters and Jason Herd when these guys came up with a Rob Tissera record they wanted me to sign. "Are you Rob Tissera? Could you sign our record? We're going to the gig tonight." I didn't think they'd realised Bobby Tee was in fact me. It was a bit of an ego boost I have to say. Very odd.

China was an amazing experience. There was a lot more VIP and hosting at Chinese clubs, which were full of very rich people; not that there weren't just straightforward clubbers there too. I was there during the advent of fancy LED screens. I remember walking into this club in Shanghai, where I had to go through this incredible LED tunnel that took me to the DJ booth. The clubbers in China were there purely for the music. There was no drug connotation whatsoever. But the people were so enthusiastic.

I remember being taken to a restaurant that overlooked the Changi River in Shanghai. We had this incredible vantage point over the entire city and this enormous river. Looking at all these high-rises and tower blocks, you got an idea of just how many people lived there. Staggering.

I loved playing Asia. Back in the summer of 2004 I released a track called *Burning* on Steve Hill's Y2K label with my friend Guyver. The track went on to be highly regarded and as a result of that I was invited to play in Japan. I played a hard house set under my own name for Frantic in Osaka, Japan. I ate so much sushi out there I couldn't see the person next to me because there were so many plates. I absolutely loved it over there. I played with this famous Japanese DJ called Energy Dai (Daisuke Sakta), which was such an honour. They put me up in one of those sleeping pods instead of a hotel, which was an incredible experience. It was all part of the trip, as far as I was concerned. It was constructed of fibreglass and had its own bathroom and all the mod cons. I loved going out shopping and spending time in China and Japan.

I had a double-up set of gigs, which involved me playing until four in the morning in Osaka, then going back to the hotel, getting showered and changed before meeting them in a limo, which took us to the train station. We then got a bullet train to Tokyo and I played at Velfarre, the most famous club in Japan. We were then picked up in another limo and ended up in this backstreet in Tokyo. We parked in this yard and got out to see a glass elevator with security guards the size of Sumo wrestlers inside. They then ushered us into this lift, which took us straight up into the DJ box. It was amazing. And about 20 minutes later I was playing in Tokyo, which felt like such an honour. I was just a bloke from Milton Keynes. Really?!

I was actually playing when I spotted some fingertips come up onto the ledge of the decks. And then all of a sudden this guy pulled himself up and it was Ben from Sundissential and Gatecrasher. Ben Thompson helped to run Sundissential and did some stuff for Gatecrasher back in the day. He was over in Japan teaching English and decided to say hello. I finished my set, came down out of the DJ box and went to find

Ben and his mates in the main part of the club. It was then that I first clocked these enormous 50ft video walls in front of the DJ box. I had no idea I was being projected across the entire club. I was thinking to myself 'I hope I wasn't picking my nose or scratching my balls or something.'

Due to the time difference in Japan I watched Greece playing in the European Championships Final at breakfast time there, drinking Asahi while tucking into Katsu Pork that resembled a giant Schnitzel. I have always loved touring Asia.

*\*\*\**

In the summer of 2009, my dog Harry Tee passed away which was really sad. I was no longer with his 'mum', my previous girlfriend, Katy. But it had been a very amicable split and we had joint custody of him; I got him every other week. And then towards the back end of August 2009, I got a call from Katy to say he wasn't too well. I went to pick him up, having not seen him for a couple of weeks because I'd been so busy and it was very hard keeping on top of my schedule.

I went to see him on this one occasion and he was just a shadow of his former self. He had lost a load of weight. He'd been to the vets quite a few times because they thought he might have some cancer issues and he was beginning to deteriorate. I picked him up and thought wow. His back legs were going as well.

I took him for a walk in the park and he got about 400 yards in and just looked at me as if to say 'I can't do it anymore. I can't walk anymore.' I just picked him up and walked him home. I knew it was the beginning of the end. I took him back to Katy and said "Look, we're gonna have to make a decision here. It's your call, but if I'm being honest, I think the time has come." And she agreed. Her new boyfriend thought the same thing and after a brief conflab we made the decision. We called the vets for the final time.

I was there for at least an hour or more before the vet arrived. Harry was resting on a cushion and could hardly lift his head. I tried to give him some sausages and he just couldn't eat them. I knew we'd made the right decision. If the tables were turned, I'd like him to do the same thing for me. And so the vet came round and put the needle in and he just went to sleep. He didn't even flinch at the needle going in and he *hated* the vet with a passion. And then I picked him up to take him outside and he did his final wee all over me, and I thought, 'You can have that one on me, pal, no problems.'

We buried Harry Tee in the garden of Katy's bungalow where she lived in Selby, about 20 miles from Rothwell where I lived. Her boyfriend had also bonded with Harry Tee and had kindly dug a fitting grave. We said our goodbyes and filled the hole with earth. I just couldn't stop thinking of all the times we spent in my studio playing and making music. Whenever an agent was acting out like an arsehole, I would take Harry Tee for a walk to calm myself down. I loved that dog with all my heart.

# The Perils Of Promoting

It was the summer of 2009 and it had got to the point where we couldn't fit any more people into Kissdafunk at Mission, Leeds. KDF was the stalwart of everything we did, the cornerstone, the total bill payer. Mission on a Friday was one of the busiest nights in the country and we were at the point where we had to think outside of the box, and so we started to look at other venues. There was a lot of competition coming through from rival nights; always someone looking to take your crown. It was quite exhausting. It felt like plugging a leaking dam. Every time you put your thumb into one hole, another leak would spring up.

We definitely took our eyes off the ball on a couple of occasions. For example, we did a gig around that time just before the students broke up. We'd always done this particular date, when all the students handed their work in and would be preparing to go home. We put on Steve Angello and his brother AN21 as well as Laidback Luke. It was a pretty massive line-up really. What an absolute gentleman Laidback Luke was by the way. I would never tar him with the same brush as some of those other people. I took them all to this fancy restaurant thinking 'This is gonna be a smasher!' We'd decided to do it at the O2 in Leeds, which held 2,800 people. However, when we got there, we thought 'Jesus Christ, it's a bit slow on footfall here!' These times were prior to a lot of ticket selling. We just had a policy of 'build it strong and they will come'. You just had to have the best gig in town and that's what we've always strived to have. But even we couldn't even have forecast this damp squib. Turned out that the students had broken up the week before because they'd changed the exam dates and so our gig was pretty much straight into no-man's land.

We had these guys booked for ages, just on the fact that it was going to be a killer of a night, but when we got there, it was virtually empty. Not cool whatsoever. I wore my shoes out backstage at the 02. I was marching up and down desperately trying to come up with a plan. We ended up getting Carly's Angels to go round town with these sandwich boards to get the numbers up. They tried to grab some bodies off the street, but there was just nobody around because all the students had gone home. We ended up with 548 people in a place that held 2,800 and we lost about 13 grand in the process. It was a proper head-in-hands moment.

It was very hard to keep a lid on everything. We did our best, but there were definitely some outside influences making it difficult to keep trading as successfully as we had before. I've always known that you can wear the crown, but you can't *own* the crown. But we had a really, really great run at it. The funny thing is that when I had a meeting with the guys from Gatecrasher and Ministry who were pretty sharky and pumping me for information and all the rest of it, the guy from Gatecrasher asked me: "What's your exit strategy?" and I didn't really know what he meant. What was an exit strategy? I wasn't arsed about that, to be honest. I was just thinking how long can we carry on for? But now I understood what he meant because the next couple of years proved to be more of a challenge than anything I'd been through.

It was so hard to keep a lid on all of that and make everything run smoothly. There were just so many problems; people who would break promises and some truly unreliable new staff members. We were making some pretty poor choices too. I would have to say that promoting is way more dangerous than having a betting app on your phone. I think most promoters will be able to relate to that. There are times you just think, 'Well, that didn't work. So, what we'll do next is something even bigger.' And we definitely took a few wrong turns where there were mistakes galore. You can increase your costs, but you couldn't charge that much more for the ticket. All the backend expenses were going up. It got to a point where we put the price up by £3 per person. But once you tried to knock it up to like £20, that represented a lot of money. People were like, 'Oh, you money-grabbing bastards!' They would be doing back-of-fag-packet maths, thinking we must be making a fortune. But what they didn't understand was that DJs had gone from costing £600 each, to a pretty hefty £13,500. All of these things were impacting on the profits

We did a couple of gigs with David Guetta at the 02 in London to 3,000 people. He had just done a track with Akon and Nicki Minaj and had been working with Kelly Rowland. David was having number one records. We had a downstairs room that was playing house and the whole thing was rammed. Sometimes the money we were making out of the good gigs covered some of what we lost on the duff nights.

The agents didn't help of course. One particular name, which I will not mention here, told us how their DJ was playing in Leeds, and then doing Creamfields before jetting off to France. On top of the humongous fee, we also had to contribute £13,500 towards the fuel for each jet. We also had to be at the airport at least two hours before the plane left and so it would have been much easier and quicker to just drive them across to Creamfields and then flown from there to France. This was making life a lot less enjoyable.

On the upside, I was doing Judgement Sundays in Ibiza, which was a great escape. I was over there every other week doing the back room at Judgement Sundays. When I say back room, you still got 800 people in there having a proper party. Every two weeks, we were the guests of Judges Jules and the beautiful Nick Turner, god rest his soul. Nick was an ally and a great friend for many years while doing stuff over in Ibiza. I met Nick through Claire Hoare who was running some stuff for Slinky in Ibiza. Nick was Jules' partner in Judgement Sunday. He really was the host with the most.

We would have separate villas for ourselves and the other DJs over there be that Lisa Lashes, BK or the guys from the *Dirty Sanchez* TV show. We had a few crazy tear-ups with the Sanchez boys who were always sliding across the marble floors, hitting each other with cat o'nine tails they'd constructed from massive twigs and branches from the garden. Micky Slim was always doing stuff with them as well. We had some great times there with Micky and all of his crew from Birmingham. They were such a good laugh. Proper salt of the earth. Our type of mates. And then one night, somebody completely on the periphery, told these girls in the VIP area at Eden that he ran Judgement Sundays. I won't name him, but he buttered these girls up to come back to the villa with us.

I'd been outside talking with Lisa Lashes, Kate Lawler from *Big Brother* and a few others, looking around at all the madness that was going on in that villa when I clocked these two girls that this bloke had brought back. My spider sense tingled when I saw them recording conversations on their phones. 'What's she up to here?' I questioned her quite closely and it turned out they were reporters for *The Mirror* looking for a drug-fuelled story of Brits in Ibiza. I just rumbled them straight off because they didn't look like they belonged there. They were asked to leave, of course.

Those guys looked after us like kings every two weeks and I could have stayed there for weeks and weeks. It was absolutely brilliant. So, thank you to Jules and Nick in particular. Always a pleasure and never a chore.

Another time back at one of these crazy villa parties I was in the kitchen with about 30 people who had managed to get an invite back to one of these legendary crack-ons when someone produced a bottle of absinthe. Up went the cry... 'Shots??!' Of course myself and Tolley were never ones to back down, so we had a huge gulp of the nasty green liquid, but then the girl who'd produced the bottle said "Have you ever drunk it the Czechoslovakian way?" So, she started melting a teaspoon of sugar with a lighter and then dropped it into the glass of Czech rocket fuel and necked it. Never one to shirk a challenge I said: "Count me in" and so she delved into one of the kitchen cupboards and rustled around until she found a jar of white stuff. We proceeded to melt it on a spoon which took ages. Eventually it crystallised and I dropped it into the beaker of absinthe. The whole thing bubbled away and then woof! I threw it down my neck in front of 30 people. There was a collective intake of breath. "How was it?" someone piped up.

– "Well, it would've been fine, except that was a teaspoon of hot salt! Wow!"

That was literally the worst taste I've encountered in my entire life!

***

People often ask me what's the craziest thing you've seen in Ibiza? I was once at a party in San Antonio after Judgement and three of my mates who shall remain nameless snorted a capful of... wait for it... tape head cleaner that they had found next to the stereo in their rented apartment. Now, tape head cleaner contains triethylamine, which will turn a rusty old penny into shining gold within seconds and so god knows what it did to their stomachs. I still can't believe to this day that nobody was taken to hospital. Utter insanity at its finest.

***

At 6am the workers in the Ibiza clubs would pile to the closest place to relax and Eden was right next to Whips Terrace, where there's a world-famous grocery store with some seating outside. A load of people would congregate there in the early hours. We'd gone over to Whips Terrace one night and met some people there before going on to this house party about 500 yards away, in a flat that overlooked the parade of bars.

My phone rang shortly after arriving and it was a mate of mine who was downstairs with a friend of his: a Spanish policeman. He said he was off-duty and cool with what we were doing. It seemed a bit odd, but I pressed the button and allowed them into the lift, still unsure as to whether this copper should be hanging around with us. My mate and the policeman arrived with a couple of our dancers who had turned up at the exact same time. When the lift doors opened, they all piled out.

This girl immediately took me to one side. "He's a wrong 'un!" They looked properly startled and these dancers were pretty robust human beings who could handle themselves in any situation. "He's a fucking wrong 'un. He took his police badge out and said, 'Take your knickers off – both of you!'" This must have happened in the few seconds it took the lift to get to the second floor. I guess this must have been his MO, because he was absolutely brazen.

My mate said, "Don't worry, I'll look after him" and he poured this copper a massive tequila. This coffee mug of tequila floored the copper, and he ended up lying on the couch in the front lounge with his hands and legs splayed open. It wasn't long before people were going up and drawing on him in lipstick. He was wearing white jeans, so that was going to be a problem for him. They wrote swear words on his forehead and drew a little moustache. Somebody placed a hanging basket on his crotch. They took some photos of him as well. And then his warrant card and police badge were removed. I looked around and thought to myself, 'I'm the oldest person here and I probably need to be the responsible one.' And so I retrieved his badge. I didn't want him returning to the party with his copper mates and those batons. So, I took the badge, had a massive 'one for the road' mug of tequila with the intention of putting it back in his pocket before he awoke from his drunken stupor. I said my goodbyes and set off back to my hotel, half a mile away.

The tequila had well and truly kicked my ass because I was crawling through the narrow back streets of the west end of San An and up the stairs on my elbows like a zombie to my hotel room. I just needed to be in that room. I then dropped the key on the floor and started to panic. Sweat was running down my back. I found the key and picked up my mini Slappa suitcase of 600 CDs and fell into the hotel room. I then crawled along the marble floor pushing this CD case with my head because I was so poleaxed. I got as far as the end of the corridor and into my room. And crashed.

I came to, a few hours later, looking like Droopy the cartoon dog or a blood-shot character from *Ren & Stimpy*. My phone was buzzing like mad. I had about 50 missed calls. I called my mate who was still with that policeman. "Rob, he won't let me go until I get his police badge back!" I told him I was pretty certain someone had placed it on the mantelpiece back at the party. "Nope, not there." I started frisking down the pockets of my cargo shorts and thought, 'Ah!' I had this policeman's badge.

I could have got seriously done for stealing a policeman's badge and so I told my mate that I would hide it somewhere for the copper to find. Now, the Hotel Sol, where I was staying, had the word 'hotel' written out in stones on a little piece of grass. "I will hide it under the 'H'," I told him. So I cleaned my teeth, washed my face and set off to bury the badge downstairs. I'd just put my flip-flops on when there was a knock at the door. It was probably the cleaner or someone. Oh no! It was the fucking copper.

The policeman looked like the angry farmer from those Public Information Films from the 70s. He was very red-faced even though the booze had no doubt worn off by now. He still had the moustache drawn on his face and his white jeans were covered in Sharpie and mascara. He was so angry his fists were clenched. Houston we have a problem.

He pushed me into the hotel room and was like, "Get down on the bed. Get down on the bed!" I'm thinking, 'He wants to disarm me, and then he can smash me into next week!' I was absolutely certain of it. 100% this was a punishment beating. And I wasn't going to have this.

I pulled the belt off my trousers and wrapped it around my hand with the buckle out and swung it around my head as fast as I could while shouting: "You're a little fucking rapist!" I couldn't have shouted any louder and it resonated around the entire floor of the hotel because, of course, there was no carpeting. My words were hanging in the air and he just looked at me and must have thought 'This boy's mad! He's mental!' And with that he took off, running down the corridor and out of the hotel stairwell, while all the time I was shouting "You're a fucking rapist!"

This policeman just couldn't believe what was going on, but he stopped at the bottom of the stairs. He did the 'I'll be watching you' with two fingers pointing to his eyes. "Room 307, yeah?!" I thought 'Jesus! I'm in deep dog shit here!'

I had to gather all my stuff together on the spot without a second thought. I knew what was coming. The door would be put through by him and his police mates. I gathered all my stuff together and explained the situation to Uncle Nick Turner. What we had in our back pockets of course, were the pictures of him behaving really badly in the party. Now, Nick was friends with people in some very influential places over there and he told me to leave it with him. 'We've got photographic evidence of your boy smashed out of his noggin at this party, and it doesn't look good for him. So, if you send the boys round for this guy, that's not going to play well. We've also got the memory card.' But I still had to pretty much go into hiding until I could get a flight home. And I didn't return to the island for two years. I didn't go back because I didn't want any trouble and so that was a real piece of negativity for me.

# Erik Morillo's Aircon

2009, Erik Morillo came over to play for us in Leeds and it cost £25,000, which I paid for on a platinum American Express. Ouch! He was due to arrive a few weeks later, and his people rang ahead to say that he was bringing his tour manager solely to transport a filter unit that you can buy for about £136. So we were having to pay a guy to come over from the US just to install this unit. The tour manager also cleaned his CDs as well, I believe. They then asked us what car we had in terms of picking them up from the airport. I said I had a brand-new Range Rover and they said, "Have you got anything better, like an E-class Mercedes?" FFS.

Anyway, they just happened to know someone in Liverpool funnily enough who owned a Merc and they booked that person to come and be a chauffeur that we obviously had to pay for. That was another £600 to get the E-Class Mercedes to pick them up from Manchester Airport and bring him into Leeds. The driver then had to wait for him at his hotel, before taking him from the hotel to the club. And then wait there until he finished in the club and then take him back to the hotel, which was, wait for it, 125 yards away. It was 125 yards from the Malmaison to the front entrance of Mission and this guy had to wait there all night for him and then take him back to Manchester because he wouldn't travel in the same vehicle as the tour manager. So, we had to get a separate car to take the bloody tour manager to fit the filter unit. It was utter insanity itself. Absolutely ridiculous.

Morillo was a very good DJ. He did a few things that made my eyes bulge out of my head like Roger Rabbit. He had some amazing skills and was by far one of the nicer DJs in terms of how he was with us, but the management team behind him were worlds apart. Morillo did a couple of mixes that night which were beyond anything I've ever seen, and that goes for Carl Cox, the lot. It was such a shame there was so much really bad baggage attached to him. A real shame. He was a flawed genius, for sure.

\*\*\*

In 2011, I was due to play a Tidy party with Ron Signum, a fantastic DJ from Holland who's done so many great tracks including *What You Got For Me* and *Coming On Strong* which are two absolutely legendary tracks in the trance and hard house fields. So I went to go and pick Ron up from Bristol airport on my way down to Plymouth. I didn't really know him that well, but we got on famously in the car. I had a really good laugh with him. Anyway, we ended up having a blowout in the car about 40 miles from Plymouth. This guy was sent to come and pick us up and so we had to leave the car where it was and get a lift with this guy into Plymouth for the gig.

This guy who picked us up said, "Listen, do you want to come to this house party after?" By this stage we'd had a good skin full of tequila and Ron was quite a party animal and so we took him up on the offer.

We got to this rather dodgy house following the gig and proceeded to neck tequila. The sambuca was out too; the whole nine yards. I was feeling more than a little rough and headed for the loo.

Now, whoever had been in there before had *destroyed* it. It looked like someone had sprayed shit all over the bathroom. It was absolute filth. I was choking so bad I sounded like a distressed goose. And then all of a sudden I could hear these girls outside wanting to use the loo. Panicking that they might suspect that I had created this disgraceful scene, I looked around for some air fresheners or deodorant. Tada! I plucked a can off the shelf and did a complete 360 circle spraying what I thought was air freshener. Only it was green shaving gel. And it literally went into every crevice and across every wall of this person's bathroom.

I then drunkenly tried to towel it down, which only smeared the green goo even further across the walls.

I had completely destroyed their bathroom. It looked like ET had exploded in there.

In the end, I opened the door, barged past these four girls and said, "I don't know who was in there before me, but they have destroyed that loo!" I quickly located Ron Signum and we legged it out of the back door laughing all the way.

***

In 2011, it finally felt like the perfect time to close the Kissdafunk chapter and seek out pastures new. Myself and Tolley had given it our all and to be honest, it had taken its toll on us both. We had been fortunate enough to have had some utterly magnificent experiences together, but there were times that we would argue like kids owing to a lack of sleep and a lack of love for how the business model was changing due to the primadonna nonsense we were encountering with the DJs on a daily basis.

It was a tough decision, but we needed to draw a line in the sand and knock it on the head. We still see each other from time to time and we get on fine. We were both gutted to pull the plug on KDF, but it was totally the right manoeuvre, as the next step of my journey has been nothing but a pleasure. This was a chance for me to concentrate on some new projects.

I started working with Simmo, a promoter from Leeds and another guy called Ray Chan. We started the brand-new night Parliament. They had access to a venue called Space in Leeds, which had been there for years. I'd always had an association with that club, living and working in Leeds.

We got some really decent artwork done by Jamie, the designer we'd previously used for KDF; bringing our various talents to the table. Simmo used to run Habit in Leeds, which was an enormous night on a Thursday that was also at Space. Habit had always been the most successful Thursday night in town. So, we consisted of three promoters from the most successful Thursday night and one of the most successful Friday nights, in Candy Pants, run by Ray Chan and me. Bringing the three things together made perfect sense. However, three chefs stirring the pot meant it wasn't always the smoothest of runs, even though we remained friends.

We were doing stuff with Steve Angello's brother AN21 who was looking like he was going to be a big deal at the time, as well as the Stafford Brothers who were enormous in Australia. The Stafford Brothers were a big EDM act 'down under' and a proper pair of lads. They were Australian Rules footballers who turned to DJing once they'd hung up their boots. They were annoyingly good looking too; they could have been in *Point Break* or something like that. They were cool characters who were getting coverage from *Mixmag* and so I put them on when they came over. It was a total blast working with them.

Simmo, Ray and I then decided to put on a bigger gig at Magna situated between Sheffield and Rotherham in 2010. It was May bank holiday and this party at Magna was Kissdafunk meets Parliament, presenting Swedish House Mafia. But the agents were becoming so overly corrosive to work with, it was becoming a torture.

The agent's role seemed to be solely based around squeezing as many pennies from people like myself as possible. It was graceless and shameless. Yet once more, heavily encouraged by my new business partners, I took the old shilling of the devil and called up the banshee agent. The Swedes decided they wanted to do some warehouse parties, which had become a cool thing again following the Warehouse Project in Manchester amid a return to 'the warehouse days of glory'. Swedish House Mafia knew my background from the Blackburn days, as we often discussed it on the many car journeys we shared and so it sounded like a good idea all round.

I booked Magna in Sheffield, which could not be more of a warehouse if it tried. Magna was on an old industrial estate; grey and gloomy – it was a huge old steel yard. You could get 4,000 people in there and another 4,000 people in other areas. It was like an aircraft hangar with machinery still inside where the dance floors were. It was pretty awesome and really inspiring. I booked this venue and we proceeded to sell it out. We were working with Russell Pate who ran Gatecrasher for a few years, and so we had some real clout behind this enormous event.

It took six months to put this event on and SHM had some huge successes during the interim; number one singles and headline shows at events like Miami Ultra Music Festival. They had also started playing Ibiza too. In short, everything was kicking off for them. As it got closer to the event, the agents started acting up. They were constantly asking for a ticket count. It got to a point where I snapped. "Why do you need a ticket count when it's not your gig? We've paid you already." It was £35,000 to get them and so it wasn't cheap, and that was mates' rates.

Anyway, we got everything set up and Magna was looking immense, with great decor everywhere that had to be installed by these cherry pickers because the ceilings were so high; 50-60 feet up in the air. We put some proper graft into making that place look right. It was a week-long experience to make that warehouse a safe and exciting home for our punters.

SHM played Brixton Academy the night before and they turned up to this warehouse and went straight up into the VIP area, which was more like a canteen for work staff, but we tried our best to bling it up a bit. We escorted them in through the back door of the venue and upstairs into this VIP area. They turned up with a full entourage.

Now, the reason they wanted to know the ticket count was that they wanted to make another demand. Three days before this event, they played Miami Ultra, which had this big pyrotechnic show. Now, SHM bought into the company that did the pyrotechnics and now they wanted to have one at Magna. And so we had to do a risk assessment for indoor pyrotechnics, which meant an extra tonne of paperwork needed to be done. "If you don't have the pyrotechnics show, they're not coming," was the message to us. By this point, I was beginning to lose the will to live. "I'm not too sure I can deal with these fuckers anymore!" Not only that, but we had to pay for the frickin' fireworks!

SHM's agent gave us all the specs for this show. We had to cough up £14,000 extra for the fireworks, hence why they'd been monitoring how many tickets we'd sold – they wanted to see how much profit there was likely to be. And then they put that cost in, which wiped out all our profit. They were pretty much using us to promote a gig that they could use as a bit of a showcase for what they were going to do at Pacha that summer. That's exactly what it felt like because they'd moved the goalposts to such a degree that this night now felt like a dry run to me.

I was doing a lot of running around that night. I always say to aspiring promoters that what you really need is a T-shirt with the slogan "I'll be back in two minutes." You will be running around like a blue ass fly all night! The stress of dealing with these increasingly toxic agents was starting to affect my physical and mental health. I was in this for the music, and that was starting to get lost as I got deeper and deeper into the business side of things.

I had always got on great with the Swedes' road manager, but because their demands had shifted so greatly, so had the stress levels. He was wearing one of those headsets with a mic. "OK, Rob. I just need you to do one thing, OK? When the guys are playing, no one's allowed on the stage. Are you cool with that?"

- "Yeah, no problem."
- "And that includes you as well. You can't be on stage."

Now, I was DJing after them. "You what?" This guy was pushing his luck. "So, Rob, you need to get all your stuff ready, so that as soon as they finish playing, you can then lift yourself up. You can put your stuff up there, but you're not allowed to be on stage at any point while they're on stage." At our own gig!

I was furious. This was a disgrace. Not long after that, the agent started shouting the odds at me in the VIP room in front of my staff. "We were in fucking Brixton last night and that was amazing. Why have you brought us to this shithole?"

- "This *shithole* is a warehouse and that's what you asked for!"

She then started moaning about the LCD video screen we installed, based on her specs. "It's like a postage stamp!"

- "Well, it's exactly the specs you asked for. But the thing is, you didn't ask us for the specs of the venue and had you done that you might have asked for a bigger screen. But you didn't."

She was shouting at the top of her voice at me and Russell Pate, dressing us down like a pair of naughty school kids. She was pointing her finger at us and going "You fuck off! And you fuck off!" and so I just said "Actually, why don't YOU fuck off and don't come back! As soon as your boys have finished I want you out of the venue and never darken our door again!" She couldn't believe it. She sat out the back until they'd finished and then off they all scuttled. And that's exactly how that all ended. I just could not take another second of the whinging and moaning and all the ridiculous nonsense I was being confronted with. I don't care who you are, that is no way to behave. And I have never ever in my entire career stooped to those kinds of levels, thinking my shit doesn't stink. It was just utterly ridiculous.

We worked on that Magna gig for months and months and we came out of it with just a few hundred quid profit. It was a huge gig. The best part of 4,000 people came along to that, but we decided to knock the big events on the head and carried on doing the smaller club gigs.

*** 

September 2011, I did the final Kissdafunk tours over in Australia with the Stafford Brothers. We did Brisbane, Perth and those guys treated me like a king. The Brothers had done their own reality TV show out in Australia and so they were like the Kardashians of Australia.

We played Platinum in Brisbane and that was full-on hedonistic nonsense. While I was DJing, Joey, the guy who ran the place, stood on the bar dancing with a bottle of sambuca. He would walk over to where I was playing and just pour sambuca into my mouth. I probably made the mistake of thinking I was bulletproof and got so drunk I could hardly see.

I somehow got back to the hotel after and stumbled into reception. I had a big 600-CD case, which was like a small suitcase. The lid wasn't on properly and as I strolled through reception like a *Thunderbirds* puppet, trying not to create a scene or whatever, I tripped over and dropped the CDs all over this tiled floor. They went everywhere. They had also been stored 'in order' for my set-lists. I also lost some. The staff helped me to pile them all back into the case and then I went upstairs. Just as I was getting into my hotel room I tripped over again and spilled the CDs everywhere. I had a great time with them over there, but I was physically and mentally exhausted; as well as drunk.

On the way back from Australia, I stopped off to play the Swiss hotel in Singapore. The Swiss was a brand-new venue with a 360-degree rotating club at the top. This place was just stunning and it looked right out over the city. You could see as far as the eye could see. The first part of the gig was on the helipad of the Swiss Hotel. I loved every second of that.

The Northern Lights in Leeds resembled an event space; a really cool building that held about 800 people. The ceilings were about 30-40 feet up and you needed to get the decor up fully assembled. Some of the production guys hadn't turned up and so I pitched in to help with all of that. I'd just come back from Singapore and didn't necessarily need this ballache, but the show had to go on. We were working with 'Burno' (Steven Burns) who went on to run the successful Prism in Leeds. Anyway, we were working with him putting a few bits and pieces of decor up on this big cherry picker crane. We had these 10ft-wide murals of the logo that had to go up into the ceiling.

I had one last banner to put up which was to go on the side of the DJ box. I'd spoken to the venue manager and he gave me this big A-frame ladder. I was putting this last banner up when I heard a click. And the ladder collapsed. I fell forward. "Wooooaahhhh!!!"

It was one of those Wily Coyote moments from *Roadrunner* where he steps off the cliff into thin air. There was a brief moment where I thought, "Ah."

I fell forward from 20 feet up and landed like a cat. I broke both my arms at the elbow, and completely smashed my wrists into bits.

My body went into total shock when I hit the deck and I could hear people screaming. Funny thing was I just sprung back up on my feet; the screaming was down to my right arm that had bent right the way back at the elbow and was now facing the wrong direction. Apparently, I calmly asked someone to call me an ambulance. And then I headed off to the loo where I passed out. The next thing I knew I was in the back of an ambulance and receiving gas and air on the way to Leeds General Infirmary.

The surgeon said, "You've cracked it so badly the bone fragments have turned into crazy paving." You know it's bad when the surgeon says, "I won't be minute," and then calls two other guys to come over and have a look at your X-rays. I'd definitely fucked up.

I was in hospital for a week on the gas and air. It was horrendous. It took a week before the swelling went down enough for them to be able to open up the back of my right arm like a chicken fillet, so they could work on the elbow.

I got a bad scar down my arm as a result of that and my elbow still sticks out at weird angles. The arm doesn't fully open up like it used to and to be honest I had about 10% power in my arms for a long while. I was on morphine for a week, which made me a bit trippy. It was like having three witches sat on the end of your bed telling you how shit you are. Pointing out all the bad stuff in your life. And then there would be moments of euphoria too. It was just so intense. I spent at least three or four months on Tramadol as well.

I'd only been seeing Anna for a couple of years by this point, but things were going great. You really know how amazing somebody is when the shit hits the fan like that. Anna helped me have showers by putting plastic bags over my arms so they didn't get wet. Anna did the kindest of acts and really looked after me. I had to take three months off due to the seriousness of the situation. But I just wanted to get back out playing.

My first gig after that accident was in York. People were coming over to me and inadvertently hugging me and shaking my hand. It was murder! I made a real mistake playing that gig. I just remember thinking, 'OK, now you need to stop the gigs for about four or five weeks because that was a really stupid idea.'

The people who looked after me during that time were Blandy, Leafy, the Diamond Posse: Nicky, Steve Dixon, Dean H, Malcolm, Anna's mum and dad and my sister. Love you all! It was a very levelling experience. And I think that just whacked the final nail in the coffin of the promoting thing to be honest. I just wanted to go out and play music, just as I had all those years ago back in Manchester and Blackburn. Promoting was killing me!

# CH. 49

# Rob Tissera Is Back!

2012, I decided to concentrate on making music and DJing now Kissdafunk was over. Of course, some of the people I'd been booking for gigs were now running events themselves and so it was always nice when people stepped forward to reciprocate. That said, I knew I had to really double down to get some hard house gigs. I wasn't on some of the line-ups I needed to be on, which meant making an awful lot of phone calls. It was a mini rebrand in some respects.

I got some fresh press shots done and bashed the phone to get some trance or hard house gigs. And that started to bear fruit within a very short space of time. I picked up about 30 bookings just by doing it myself, even though I had an agent who was doing some stuff for us based around Kissdafunk.

I was so glad it panned out as well as it did. A lot of people were like, "Why haven't we put you on in such a long time?" I managed to pick up a lot of work, which was absolutely great.

I'd been getting tonnes and tonnes of offers to do old skool gigs when I was doing Kissdafunk even though the set-lists were veering more towards EDM than house. Because of the demands of promoting I'd put the old skool on the back burner for 10 years or so. But I was now determined to reinstate my love of house and old skool.

I'd been listening to a few old DAT and cassette tapes from back in the day; TDK and Maxell Metal tapes from Richer Sounds. I dug them out of the loft and was listening to them with Adam and a few of my mates. And then boom! Out of nowhere, I got a call from Brad Kells at

Joy in Leeds, a night borne out of his love of Ark. Joy closely resembled the line-ups and artwork of Ark and of course, the crowd was the same too even though it was not on the same grandiose scale; this was a more intimate affair. Anyway, he asked me to come along and play in March 2012.

And then out of nowhere, I got a call from these guys who ran an event in Chorley Park Hall, Lancashire who were putting on this really big party at Bowlers, which I hadn't played since '97 or so. It was a Bowlers reunion.

It was September of 2012 and this party was rammed to the gills. It was like stepping back in time. I went with my mate Wilba and a couple of friends. You had to go over a tram track into this proper old industrial estate in Trafford Park, Manchester. You turned left into the road and Bowlers was about 200 yards further down. We turned the corner and it was just like the old times. It was mayhem! They were queuing right around the block. 'Why have I not been doing this?'

I was waiting to do my set, just stood on that stage looking at MC Energy who used to do Fantazia really giving it some! That night really went according to plan. I brought my third CDJ with me, so I could do my best. Whatever the set-up was, I could add my third CDJ to get that USP of being able to do some of the stuff I'd learned over the years from watching Carl Cox, Erik Morillo and Swedish House Mafia, who all made a name for themselves on three decks. That was a great night!

I actually went to a couple of old skool nights as a punter to get properly into 'the zone' for these gigs. I would pay to get in, no guest list, and just watch what people were up to. What struck me was that a lot of people were trying to do it all on vinyl, which was all good, but I wanted to create my own reworks and edits and needed access to acapellas galore. I could do stuff on the third deck that I wasn't hearing other people doing at the time and that really helped to set me apart in some respects.

I would never say I don't love vinyl because I do, but it's not the be all and end all. It's a vehicle through which to communicate with people and if a better form of communication comes along, then embrace it. You can now stream music straight to the decks with Rekordbox, something I don't have a grip on just yet. But just being able to have stuff on USB makes the travelling a lot easier. I've got a small bag holding 20 USBs with 500-600 tracks on each one. Moving about the globe with a record

In action, Liberation at Fabric London, 2022. Picture by Marc De Groot

Paul Priestley (RIP)

Me and Wilba at Rejuve, 2018

Me and Steve B2B Frantic at Koko, London, 2018

Mark EG, BK, Billy Daniel Bunter, DJ Vibes and me at Unity In The Sun, 2019

Billy Daniel Bunter and me at Clockwork Orange, 2022

Dean Hyden

Me and Ben Amponsah

Me and Ian Bland, Slipback In Time, Ibiza, 2023

Me and Colin Elson

Me and Scott Vinylgroover

Me and The Mighty Ian Bland

Me and Gary Simpson from Housework, London

Me and Marc Leaf

Me with Sam Townend and Dean Ashraf aka
The Tidy DJs

Me, Stu Allan (RIP) and The Fat Controller

My mate Mark Wilba Williams

Ru Curthoys (RIP) and Sam Townend from Tidy

The Tidy Boys, Sam Townend, Anna Tissera,
Dean Ashraf and Steve Lidd

Tommy Smith, Boomtown, Blackburn raves

Uncle Nik Turner and Susana from Judgement
Sundays, Ibiza

Uncle Mo Choudry, Amnesia and Cream, Ibiza
RIP

Writer Andrew Woods and Richard Raindance

Quake - *The Day Will Come*, 1998

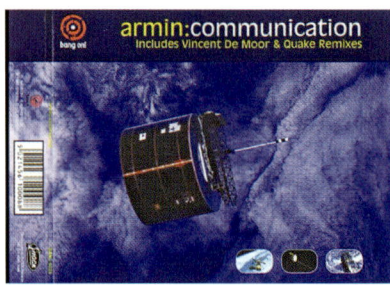

Armin, *Communication* cover

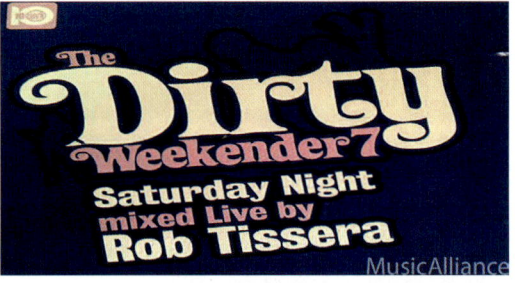

Dirty Weekender

Asha - *J.J Tribute* front cover

Goodgreef, Creamfields

Goodgreef album

*Ideal Weekender* album

Kissdafunk album cover

Rob Tissera - *Kick Up The Volume* cover, XL Records

Sundissential North 10th birthday

Rob Tissera, Vinylgroover & The Red Hed, *Stay* cover

York *The Awakening*

*Clockwork Ibiza, 2020 flyer*

box was an absolute ballache, let me tell you. But now I can travel with a portable studio sat inside a little bag.

The third CDJ brought a fresh coat of paint to the old tracks because you had to be really careful not to fall into the same trap I kept seeing some other DJs do by playing the same stuff all the time. You would hear 2 Bad Mice's *Bombscare* four times a night at some of these old skool nights. Even though I absolutely love *Bombscare* there would be loads of other tracks that people would always want to hear at those events. So, I was trying to think a bit outside the box and edit things a little differently to bring something fresh to the party. Lo and behold it seemed to bring something that people really connected with and from doing that lots of other things started to pop up.

The line-up that night was Rhythm Quest who did *Closer To All Your Dreams*, N-Joi, Awesome 3, Rat Pack, and a whole bunch of local legends. There was also Matt Bell, who I used to DJ with, all the way back in the Zone days in Blackpool where I first met Flipped Out and another guy called Andy Pendle (a Northern legend), plus John Jepson who used to play at the Blackburn raves and Slipmatt and Vertigo from the Ark days. That was a huge line-up. And so now people wanted to book me for the old skool tunes, which set me off on a completely fresh path.

As a result of doing those two gigs, Brad Kells from Joy booked me on a regular basis for his event, every two or three months alongside DJ Sy and Vertigo with Flipped Out on the PA. I've played every single Tidy Weekender and the location was Southport that year. And that was awesome! I did a mix CD of brand-new music for those guys, which was quite a significant thing at that point in time. I'd made a load of hard trance with Tidy, Guyver and Steve Hill along with Technikal (Alf Bamford) and so I had some super fresh stuff to bring out for that as well. I also continued my long-term love affair with Goodgreef as they were booking me every year for their birthday celebrations and any other special events they were staging.

Eat Your Words was a great night in Hull that I also played for donkey's years and Neil Collingham who ran it became a really good friend to me; just a salt-of-the-earth kinda guy and not too shy to get dressed up in a Star Wars stormtrooper outfit or any other kind of costume for these parties. Just a really fun guy. And I loved playing those nights.

There were also Frantic and Sundissential reunions going on in 2013. And there were also nights like Rave On too, which was run by a whole bunch of people involved with Tidy: Ben Stevens, Sam Townsend and Irish Dave. Rave On was brand new and picking up some significant interest with acts like Tidy Boys and myself, plus the usual suspects. The parties were absolutely crackers and all themed. There was a Bad Taste Ball where people turned up as Josef Fritzel and Jimmy Savile to raise money for charity.

On the hard house front I was playing Frantic and Timeless at Scala in London; a great little venue. I was also starting to pick up a few more bookings with the boys who run Xstatic who were running yearly events in sunny Ibiza, plus, I was doing more of the old skool stuff at Bowlers and Fantazia with 808 State, Billy 'Daniel' Bunter and Slipmatt. The old skool thing seemed to have suddenly caught alight, and there were gigs on a fairly regular basis. I was chuffed to bits that it was going so well.

***

In 2013, I hooked up with my old buddy Steve Hill. I explained to him that I was looking to get back to doing what I loved the most, which was writing more music. He was over from Australia for a few weeks, so he generously offered to get me involved in a few projects he was working on with Klubfiller. I rolled over to Southport to Klubfiller's studio and we banged out two tracks: *Sunrise* and *Things Can Only Get Better.* Both of these were released by Steve on his Masif label and they promptly sailed into the Toolbox digital chart at number one. I'm putting Steve Hill at number one in the generosity stakes. There really isn't anyone like him. He goes out of his way at any given opportunity to help me and everyone else around him. He's also one of the most driven people I've met in my entire life. I thank my lucky stars for having a mate as kind as Steve.

After the success of those two releases, I followed up with another number one in the Toolbox chart with my old mate Guyver as we remixed our track *Burning* from 2004 and all of this had a huge impact on the amount of hard house DJ bookings I was being offered. I was back in the game thanks to my mate Steve Hill. Thank you, brother.

Steve had started running gigs in Auckland, New Zealand called London Hard House Reunion with a wonderful lady by the name of Janelle Kleinhans Matchett. There were loads and loads of workers in London that went to all that stuff when hard house was massive in 2003/4/5 and even 2006. A load of people that went to all of those gigs were from Australia and New Zealand. And then there was a change in the visa rules, which meant that you could only stay in the UK for four months or something rather than two years and as a result of that the numbers dropped off a cliff in hard house. So when they put this party on in Auckland, all those people that used to go to those nights in London converged on the centre of Auckland. And they had this huge party which was like going back in time. 2,000 people in a club listening to hard house. Janelle and her team would give anybody a run for their money in the generosity stakes too. She literally leaves no stone unturned in how she cares for her guest DJs. I've never known anybody provide the insane level of hospitality that she does. Wonderful stuff!

Tidy, Frantic and Xstatic put on some big nights, but the numbers had definitely dwindled down to only a few hundred at some hard house nights in the UK. And so it was something special to be on the other side of the world where it was rammed to the rafters. I went over with BK that same year too. We'd done a track together called *So Good* which also went to number one in the Toolbox charts. We also did Sydney, Australia and had a great time there.

I got a call from Neil Green who ran More Cake at Park Hall around this time and played at their night at Camelot, Chorley, Lancashire. Camelot used to be a mediaeval banqueting place with a few amusements for the kids, plus a hotel. Inside, it was like every 80s/90s nightclub, except you could get about 900 people in there on two levels. The crowd was four feet below stage level. It was a little like Uropa in Leeds in as much as it was a multifaceted venue with people all the way around the top level, hanging over the balcony, and people dancing below you and to the sides in raised areas. Camelot was an absolutely brilliant venue, right next to the M6 Services at Charnock Richard. There were all kinds of crazy action going on there before, during and after the event. Just a full-on rave with everybody all dressed up in crazy gear. I was stood on the stage there thinking 'Why did I ever give this up?' But I guess everything has a time and a place.

That whole scene was really burgeoning because lots and lots of people going to those events had kids that had possibly grown up and fled the nest, leaving mum and dad free to party again just as they did back in the day. I never thought for one minute when I was doing that stuff in the warehouses that I would still be dining out on that period and having such a great time doing what I loved. I was truly grateful for that experience and that rekindled my relationship with Paul Taylor (formerly of Angels) and his Retro brand. Paul was doing massive events at Bowlers, including the History of House Music in 2014. I just felt so blessed to be back out playing with legends like Jon Pleased Wimmin, Danny Rampling, Alastair Whitehead and John Kelly.

***

I played EDC at the Milton Keynes Bowl in July of 2014, which was quite a significant moment for me. To play EDC, one of the biggest festivals in America, in my home town, was very humbling. Another pinch-me moment. EDC was a huge carnival affair, involving Swedish House Mafia and all these huge acts. The last time I was there, I was watching David Bowie and Queen; still a teenager! I lived about a mile from Milton Keynes Bowl. So, I'm now up on that stage and I'm thinking, 'Oh my god, I remember jumping over the fence to see Bowie!' It was truly mind blowing to play Milton Keynes Bowl and I will be eternally grateful for that.

***

2014 and I was spending a lot more time with my mate Wilba, going back and forth to Manchester and any other gigs I did in the north. Then we'd go back to Wilba's afterwards and make music until Sunday afternoon. We were making quite a lot of house music under the name Bobby Tee & Mark Williams again, which was beginning to bear fruit in 2014. We went over to the Amsterdam ADE and made some connections there with a couple of record labels. We made a good contact in Jonathan Ulysses who I hadn't seen for five or six years; I used to go and watch him at In Bed At Space, Ibiza on a Tuesday morning after we'd done our parties. That man is a phenomenal DJ.

Jon had started a record label called Ulybug and so we put some stuff out on his label that started to get a little bit of interest with some new house fans. I was just happy keeping my toe in the water and I didn't want to completely die on the vine in terms of playing upfront housey stuff. That alliance gave me a really decent, creative outlet.

I did another track with BK in 2014 called *So Good*, which we did on his label Slam. And that track seemed to go down so well, all the time. It's one of those tracks that the crowd don't seem to get tired of hearing, which is a real pleasure for us both.

I finished my set at Bowlers one night in 2014 and Ryan Galloway, who I knew from the Ark days, came over. "I want you to meet a mate of mine." He took me down to where the fairground rides were out the back of Bowlers. He introduced me to this guy called Si Frater. "I run a thing in Leeds called Rejuvenation. We've done a couple already at this venue in Leeds called the Beaver Works, and they've taken off like a house on fire." This guy was just a lovely bloke and he invited me to go and play for them. Shortly before that gig I went to Thailand for a holiday. I was away in Thailand for a couple of weeks with Anna, my now fiance, and looking at all the posts and mounting excitement for this event, thinking 'Bloody hell, I'm gonna need to get my act together for this and do something really special!'

It is really important to me to not play the same stuff every set. I've got to turn up with some big guns. I spent a good five or six days working my stuff out when I got back from Thailand.

The Beaver Works was the perfect venue for a full-on warehouse party like Rejuve. An old mill that sprawls out over three rooms with a dark and dingy basement, where you can feel the damp in the air. The number of times we came out of there coughing like champs. You would also speak to people after the parties who claimed to have 'Beaver Fever'. I played '91 hardcore tunes there, the kind of stuff Carl Cox taught me to play all those years ago, as well as the big piano tracks like Asmo's *Jam The Dance* and a new remix of Bassheads' *Is Anybody Out There?* that I'd made with Wilba and Blackburn legend DJ Shack. It was full-on fire and a moment in time where a whole bunch of new friendships were born.

Si Frater and his wife Suze Frater were just solid gold from the off. I've never met anyone like them in terms of how much love everybody has for them and how much love they have for everybody else. They meet everybody at the door and Suze hugs every single person that comes in. She is really really funny and not afraid to speak her mind; an absolute diamond. If she doesn't like the look of somebody, she just turns them away because they have to be a family. It's that kind of atmosphere where everybody's family.

And as a result of that dedication, I was just talking to all these people, unable to believe how many good eggs were in there. It was just brilliant and I went off to the after-party with them and stayed for a good 10 hours with all my new best friends.

They do two or three parties a year and I nearly always play if I'm in the country. Without a shadow of a doubt it was one of the best things I've experienced in a club, because you got that collective spirit and that roar when you played a track. Their brand was just flowing and watching them grow has been a thing of beauty. You could draw a comparison between the way Si Frater branded his stuff and when I first saw Cream, Gatecrasher and Tidy. Everything was growing beautifully for them and they just kept getting bigger and bigger; 1,000 people through the door every single time without fail.

Also in that year, myself, Ian Bland and Anne Savage started a small night called Flashback which we did at Stinkie's Peep House in Leeds, run by Roger Faversham from all those years ago when Ark used to do their after-parties at his place. Dave Angel, Frank De Wulf and various other characters would play the Ark after-parties. I remember they couldn't pay me one night and so I asked for their foosball table instead. I got my mate Ian E to go around and collect this glass-topped fussball game in his van. I put it in the downstairs dining room. I used to love playing that thing.

We only did a couple of Flashback events at Stinkie's, but they were pretty well attended and we had a great time with them. But there were so many other good things going on in Leeds at the same time, it felt like a bit of an encroachment on the guys who did Rejuve and Steve Luigi who was now doing Gallery reunions. There was no necessity for us to be doing that. I would be better off playing as myself or with Ian from Dream Frequency rather than trying to compete. Plus, dipping my toe back into promoting made me shudder. I was enjoying myself way too much to get involved in all that nonsense again.

I started playing at Hidden in Ibiza run by Sam Mitcham. Sam ran Wax Format, a vinyl-only night and he asked me to come along and do some trance and hard house. We struck up a friendship that's still strong today and I've played for Sam loads. Sam teamed up with a guy called Kirk Field; another lovely character who's done loads of stuff in Ibiza over the years. He's written books and was a roving reporter for *Mixmag* for donkeys' years too. Kirk was involved in the infrastructure of the world of Tonic and Club 18-30 and more. They would do a week-long event over in Ibiza called Trance Week, which was incredible.

I was also working with Xstatic back in the UK, run by JP & Jukesy and Jimmy Dean who teamed up with Sam Mitcham and Kirk to do Captured Festival at Benimussa Zoo. Benimussa Zoo had shut down as an actual working zoo in the 90s and so this abandoned site was perfect for parties. There were seal pits, exhibition areas and a bear cave; I remember DJing in there. There was a really big stage in the middle of it and loads of other little side arenas. You went through a little door, which opened up to where the bears used to prowl. We would go and do the Sunday night at Captured Festival in the bear pit or an aviary, which opened into a little amphitheatre area where everybody stood in front of you on raised platforms. I'd come a long way since those Blackburn warehouses!

In May of 2014, we went over to Ibiza to do a party called SOS, an old skool promotion where I got to meet loads of peers and heroes: Billy 'Daniel' Bunter, 2 Bad Mice, Stu Allen, Fast Eddie, Jonay Amador, Mark Archer and tonnes and tonnes of people I'd worked with over the years; sometimes passing ships in the night. I brought the third CDJ again as it seemed to hit the spot with a lot of people who hadn't heard me play that way before. Out of the back of that came my long association with Daniel Bunter, Stu Allan and all of those guys. We had loads of chats and lunches sat around the pool with all those guys discussing our journeys. I loved talking to 2 Bad Mice about their role in the development of Moving Shadow and having long conversations with Stu Allan, expressing what an influence he'd been on me when I first moved to Manchester. I remember trying to find those records he played on Piccadilly Radio at the Vinyl Exchange in Manchester and Eastern Bloc. What a hero. I chatted to Stu for hours about soul music and his connection to the soul scene in Manchester. In true Stu fashion, he was as humble as the day was long. What an absolute gentleman.

Stu asked me if I would be interested in doing a radio show on OSN radio, which I've been doing right up until now. And you know, it's not the biggest station in the world, but for the people that listen to it, it's perfect. It has 'listen again' links which are popular. Lots of people listen to it via Mixcloud. It's such a shame that Stu is no longer with us. But I will keep on honouring his legacy on the first Saturday of every month.

As a result of doing the radio show, I met another couple of amazing people in Paul Draycott, who was Stu's partner in OSN and another fantastic chap called Mike Breakbeat Brook who selflessly posts my shows onto all my social media sites and various portals to give the show maximum reach. He is definitely part of the mighty, ever–growing Diamond Posse!

I was still doing Ibiza boat parties and Kanya in 2014, which now had an outdoor swimming pool at the bottom of the bar. I was only supposed to play for an hour this one night, but Pepe and Salvador allowed me to go on for three hours, covering all the bases from old skool like Joe Smooth's *Promised Land* and Phase 2's *Reaching* to a bit of electro and trance. There were about 300 people in Kanya and it was electric. Truly a moment in time where you just get to do what's in your soul. I still get people coming up to me saying they were there for that party. As Inner City sang: "We don't really need a crowd to have a party!" You don't need 2,000 people in front of you. All you need is a few hundred of the *right* people.

And then my friend Ru Curthoys, god rest his soul and his then partner Jamie, put me on at a We Love Hard House night where I played stuff from '89 all the way through to the hardest of hard house over a six-hour set held at a small venue called Pure just off the Holloway Road. Andy Farley, another great friend of mine from the Sundissential days played there too.

I also started doing a few events where it was Rob T & Friends that would have me playing with Steve Hill, BK, Ilogik and Sam and Deano (part of the Tidy crew). We would play back-to-back throughout the night. Anne Savage also played and they were great nights.

I also played a Tidy versus Nukleuz party at Fire in Vauxhall, London. That was a three deck, vinyl set, which was absolutely awesome and one of the beautiful things that came from that was hooking up with Steve Hill who was involved with it. He'd come over from Australia and it was great to catch up. Such a wonderful night all round.

# CH. 50

rob
Tissera

# I Do!

Owing to all of my dealings in Kissdafunk, my pension pot and savings had definitely taken a bit of a hammering. If I'm being totally honest it had taken the wind out of my sails. Kissdafunk was just exhausting and it had been so stressful keeping all that going. There were times when I just felt that I had no energy left. Looking back, I was at a pretty low ebb and needed a rest, but I didn't want to take my eye off the ball. It was certainly a bit of a leveller, I have to say.

Steve Hill was solid gold that summer and just super helpful in what was a really difficult and dark period for me. Some people really surprised me with how they helped out. Steve restored my faith in human nature in terms of just how helpful he was and how much great advice he gave me when making those tracks the year before, which he paid for. He always said to me that he felt he was backing a decent horse and that everything would be all right.

And everything was roses in terms of my relationship with Anna. We were so connected and just loved each other so much and have done from the moment we met. Her love and support and the kindness of Steve Hill and all the usual suspects like the Diamond Posse namely Nikki Hainsworth and Adam and all those guys as well as Ian Bland kept me positive. They've always been my solid rock friends and they helped me out hugely during a really shitty period. There were definitely some good things going on during that time, but they were tainted with a backwash of dog dirt.

On a happier note, I asked Anna to marry me. We went to Dubai for a few days in 2014 and I proposed. She said yes. The book is called

*The Smiler* and although I'd had my 'off days' Anna has kept me smiling since the day I met her.

***

August of 2015, I was back on track and playing Creamfields at Daresbury, Cheshire which felt phenomenal. It was a beautiful summer's day playing another World Cup Final.

That same year Slip Back In Time and Unity In The Sun took over from SOS in Ibiza. SOS was a strong concept, but you had to be well organised in order to do that successfully. And unfortunately SOS couldn't cut the mustard in that respect. However, out of the dark comes the light and Slipmatt, Rachel Hill and Terry Ashton brought it back, sharply rebranded as Slipback In Time, which has proved to be a roaring success. That was when I first got to really talk with Slipmatt. I can still remember when SL2 used to do those Dream events. It was great to be able to talk to him. Matt used to play Ark as well.

Around the same time I became great friends with the Unity In The Sun guys: Billy 'Daniel' Bunter, Sonya Steele and Jay Folly aka The Fat Controller. It was lovely seeing Daniel Bunter and Sonya. I'm very thankful to Daniel, because he then connected me to Raindance. Playing Raindance was a huge honour for me. I got on like a house on fire with Richard Raindance, Daniel, Sonya and Jay Folly.

And as you can see, my path has stuck around the old skool and it's a breath of fresh air. It felt much more like winning again. There are dark days for everybody, but you've just got to hope that the best days are ahead of you.

I loved doing hard house for Tidy and did Koko for Frantic; it was rammed solid. Koko (formerly Camden Palace) is literally a theatre of dreams; it can't be described as anything else. It was like playing the best stadium in the world. The roar from the crowd with everybody looking down from so high above you, and the dance floor sprawling in front of you and people down the sides, was incredible. It gave me the same feeling as playing The Sanctuary in Birmingham; the spiritual home of Sundissential. Playing Koko connected me to my younger self who was dancing there as a teenager to Eddie Richards. It was such an emotional experience for me.

2015, the Tidy guys put on a party at The Warehouse in Leeds. It was a venue of some vintage, but had recently been revamped. I did a three-deck set at Essential Tidy and it was a blinding night. Being 'The Closer', I went on after everyone had smashed the granny out of it, and so it was up to me to deliver the killer blow, as they were wiping tears from their eyes. Up and down the rollercoaster.

\*\*\*

I turned 50 in 2016 and felt so blessed to still be doing what I loved. I never thought I would get that many years out of DJing. Rejuv nearly always fell on the same weekend as my birthday and I often had my birthday celebrations with those guys. I was extremely grateful to them for having me on. I got to play in the old skool arena as well as the hard house room. At this point it was fast becoming one of the best hard house parties in the north. People came from all over to see these technically fantastic acts. I also started playing for Dale Castell who had done lots of stuff in Leeds through Bar Fibre. Dale started a night called Our House at the Mint Warehouse in Leeds. There were some great seeds planted back then that just grew and grew. Dale's a real gentleman and a really smart operator with a truly creative spark.

\*\*\*

Anna and I got married in January of 2017 in Sri Lanka, so that was a really enormous thing. I can still remember the butterflies in my stomach. But we are so tight and it's a thing of great beauty. I'm eternally grateful to Anna for being there through thick and thin especially when I was lying on the operating table. She would bring me Thai meals when I was hallucinating on morphine. If I hadn't gone up to that party with the bag of 50p pieces back in Leeds all those years before, I never would have met her.

My dad is from Sri Lanka and so that wedding location had such significance for me. All of Anna's family and friends came over. Danny, my old school mate from way back, was my best man. Seeing my mum and dad looking so proud and also seeing all of our families happy together was a complete and utter joy. We had a beautiful time.

# The Old Skool Teacher

I played TDV – the Tony De Vit Memorial Party – for Tidy in 2018. They did a huge party in honour of the great man and I was asked to do the closing set. It had been one of the hottest days of the year. It was such a great evening. They even had a symphonic orchestra playing Tony De Vit tunes to begin the night.

I was stood out the back of the venue trying to keep cool when Lisa Lashes, who'd been a friend of mine for donkey's years, came over for a chat. She's one of the funniest people I've ever met; just lights up the room wherever she goes. She's hilarious. I hadn't seen her for ages. She said she was about to start a school of music, which sounded amazing. Earlier that year, I'd started doing some tutorial and teaching stuff for a friend of mine called Claire Melody at Melody's Academy in Leeds. I taught people how to use Ableton and so I'd definitely dipped my toe in the water and had a few clients who used to come to me so they could learn more about making music. I asked, "Do you have anybody who teaches Ableton?"

–  "No I don't, but I am looking for some tutors. Hit us up some time if you're up for it."

–  "I'm up for it."

And so I started working with the Lisa Lashes School Of Music. I was totally committed. I needed to explore some other avenues and imparting all that knowledge I'd gleaned over the years was mega important to me and those people who wanted some decent guidance.

I remember going in there for the first time. It was nerve wracking talking to 40 people across such a broad age range; students aged from 18 right the way through to 60. It felt great being able to convey my experiences and talk about going to jail for acid house and all that. I think the youngsters could relate to that. And so I taught people how to use Ableton and how to DJ and how to put sets together. It just went swimmingly and I ended up working with those guys every week for a long time.

Lisa also managed to forge a connection with a government grant scheme to do the same kind of course model in Manchester, which she asked me to run. One year later, it was a proper concern where I was marking exercise books and sifting through these huge manuals; it was all Ofsted regulated. And to be honest, I absolutely loved it. It felt great to make a meaningful connection to some young people who had come from the most awful backgrounds.

There was a whole bunch of people that taught at the school: Lisa Lashes, Anne Savage, BK and Murphy's Law, who were much younger DJs now doing well in the tech house scene. They were a huge inspiration to the people on that course and loads and loads of them have gone on to run their own nights and record labels. Some have become successful DJs and musicians. There were some real bright sparks there and it was great unearthing those talents.

I loved showing the students how to use the new technology and then sitting back and watching them embrace it. It was a thing of true beauty to be able to pass on my knowledge and experience.

***

It was around this time that I first met Paul Priestley, through my good friend Claire Melody, while I was teaching at her academy. Paul came to me to be taught how to use Ableton. He was just one of the funniest guys I'd ever met and just a lovely man with a fantastic nature. A real gentle guy. He was also a troubled soul and highly vulnerable.

The course ended up almost being a therapy for Paul and for myself, because he felt he could open up and talk to me, whilst we were learning Ableton. He started telling me all sorts of stuff about his past and some of the problems he'd had. If I said that life had dealt him a tough hand, it would be a total understatement. I wouldn't ever share a person's problems in a book, but he'd had a rough old ride. What a funny, beautiful soul this man was. I would honestly count him in probably the top ten people I've ever met. That guy was rock solid and definitely 100% part of the Diamond Posse. Just such a beautiful man.

It became quite apparent that Paul really wanted to do more than just be able to use Ableton. He wanted somebody to become an engineer for his music, because he had all these ideas in his mind. Paul had been diagnosed with autism along with PTSD, but he seemed to be able to relate to me, and he knew my history and everything. And so we started making music together at my own studio. So, we embarked upon working on this track together.

Paul wanted to remix *Rapture* by iiO, which came out on Ministry of Sound Records. Paul absolutely loved all forms of music, but he particularly loved trance; it amped him up. And so we got some great examples of the kinds of stuff he wanted to make. I hadn't really made that much trance over the past few years and this gave me an awful lot of impetus to get back into making more with all the skills I've learned over the last few years from Ian Bland, BK, Technikal and all those guys.

I started playing out this remix of *Rapture* and it went down very, very well and it prompted us to do more music together. And we ended up working every other week, for the next five years or so. And it was definitely a form of therapy for him and part of his journey. We would speak at least four or five times a week and he definitely had the same sense of humour as me. We just became firm, firm friends.

We set about making a track called *Aspirations*. He found this speech Denzel Washington had done at college and we sat there for hours listening through it. And then between the two of us, we said, 'That's it. That's the killer bit.' It was a 45-minute speech and we found this little three-second clip and we stuck it over some music and it was a marriage made in heaven. It ended up getting released on Tidy Trax by Ammo, Andy and Sam. They all loved it. I played it out absolutely tonnes all over the place and it picked up a huge response. And then out of the back of that, we did another track as well, which featured another very inspirational speech by Alan Watts. And that track was also picked up by Tidy as well. For Paul to release music on Tidy Tracks was like a dream come true. And to be able to give that gift to him was golden.

Paul was a troubled soul during Covid. It really wasn't easy for him, but he got through it. But he really suffered with his mental health. And

I'd like to think I did my utmost to support him on that front. And then we did another track called *Home*, which featured another famous poem, that I'm going to release as part of an EP we're putting out in his honour. Because unfortunately he had a little bit of drinking problem, and February of last year, I got a call to say he'd passed away. He'd come home one night and unfortunately, just had too much to drink and passed away in his sleep. Paul had left this planet and it was heartbreaking.

Paul didn't get on very well with his family, which was sad, but I got up and did a eulogy at his funeral. I celebrated his life because unfortunately, with the exception of his lovely partner, Leanne, there were some major issues with his family. It makes me very, very sad to think that that guy is no longer around. I absolutely loved him, and it makes it me sad every single day. I've got two computers and I only have to type the letter P in anywhere and boom, I get a thousand Paul Priestleys appearing as file names. And, yeah, I will never forget him. And I always think about him. And that's why I'm going to honour him by using one of the tracks we never released and donate some of the funds to his lovely wife, Leanne.

***

2018, I got booked to play Clockwork Orange in the UK. That was a real game changer for me. I sailed down to 338 in Greenwich, London with a couple of my really good mates: Steve Gaster and Colin Elson, who'd been out clubbing with us right back to the Sundissential days.

I used to go to Clockwork in Ibiza when it was at Es Paradis in San Antonio. I used to marvel at how massive the queue was. To this day I've never seen anything like it in San An. The queue used to come right down to the main road and then it would go off in the direction of San Joan all around the corner paths to the massive slingshot and all the way up to the Bull Bar. It was a 400-yard queue; people were fighting to get into the place. Clockwork Orange would be full to the brim every single week for years. And then for whatever reason they stopped doing it.

I knew Andy Manston purely from meeting him there. I would find my spot in the club right at the top and look down at that beautiful ornate all-white, sparkling club. It would be teeming with people and I used to think 'My god, I'd love to play for these guys.' And then out of nowhere, I got a call from Danny Gould and I was extremely flattered. I think Colin Elson and a few others had mentioned my name to them.

Colin Elson was a guy I just clicked with as soon as I met him. He's been all over the place with me over the past six years or so; he is as genuine as they come and not afraid to speak his mind. I've said before, I don't like yes men. And he's definitely not one of those. He's so knowledgeable music wise and one of the best vinyl DJs I know; our car journeys are nothing but a pleasure.

And so back to Clockwork Orange who had sold so many tickets they filled three arenas. It was March time and they put a marquee outside 338 because it was that busy. It was mobbed and I was booked to play the old skool arena.

I had this real nervous energy before playing there. I worked hard on the practice ground to get some ideas together. I'd randomly loaded a set of funk and soul tracks onto one of my USBs for some reason and so I played a set with those tunes I'd put together over the summer of 2017, but never had a chance to play. This place was absolutely buzzing with a huge queue outside. I walked through the main area and down a corridor and through some open doors and out into a courtyard. And it was snowing!

Paul Trouble Anderson was playing; just the nicest, nicest guy. Paul was playing proper '88/'89 tunes from Fast Eddie into Jungle Brothers. This older crowd was pretty much up for anything. I went on and started playing my acid house stuff. I then dropped the Dancing Divaz remix of Alison Limerick's *Where Love Lives* and then it dawned on me: why not drop down out of nowhere into the funk and soul tracks I'd loaded onto one of my USB sticks? It just felt right for some reason. So I mixed in Rob Base & DJ E-Z Rock's *It Takes Two* and the whole place just exploded. I also played Chaka Khan *I Feel For You* into D-Train *You're The One For Me*. It was such a beautiful moment in my life and it was my birthday weekend too. Then Steve Gaster and I drove back in the teaming snow. It was an out and out blizzard to be honest. We couldn't even see the white lines in the road. We got all the way to Rejuv and then carried on from there. What a magical night.

I played for Clockwork Orange at Koko in London too. And that was also phenomenal. In fact, that same year, I also played the Frantic birthday in Koko playing full-on hard house; the two styles couldn't be more poles apart. Again, I am eternally grateful that I chose the path of being very adaptable. And if I could give any advice to an aspiring DJ, it's don't box yourself off to one thing because as one thing recedes another one takes off. The beauty about Clockwork Orange is it's not just about the old stuff; they like the new stuff as well. They love a bit of tech house and anything with a slightly modern edge to it, and then you can fuse the two things together.

I was playing at the Zoo in Ibiza for Clockwork Orange one time and we went for some breakfast. Coming back from the fry-up, we went to this beach shop and for some reason I bought this 4ft inflatable seal. The rotters wouldn't give me one that was already blown up and so I spent a good half hour blowing this thing up.

When I finished my set in the seal pit later, I brought out Sammy the Seal to the crowd. Everyone was dressed in orange and the intensity of the atmosphere was astounding. Everybody was having one of the best days of their lives and when I put Sammy the Seal into the pool it got the biggest cheer. It was a proper moment, with *Follow Me* by Aly Us blasting out.

Housework in London was another great house event; such beautiful people. I ended up forging a very long relationship with those guys as well. I also started doing some closing sets at Cream events that were springing up in Leeds at The Church, which still had all the stained-glass windows. The DJ booth was up in the pulpit, so it was a case of playing above the dancefloor. What an impressive place to play, especially when it was backlit. Just a phenomenal sight. I went on after Seb Fontaine, Jeremy Healy and Dave Pearce to do the closing set. Tidy also did an event there and I did the closing set for that too.

This led me to the Cream Weekenders at Butlins, which were absolutely awesome; everybody was right up for that. Such knowledgeable crowds. I started playing at family raves too like Big Fish, Little Fish and Raver Tots. I would never have had myself down for that kind of stuff, but it was such great fun. You got to see tonnes of people who'd gone 'missing in action'.

October 2019, I did a Reunion party in Blackburn at King George's Hall, which was sponsored by Adidas. The night was run by Tommy Smith who was heavily involved in the parties back in the Boomtown Blackburn days. The old crew had been asked by the Council to be involved in this party through a grant. The Hall was really ornate with a big wooden ballroom dance floor. It had the same kind of feel as the

Opera House down in Bournemouth and the Sanctuary in Birmingham. On stage you're looking down to at least 1,200-1,500 people that you used to rave with, back in the day. Quite ironic that the Council was putting this event on when it was them and the police who tried their best to smash the parties back in the day. That night was special though, and me, Graeme Park and Jay Weardon who used to do the Thunderdome back in Manchester, played that. There was also Gilly and a few of the other DJs who used to play back in the warehouse days. Sadly, since the good old days, the old faces had split up into different factions and it was such a shame that not everybody could be there.

2019 was Raindance's 30th birthday at Heaven in London, which was a hell of an occasion with all the usual suspects: Billy 'Daniel' Bunter, Slipmatt and Ellis Dee and many more. Heaven was another one of those landmark venues I used to go to as a raver. I've still got a Rage membership card from 1988. That venue really was something special and that was a great party. So nice to be taken on board by those guys.

*** 

2019, I had the biggest debacle ever trying to get out to Auckland, when they changed the Visa forms. In short, I had to disclose my criminal past. I detailed all the events and charges in as much detail as I could and when I read them back I realised that one of the charges was only two down from Incitement To Riot. It didn't look great. I still had about six weeks before the gig, so I thought I would be fine.

They came back to me and said I couldn't have a visa, which meant I then had to submit a plea. I got some backup from Janelle and Steve Hill over there and the guys from London Hard House Reunion. They kindly wrote a letter, giving me an endorsement to allow me in. Then I had to wait to see whether they would approve it.

I didn't hear back for ages. Because they were 12 hours ahead of us I was having to call them in the early hours to try to get some response. I called the Embassy every single day and was on hold constantly and then they'd put me through to a different department. Then I'd get cut off and you'd go back to the end of the queue. It was an awfully stressful few weeks.

It got right to the final week and I pretty much had to stay up all night to keep phoning them. Eventually I got to speak to somebody who said they would talk to their supervisor. And then eventually, I got to plead my case to somebody in person, on the phone rather than over email.

They were supposed to come back to me with a solid answer, but of course, there was nothing. I didn't really want to have to do this, but I wasn't going to let anybody down at this gig, and so I winged it. I waited until the final possible moment prior to the flight and then set off on the train to Manchester Airport. I got as far as Huddersfield and for some bizarre reason the train stopped in a tunnel where there was no signal whatsoever. I was seven or eight minutes out of the station, but there was zero signal. Anyway, we got off that train and boarded another. I was just getting onto the second train when my phone rang. It was a private number I thought I recognised. I spoke to this woman from the Embassy and she said, "We're giving you your approval." I let out such a massive sigh of relief. I was about to fully get myself into a situation where I was likely to get deported at the other end if it hadn't all panned out. But I had to make that call.

I didn't feel too well while I was out there and had a really sore throat. It was the longest weekend ever in terms of how many hours I was awake. It was a really painful experience. But on the way back, I got what I believed was the beginnings of Covid. This was October 2019 and when I landed in Bahrain airport, I had an eight-hour wait. I was coughing so much in the waiting room that people were walking out. I actually coughed myself to sleep on one of those little seats.

I tried to check into a hotel, but they wanted $300 for five hours sleep or something crazy. So, I found one of those little seats at the airport and curled up in my plane blankets from the previous flight. When I woke up there was absolutely nobody sat around me. It was like I had bird flu or something. I was ill for about five weeks after I returned to the UK. I was so ill.

Lo and behold, only a few months later, Covid-19 entered our lives. A lot of people said they'd also had something that was really bad only a few months previously and I don't know what I had other than it was real bad. *Real bad*, like a potential-forerunner-to-Covid bad.

\*\*\*

The first three months of 2020, everything was cooking on gas; a blooming whirlwind. Clockwork Orange did this event with myself, Todd Terry, Jeremy Healy, John Kelly, Andy Manson and Danny Gould from Clockwork all in one room at Magazine near to the London O2. It couldn't have gone any better with 5,000 punters. It was a great event. We got back to Leeds just in time for my sets at the mighty Rejuv and we then went 'out out' until Sunday afternoon. It's a birthday I'll treasure for forever and a day. I've done countless phenomenal gigs for Clockwork Orange and I am truly grateful for all that they've done for me over the past five years. Both Andy and Danny are masters of their craft and together they are an unstoppable force. The Clockwork crowd is breathtaking to play for every single time. And so it was just a brilliant weekend.

And then on the following Monday we got the announcement to say the country had gone into lockdown. We'd heard bits in the news about the Covid thing coming along, but I never expected them to shut the entire country down. It just seemed like an alien concept to me and to everybody else. And what a low moment that was for everybody with all the horrors it caused.

My friend Nikki is a sister in the ICU at Leeds' St. James's Hospital and she was right in the middle of it all from the very beginning. She was with the families who couldn't say goodbye to their loved ones and it was heartbreaking seeing them FaceTiming their final goodbyes on an iPad.

Obviously clubbing took a massive hit and many DJs simply put their feet up for a few months, but I couldn't even consider that. I didn't qualify for furlough, but I still had other elements to my business that I could make some money out of, including making music for people. Blandy kindly helped to set everything up so that I could Zoom people and we ended up having this really creative period.

I worked with Steve Hill and a couple of other DJs making music for some clients down in Australia. Alf Bamford, aka Technikal was now living down in Australia and so I was working with those guys at 6am and making music until 11.30am. I also started making music for Rob Moore who I met through the Housework guys. I did loads of stuff for him over lockdown. Not knowing how long lockdown might last, I decided to really double down on my efforts and so began a very fruitful period for me. I was putting in 12 to 15 hours a day making music for people.

I was sat working on my computer one day when I felt a strange tingle in my right eye. I was struggling to blink. I sneezed and then my right eye just seemed to not close like it used to. It was very odd. I'd never experienced anything like it before. I just completely ignored it. 'It will go back to normal in a while.'

I carried on working for another few hours, but my face still felt a bit funny. I went to bed that evening and woke up feeling like shit. My eyes hadn't shut all night. I was due to do some work online with Lisa Lashes' School of Music with my mate BK and 18 students. We had a Zoom call before the online tutorial and Ben immediately clocked it. "Mate, you need to go straight to A&E. What is going on with your face? It's all fallen down one side. I think you might have had a stroke. Get yourself to an A&E immediately!" My face looked like a Halloween mask or that ghoul out of *Scooby Doo*. I went downstairs and told Anna that we needed to get to the hospital.

It turned out it was Bell's Palsy and not a stroke, thank the lord. But they shared so many similar symptoms it was hard to tell. So, listen to your body! I then had six weeks of pretty much laying on the couch all day, every day, thinking, 'Oh my God, is my face ever going to go back to normal?' Thankfully, it did, and I ended up actually helping other sufferers to identify and cope with the condition.

***

Sam Townend helped run the Music Factory Entertainment Group with Andy Pickles of the Tidy Boys and they'd done all sorts of music for the fitness industry and Covid-19 saw an acceleration for their company Pure Energy Music. Pure Energy Music supplied royalty-free tracks that sounded like big dance tunes we've all heard before with that same kind of vibe. They asked me whether I'd be interested in doing an old skool album for them. And so I enlisted the help of my good friend Ian Bland and embarked upon this album of 90s rave tracks that sounded like Robin S and Sonz Of A Loop Da Loop Era. Sam and the boys loved that and so they asked me to do a trance album that covered the same terrain as the Quake material in the late 90s. We delivered that album a few months later and they loved that too.

And then the work just kept on coming throughout Covid. I'd gone from being so worried about what was going to happen work wise during lockdown to having too much stuff on. It had been years since I was able to make money out of music, but here it was and it took a global pandemic to trigger it. The royalty-free music I was creating was content that could be played by fitness instructors on YouTube, or Zoom, or any of those open formats where they normally take down copyrighted music. Sites like Loop Cloud and Splice meant that there were lots of newer sample sources that were never available before.

I would sit with my chin on the table for about four hours, losing the will to live, until I found that one sample that changed everything. You could also listen to the samples 'in key' with the track you were making. We made the tracks around these massive royalty-free vocals. It was quite a laborious task, but there was definitely gold in them thar hills. Then I did another 90s album, this time a funky house affair that encompassed all the Kissdafunk stuff. I loved working for Pure Energy Go and still work for them now.

I made full-on breakbeat albums and some downbeat chill-out stuff too. It was such a brilliant and creative outlet, just great to wake up every morning and make some music; rejoicing in the fact that I was still doing it after all these years.

Covid-19 also meant I spent a lot more time with Anna who was working from home like many other people. Suddenly, I was home on Friday and Saturday nights. It was an awful time for so many people, but with little moments of positivity. We ate so much cheese! Cheese dipped into molten cheese. Cheese on cheesy toast. Cheese! Cheese! Cheese!

## Amadeus Mozart, Tidy Boys

*"Obviously, all events stopped during Covid and producers didn't want to produce, because there was nothing to produce for, and people like Rob Tissera and all our producers and DJs thought 'Shit, what we going to do? If this goes on for too long, we're buggered.'*

*Music Factory had this company called Pure Energy Music, which did aerobics music for instructors. We got a blanket licence so we could, for example, mix Rihanna with anything. A bit like the Disco Mix Club and so we did that for aerobics instructors. And we got to the point where we had 10,000 aerobics instructors subscribing to it.*

*Then in 2020 the instructors couldn't work, so they all went online, on Facebook, Twitch and Twitcher. However, they were getting muted, because you're not allowed to do aerobics to Rihanna or to Earth, Wind*

*& Fire, or ELO or anybody's music, because Facebook mutes the music – you can't do an exercise program using other people's work.*

*So Andy Pickles said, 'OK, what we'll do is get all the producers that are doing nothing right now and looking for work, and get them in the studio to make lots of music. And we'll do it licence-free.' So, no copyright which means, it won't be muted online.*

*So we got all the hard house producers, all our friends and colleagues and said, 'Right, make as many tracks as you can. We're going to pay you per track. Just make music as quickly, but as good, as you can. We don't want shit' – because licence-free music's got a reputation for being shit. Now, we know that all our producers have got OCD. They can't make shit. They have to make good stuff. And one of the first people we rang was Rob Tissera and he said yeah.*

*So, Rob started making music and the aerobics instructors were loving it because it was so credible. They could now do it online, and so we set up Pure Energy Go as a new company. And then it became an app and now it's a very successful business, only doing licence-free music. We've produced over 2,200 tracks in the past three years. And the good thing is that Rob can do any style you want. 'Can you do us an Ibizan chill-out track at 116 bpm?' No problem for Rob because he can do so many different styles."*

***

Dale Castell started the online Home Rave nights in 2017-2018 featuring myself, Marc Leaf and John Marshall with external guests like K-Klass, Seb Fontaine and Julia Knight. It was a small concern, but very good pre-pandemic. Once lockdown started Home Rave became an internet sensation. *BBC Look North* did a feature on Dale and this phenomenon. Dale first set it up in his son's bedroom. Initially, it was the people who actually went to Our House who joined the live streams, and then out of nowhere, tonnes and tonnes of other people started joining in. Dale's a charismatic and funny guy and you couldn't wish success on a more fitting person. He says what's in his heart.

Lockdown saw loads of older parents and veteran ravers who hadn't been going out for years, suddenly getting their virtual fix on a Friday night. And the show became a literal sensation with thousands of subscribers. Home Rave is an app that for £5 a month gives you access to Judge Jules, me and Danny Bond, a huge baseline DJ from Leeds who's also got an enormous following. Plus, Simmo from Leeds and Paul Taylor from Retro who had his own show on there. It's all live, plus you can have the recordings too.

My show was directly after Dale's and so I got a lot of people staying on to listen to me. Home Rave just exploded and it kept me really current during difficult times. I was also doing some streams for Tidy and Audio Addiction who put on London Hardhouse Reunion down in New Zealand. There was so much good stuff going on. All of those things paid off because all the people I'd done the live streams for ended up supporting me post-Covid too. Tidy, Clockwork Orange and Our House in particular, just went insane.

# CH. 52

# A Strange New World

Our House's first gig after the lockdown was at the Mint Warehouse, Leeds with one of the biggest Function One systems I've ever seen. It was twice my height. The ceiling of the club was lights all the way along with different LED displays synced in time with the music. It really was state of the art. There were at least 1,500 people in the Warehouse when we were only getting 300 before lockdown. We had all these brand-new people who'd never met each other, but had been interacting online during lockdown.

I played for Clockwork's Garden Party right after lockdown down in Chelmsford at the racecourse for 2,000 people or so. I got down there, played and was on my way back, feeling very tired. You completely forget how tiring these gigs and all the travel can be. I'd been used to going to bed at 9pm during lockdown in order to work with the Aussies early in the morning. I definitely lost a layer of toughness during Covid.

And anyway, driving back from there, 240 miles or so, I pulled off the motorway. I must admit, the last hour of the journey had me flagging. I was really feeling the pace just thinking I needed to get out of the car. I got all the way home, came off the motorway and just as I was one mile from the house I looked at the petrol gauge and realised it had been flashing for quite a while. It did a cursory orange flash with 100 miles to go and I had completely ignored it. Now it was flashing incessantly. I was running out of fuel. Would I make the last mile home? I was right next to a roundabout and I could see the petrol station was not too far from the house. I knew I was gonna have to go down and put some fuel in it in case I ran out on the last mile.

I turned the corner to drive down to the station and the windscreen lit up like a Christmas tree. They put a bloody new speed camera in just round the corner from the roundabout. The camera was partly hidden by a tree. Another ban was on its way.

This was the first gig I'd done following lockdown. I had to go to court and plead my case and to be fair the two magistrates were really kind. It was one of the first times in my life where I thought 'Wow, these two lady judges are as nice as pie!'

I decided to represent myself as no one was going to do it better. I laid it on real thick that I'd worked all the way through Covid and mentioned the Bell's Palsy and all that. And they gave me a one-month ban (and a pretty hefty fine) which was unbelievable. It certainly felt like I'd dodged a bullet. It was my fourth ban, all for speeding and totting up, as I never ever drink and drive.

I was only out of action for a really short period of time too because I was on holiday for two of those banned weeks.

*** 

It was November 17th and it was snowing when I set off to Heaven. Out of nowhere a blizzard just blew up. It was pretty odd for it to snow around that time. It had just started to dump it down when I hit Sheffield. There were cars skidding off the road and a huge queue of traffic. I was thinking 'Jesus Christ, I will never forgive myself if I don't make it to Heaven.' I raced on into the centre of Sheffield and whilst sat in the queue I looked over to the tracks and saw a train that would be going to London pulling in. I was right next to a junction and so I went down a tiny bit of a hard shoulder and then off the motorway. I got down into Sheffield, parked the car about 500 yards from the station and ran. I cursed every single step, thinking 'Why did I eat so much cheese over lockdown?' I had become so unfit.

I got to the station just as the train pulled away. Shit! I huffed and puffed back to the car using every expletive known to man and drove to the far side of Sheffield making sure I didn't go back into that traffic and set off down to London. I was thinking 'This is going to be close.'

I had to do some of the most creative driving I've ever tried to fight my way through the traffic. I parked the car up at the first available opportunity – St John's Wood, I think – and got on the Tube. I ran out at the other end at Charing Cross and got to the venue with one track to spare, sweating like a sumo wrestler. It was a fantastic gig though. But my drives to and from gigs were still no less stressful. I'm not sure I'll ever avoid that to be honest.

***

My wife Anna had never had a dog before. And over the years, we would pretend that we had an imaginary pooch. But we never seemed to want to commit and quite rightly so; it's a big commitment. And so Anna dreamt up this imaginary dog called Doggis.

There's a beautiful place near where we live called St. Aidans, which is a bird reserve just out the back of the house. It's about 400 yards walk from where we live - boy was I glad to finally leave the flood–damaged cottage. You go down through some bushes and then you come out in front of what used to be coal mines; the land has been reclaimed. They've turned the coal mines into reservoirs and birds travel from all around the world to stay there. You get Canadian geese and crested grebes and all these beautiful birds. We would go there a lot during lockdown, walking around these stunning lakes and we couldn't help thinking, 'Wouldn't it be great to have a dog?' I was getting broody for a pooch, having not had one since Harry Tee died. I came back from a gig one day and said to Anna, "We need a dog, simple as that."

I went on this site called Pets For Homes and trawled through about four pages and then boom, out of nowhere, there he was: this utterly gorgeous little black cavapoo. He was the spitting image of the puppet Sweep from *Sooty And Sweep* that Anna has an infatuation with and so it was just meant to be. I said to Anna: "Look who it is!" She studied the picture and then looked at me and shouted, "It's SWEEP!"

We drove down to deepest, darkest Lampeter in Wales, which took us about four and a half hours and met the breeders. We had a really nice chat with them and got introduced to the puppy for the first time and it was love at first sight. He was about the size of the puppet Sweep too, just a handful with little floppy ears.

Feeling his little heartbeat in my hand on that first meeting was the most precious thing; one of the most uplifting and happy things that has ever happened to me. Truly magical. Sweep has since become known as 'The Stealer of Hearts'.

\*\*\*

Ibiza 2023 and I was with my best mate Adam and another good friend Eddie Walsh. I was playing Slip Back in Time and we went to this bar called Itaka to see Luton play Sunderland in the Play-off semi-final second leg. And we tore them apart. Luton were on their way to Wembley. I mean, Luton had had a rough old time following our 30-point deduction in 2008 and now we were on the verge of the Premier League having been non-league not that long ago.

I couldn't go to Wembley, but I watched it at home with Anna and Sweep. It was such a high-pressure game – one of the world's richest – but Luton were as cool as cucumbers and slotted every single penalty home to overcome Coventry. We had come so far since my Dad first took me to Kenilworth Road in 1974. But no matter where I am in the world, my heart will always be at that much maligned ground. And so at the time of writing, we are in the Premier League, although by the time you read this we might already be relegated. Ha ha.

2023, and both Luton Town and Rob Tissera are doing OK. I am still so humbled to be asked to travel all over the country and beyond to play the music that has soundtracked our lives. I have another sell-out tour in NZ and Australia, a week in Ibiza as we take the Our House brand on tour and more great parties with my good friends at Tidy and Clockwork Orange to come. I am truly blessed. In fact, I'm currently sat in a hotel room in Ibiza and tonight I'm playing an almighty party at Amnesia; one of the most famous clubs on the planet. I'm truly humbled that these opportunities keep coming my way.

It's mad to think back to those early raves as a punter and the first few weddings I played out at. And there was that moment when I came out of prison and was seriously considering giving all this up. But I'm so glad I didn't. The journey this music has taken me on has been beyond my wildest dreams. And to still be making music at my age is such a pleasure and a joy. I feel that I've had a charmed life thus far and should you bump into me at a party, I'm sure I will have a smile on my face. Hopefully, I've put a smile on your face too. So, don't give up on your dreams. Work hard, love what you do and surround yourself with great people.

## Ian Bland, Dream Frequency and Dancing Divaz

*"I wouldn't say Rob is the best DJ in the world, but he's in my Top One. I mean, the level of dedication he puts into his sets and craft is incredible. And that's down to his passion and love of the music. It's been an honour and a privilege to work with Rob for a long time now.*

*Even now, after 30-odd years of producing, I still send Rob a track and say, 'What do you think of this?' We know each other so well, it won't wound an ego to say, 'Do you think you should do it like that?' It's a trusting relationship.*

*I played on a bill with Rob in a forest recently and it was a small event. There was me and a couple of other DJs and Rob was on last. I thought I did pretty well. It was in a forest, in a tent. It was proper old skool. It was the original people who did the Blackburn parties, Tommy Smith, and the Revenge parties. We both did this gig for free. Some you do for dough, some you do for show. We wanted to give something back. We loved what these guys did with the Blackburn parties and all the free parties they put on. You just want to play good gigs sometimes.*

*Honest to God, there were only about 5-600 people, but it was electric, I'm telling you. I thought I'd done well, and then I came off, and Rob was behind me, and he went, 'Mate, that was ace. I'm going to give you a solid four.' Rob then went on at the end and he absolutely smashed it. I'm not just saying that. I think that was maybe one of the best sets I've ever seen him play. He was absolutely on fire. You know when you just think 'He's the man!'*

*Rob just has the ability to read the crowd, and that's through careful preparation and experience. He just knows when to drop the right track. Even now, after 30 years, and I am still waxing lyrical about him. I was watching him a couple of weeks ago, and he was playing an old skool gig, but he was playing some classics. And then all of a sudden he just dropped this remix of French Kiss that I hadn't heard before. It was a modern remix, but it really worked. It's just that ability to alter the direction and change it up. He just had them eating out of his hands. I think that's his greatest strength, his preparation, his experience, and his ability to read the crowd. He just brings the party. I've never seen him play a set where you think, 'I'm not into what he's playing here.' He always delivers. That's something rare. He's just got that spark.*

*Rob lights up a room and has this infectious sense of humour. He's always got a smile on his face. He's very charismatic. He's an absolute gentleman, as well. I'm paraphrasing another good friend of ours Marc Leaf. We were on about Rob a few years ago, and he just went, 'Rob Tissera? Machine!' That's it, he is an absolute machine."*

**Tommy Smith, Blackburn rave promoter**

*"We were putting on a Blackburn reunion night and Rob phoned up and asked, 'Can I play?'*

*– 'Of course.'*

*I advertised it and all the tickets sold. We've got a couple of Facebook pages and Instagram and it went ballistic. There were 1,000 hits within three minutes when the word spread that Rob was playing. 'Don't be telling me Rob's playing. Don't be making up these stories.'*

*– 'He's coming, I'm telling you.'*

*Rob is a talent from the gods, but his feet are still firmly on the floor. He knows where he came from; he knows what he represents. So many DJs we've had before are like, 'Oh, speak to my manager,' and all that. Rob's on the phone any time and he'll talk to you all day long.*

*Talent from the gods, feet standing firmly on the floor, that's Rob Tissera right there. The Smiler!"*

**Mark Archer, Altern-8**

*"Rob is from the Stu Allan school of gentlemanly behaviour. He always makes the time at least to say hi/bye whenever our paths cross. One of the good guys!"*

**Graeme Park, DJ and musician, Haçienda, Cream…**

*"I can't think when I first met Rob, but I've known him for many, many years. I remember doing a lot of the Sheffield Love To Be nights and Rob would often be there. I often see him at Clockwork Orange events too. One particular thing I remember – and this would've been late 90s, I think – was when Pete Tong wanted me to do a Haçienda mix; probably after the club closed. He wanted a mix of big Haçienda tunes for a CD as part of this compilation he was doing. And I'm like, 'Yeah, OK, Pete, but I'm moving house and I'm not sure I can put my hands on all those old records right now.' And I remember Rob, and I don't know why it was Rob, helping me out and lending me those records just so I could do this mix for Pete Tong. And that was such a kind and helpful thing to do.*

*When I first met Mike (Pickering) I didn't know he was 10 years older than me. When I found that out, I was truly shocked. But then I realised, 'Ah, hang on a minute. That explains why he's so fucking grumpy all the time; he's 10 years older than me.' And then, literally, every decade, I'll say something and think, 'Oh, fucking hell, I'm 10 years more grumpy than I was,' because it's a fact, if you're a man, that you do get grumpier as you get older. Maybe not grumpy, maybe less tolerant. When you get older, you go, 'What? No! I'm not fucking doing that!' Unless you're Rob.*

*Rob has this really infectious personality. He's never not pleased to see you. You never know if he's tired or fresh or anything in between. He's always really pleased to see you and there's a real skill to that because sometimes he'll be on a punishing schedule. I can get quite tired and grumpy when I'm on the road, but with Rob, you never know how tired he is because he's always got this massive smile on his face."*

# Acknowledgements

I would like to thank the following for doing what you do so well....

My awesome wife Anna and our furry son Sweep.

My mum and dad – I'd be absolutely nothing without you Auntie Queenie and Uncle Sid (RIP), Auntie Pam and Uncle Ron (RIP), my sister Diane Pinto, my nephew Matthew Pinto, my cousins Iyoni and Ivan, Auntie Latha, Uncle Robert (RIP), Uncle Neville (RIP) and Auntie Cathy, Uncle Frank and Auntie Marge (RIP), Ken, Karin and Magnus Gledhill, Leon Gledhill (RIP) ,my best mate Dan James and his wonderful mum Veronica, Mr Clarkson my long suffering but brilliant English teacher and Mick O'Leary the best football coach ever!

And thanks to... Steve Hill and Sasha Barber, Janelle and Luke Matchett (LHHR New) Zealand, Eamon Fevah, Damo Pennells, Dean and Niki Hyden, Malcolm Ladkin, Wayne Smart, Skol Kelly and Rosie Redmond, Deborah Hewitt, Lisa Lashes School Of Music, Rob and Saskia Oakley, Barry Amphlett (Fresh Artist Management), Ian Bland (Dream Frequency and Quake), Charlotte Bland, Tommy Smith From Boomtown for your awesome support in the Warehouse days of glory, Ben Stevens, Amadeus Mozart, Andy Pickles, Angie Mozart, Lee Haslam, Sam Townend, Leigh Green and Angus at Tidy HQ, Debbie Sharp, Scott Vinylgroover, Jay Folly aka The Fat Controller, Dave Gray, Tim Simmons for 40 years of friendship and advice, Amanda Michalak and Andrew Michalak without you, there'd be no Blackburn days of glory, Neil 'Shack' Shackleton for your love and support when I moved to the north, Anthony and Chris Donnelly (Gio Goi), Adam Falkingham, Pat Falkingham (RIP), Pete Falkingham (RIP), Justin Hainsworth, Nikki Hainsworth, John 'Skinny' Hainsworth (RIP) , Lis Johnson, Dawn Jessop, Catherine, Helen Lewis and all of the Diamond Posse, Drew

Hemment, John Jepson, Kevin Walsh, Rex Sargeant (RIP), Jordeb Hodgson, the boys at Dat To Dat, Adrian and Mark Luvdup, Mark Wilba Williams for being there through thick and thin through ought my career, Julius 'Jools' Newell, Chris Duff, Big Chris from Kissdafunk, Katy B and Stella Smith, Shaun Wilson, Judge Jules and Amanda O'Riordan, Graeme Park, Mike Pickering, Carl Cox, Slipmatt and Rachel Hill, Emma Frisco, Ian Emberton you crazy fool from way back, Helen Cox (Judgement Sundays), Lisa Lashes, Deborah Hewitt, Jon Paul Montgomery, Adam Jukes, Andy Farley, Craig Booth, Dave Booth (RIP), Hue and Rikki Garry, Barry Mac, Tim Sheridan Kiss FM, David Dunne Kiss FM & Galaxy, Andy Durant, Nick Riley , Si and Suzanne Frater (Rejuvenation, Leeds), the awesome Sunshine Crew in Leeds, Brad Kells (Joy, Leeds), Tony Hanon (Kaos and Up Yer Ronson, Leeds), Jacqui Ward (Minstrels, Blackburn), George Smith, Glen Grant, Bry The Snail, Dave P, Preston Bob (RIP), Flash and Pete (Rhythm Foundation), the boys from Eastern Bloc, Kenny Grogan, Paul Walker, Mark XTC and the team from Spin Inn, Manchester, Richard Moonboots, my great friend Paul 'Huggy' Huggett, the mighty Stu Allan (RIP), Alison Allan, Paul Draycott (OSN radio), all of the incredible OSN radio crew for tuning in since 2016, all of the Slinky Kids, you know who you are, Richard Raindance, MC Natz, Top Buzz and Mad P, Sally Newton, Emma Fletcher, Vic from Flipped Out, Gleave and Mark Dobbin, Mark 'Jacko' Jackson, Ian Jackson (RIP), Paul P (The Point Inn), Colin Bass, Charlie Dillon, Billy Dunseath, Rob Tyrell (Ark), Tom Edge (ARK), Glyn Tolley, Carly Hammond and all the Carly's Angels – you were amazing!, Annabel Marner, Gavin Herlihy, Nick Stevenson, Tracy, Cathy, Miranda, Becky, Paul, Duncan and all the staff at *Mixmag* for so many years of support, *DJ Magazine*, Kevin McFarlane and Euwen at *M8 Magazine*, Maggie and Jess O'Sullivan for being my saviour on so many occasions, Paul Taylor, Irish Dave, Ben Stevens, BK, Janelle & Luke Kleinhans Matchett, Jason JFK Kinch, Jimmy Dean, Arthur and the boys at the Emporium in Coalville, Fraser Barraclough (RIP), Tony De Vit (RIP), Paul Priestley (RIP), Fergie, Neil (Godskitchen), Jason Herd, Billy Lewis, Catherine, Katy Mustill, Jayne Heales, Jo Knowles, Aaron and Maxine Saunders, Dawn Jessop, Big Wayne, Gary and Kelly Simpson, Matt May, Mark Anderson, Matty and Lois Robbo, John Kelly, Barry Almond, Uncle Steve Almond, Lisa Lashes, Mike Knowler, Andy Owen at Cream, Gavin Brennan Smith, Beth at Vision Talent, Jo Usher, Glen Walker, John and Amity Watts, Andy Carol, Dermot Condon, Pete Gooding, Jason Bye, Danny Gould, Andy Manston, Billy Bishop, Simon Colderley (Bowlers), Stu Peet, Darrell Wilde, Danny Walsh at More Cake,

Mark and Nikki Archer Altern-8, 2 Bad Mice, Mark Hadfield, Stephen Wood, Nikkie Riozzi (Pure Energy Go), Anna Murphy, Pepe (Kanya), Salvador (Eden), Dexter Jones, Marc and Jen Leaf, Denver and Pete Ellis, Ben Spier, Simon Halliwell, Eddie Halliwell, Jo Halliwell, Danny Kirk and Madders (Sundissential), Neil Moffat (Godskitchen), Sam Mitcham, Eddie Walshe, Shaz Taylor, Matt , Jo and the team (Itaca, Ibiza), Richie and the team at the Garden Of Eden, Nik Turner, Kev (Judgement Sundays), Rob Farrell, Dan Prince at DMC, Marc De Groot, George Dillon, Seb Fontaine, Tall Paul Newman, Jon Pleased Wimmin, Ru Curthoys (RIP), Steve Wise, Lee Jeffreys, Jenna West, Craig Jones, Simon Frantic Gordon, Graham Gold, Tariq & Ziad at Pure Groove, Steve Luigi, Rich Simpson, Natalie and Ryan Walker, Guyver, Skinny and Lee at Boomtown, Gary and Kelly Simpson, Damo Gelle, Dawn Dale, Jason Fubar, Paul Bailey Hague, Pete Croney, Julia Pinkney, Julia Warrington, Jane Winterbottom, Paul Oakley and Sarah Madden, Steven Gaster and Corinna Wardman, Terry and Kerry Ann Gosling, Martin Nitram Thomlinson, Jan Thomlinson, Ben Trengrove, Mike Devlin and family, Paul and Jen Hutchinson, Paul Bagley, The Clockwork Orange Army, Juanito Chanclas, Kelly Whitehead, Paul Rimmer, Chalkie White, Natty 'Natz' Congo, Adam Simms, Adam and Jo Jo Martin, Terry Ashton, Jacqui Bennett, Zoe Gillie from Slip Back In Time, MC Strict and the Unity In The Sun Posse, Marcia Ray, Paul Shaggy Wilson, Shaun Lever, Gary Hibbert, Daz Hick, Mark Wilson, Jason and Rachael Hurt, Jon Da Silva, Rod & Esme (Trades Club), Phil Easy, Graham Higgins and family (Beaver Works) , Sash Van Wah, Danny and the Pam's House family, Clare Melody, The Utah Saints, Chris Duff, Russell Pate, The Zone Crew, Sam &and Sinéad White, Leanne Priestley, Barry MacDonald, Paul Knaggs, Chris Waddleton, James Sammon, Steve 'Eppy' Heptanstall, Shaggy (Ibiza Properties), Jon Davies, James Perkins, Dale Castell, James Parker, everyone at Boomtown, Tim Bins, Nick Halkes, Steve Kelly (Universal Recs,) Pete Tong, Doug Olson, Dave Beer and the Back To Basics Crew, Carl Finlow, Billy 'Daniel' Bunter, Sonya Steele and Andrew Woods (Music Mondays), Tony Oneto (Amnesia Ibiza), Lisa Barraclough (Do Not Sleep Ibiza), Alex P, Brandon Block, Kenny (Drop The Beat, Burnley), Madge Nawaz (Penny Black, Burnley), Jamie Burley, Dean and Kirsty Smahon, Daz Hick & Mark Wilson, Ricky Istead, Paul and Liz Brace, Lee Drake and Joe Wilson (S2S & BBDD, Manchester), Chris Waddleton, Caz and Waine Johnstone, Dean and Daniella Ashraf, Gordon Wizzkid May, Shades Of Rhythm, Sonny Donlan (Dirty Secretz, Leeds), Mark Simon, Lee Butler, Ebo Richo and Lynne McNulty (Twisted Tunnels, Liverpool), Scott Barton,

James Barton and Andy Owen (Cream, Liverpool), Pete Mac, Jon Ullysess and Camilla, Darren Harvey, Chris Morgan & The Team at Golden, Stoke, Pete Wye (Progress, Derby), Paul Morrell, Chelsea Singh, Mick Singh, The Luvdup Twins, Leyna and Rebecca Coates, Ben Davis (The Vibe, Peterlee), Billy Emms RIP, Anna Margretts, Mark Holliday, Gary Van Norman, Gary Woodhouse, Rob and Saskia Oakley, Paul Rimmer, Ben Stevens, Dave Jackson, Mike Hooper, Tache, BK, Tony & Ruthy Hunter (Shine, Birmingham), Vicky Devine, Brett Taylor, Martin Shaggy Makepeace (Ibiza Property Shop), Karn West, Mark Lewis, Ce Ce Sunshine and The Amazing Sunshine Crew, Leeds, Jeff and Serena Booz, Steve Thrower, Matt Bell, Mez La, Alan Nixon and The Boomtown Massive, Carl Smales, Gavin Barker, Jay Funk Danny Banthorpe (Pam's House), Phil Gifford, John Hollis and The Crunch Crew, Birmingham, Jason Shock Taylor, Leeds , Gavin Mhuineachain, Jason Willans, Sharif (Mint Club) RIP, Martin (The Gallery), Gemma Smith, Isle Of White, Alan and Emma Hartley, Geoff Peters (Talksport), Trevor McLachlan, Phil Reynolds and The ATT Crew, London Lyds, Good Vibes, Leeds, Steve Panda Cooper, Lee Monteverde and Johnny (Development Corporation, Manchester), Lee Crank, Billy Ogden and Emma Robinet (Cloud 9), Calvin Miles, Sammy Dean, Paul Reid, Jack Hart, Sacha Wall, Filthy Rich Wakely, Drew Scott, Luke Pompey & all of our Kissdafunk resident DJs, The Kissdafunk Crowd, Ben Harding, Clare Hoare (Slinky), Dave Lee (Slinky), Vicci Lee, Jon Langford, Stephen Porter, Steve Lid, Rich Miller (Anomaly), Davina Cox and Sally Wiley, Mikaela Anderson, Johnny Mac Ibiza Legend, Alan Luv Dup Stephens, Burger Williams, Mely Sanders, Rachel McGuiness, Dom Noble, George Smith and Glen Grant (Boomtown) and Daz Quayle -thank you for years of help and advice with my Mac. I'd be lost without you! And Vicky Gledhill and family and Tristran Ingram (Judgement Sundays)and Leon Gledhill (RIP)

And thanks to the crowds at all of these events: Audacity, Ark Leeds, Hi Flyers, Leeds, Rejuvenation, Leeds, Zone, Blackpool, Boomtown in Blackburn, Minstrels Blackburn, Carlos 2, Angels, Burnley, Bowlers, Manchester, Sundissential, Godskitchen, the Tidy crew, Hippos in Middleton, Empire, Middlesbrough, Clockwork Orange Army, Housework, Goodgreef, Richie and the boys at the Garden Of Evil, London Hard House Reunion, Frantic, Storm, Passion, Hotdog, Lashed, The Coach in Banbridge, The Point Inn, The Network Club, Tall Trees Yarm and all the venues who have looked after me through the years.

Apologies to anyone who I may have unintentionally missed off this list. Thank you all for helping me along the twisty turny journey.

# The Love Dove Generation

BILLY *'DANIEL'* BUNTER
with ANDREW WOODS

'One of the most entertaining histories of rave I've ever read'. **Ian McQuaid, Ransom Note**

'The Love Dove Generation, one of the most honest — and indispensable — accounts of the early 90s rave scene you will ever read'. **Mark Kavanagh, Buzz.ie**

'An instant classic'. **Kirsty Allison, DJ Mag**

'Britain's biggest raver Billy 'Daniel' Bunter on a life of thrills, pills and more pills'. **Tom Fenwick, Fact Magazine**

**The Love Dove Generation** centres around the east London rave scene of the late '80s/early'90s and is the autobiography of Daniel Light, professionally known as Billy 'Daniel' Bunter who started out as Britain's youngest rave DJ aged just 15. Daniel rose to the top of the pile at the legendary Labrynth, 12 Dalston Lane, E8 before embarking on a global career in music that continues to this day.

**Paperback books available from www.musicmondays.co.uk**

# Big Bad & Heavy

**Big, Bad & Heavy** is the story of legendary jungle DJ Jumpin Jack Frost; a man who lived his life at the break-neck speed of the music he played.

Raised on the tough south London streets of Brixton, Nigel Thompson was saved from a life of crime and punishment, by music. A pirate DJ on Passion FM, when acid house broke down virtually every cultural boundary in the UK, Frost was right there at the forefront of the British rave revolution. Then, when hardcore splintered into jungle in the early nineties, Frost became one of the figureheads of this uniquely British phenomenon; releasing many of the tunes that defined this scene, on his and fellow DJ Bryan Gee's hugely influential record label V.

But no matter how hard he tried to evade the criminal lifestyle that had taken many of his friends down, prison, guns and violence were never far away. And when his drug use started to spiral out of control, Frost faced a battle that threatened to take everything he had.

# The Smiler –
# A DJ's Life

*I seriously can't thank you all enough for nearly 35 years of love and support. Without you all, I'd be absolutely nothing. I never forget it.*

*Here's to years more fun together. Like I've said a few times in the book, the best days could still be just around the corner for us all.*

*Love Rob Tissera XxX*

A.LINCOLN BIGGS

Abigayle Blood

Adam

Adam Bellew

Adam Hallsworth

Adrian Jackson 'Adi J'

Adrian Russo

Alan & Emma Hartley

Alexa Burman

Alfie Bamford (Technikal)

Alfie Hoole

Ali McDonald

Alice Bailey

Alice O'Connor

Alison Finburg

All the Slinky Angels

Amanda Pulford

Amber D

Amy Hackett

Amy Smith

Andrew Galliet

Andrew Neenan

Andrew Rowsome

Andy

Andy Bear Roden

Andy 'BopH' Barber

Andy Cummings

Andy Rise

Andy Roden

Andy Slater

Andy Stainsby

Angela Winton

Anthony Reynolds

Bam Bam and Pebbles

Barry Holland

Ben Amponsah

Ben Davies
Ben Stevens
Billy Sispal
Brad B-RaD Johnson
Breakbeat Dags
Brendan Corr
Brian J Young
Brian Laurie
Cameron Chapman (Grubby!)
Carl Hetherington
Carrie Wilson
Cassie Bond
Chris Angels
Chris Glover
Chris Marsden (Dj Slouch)
Chris 'marshionist' Marsh
Chris McNicoll
Chris Singer
Chris Waddleton
Chubby
Chuckmeister
Claire Calder
Clare Hulse
Colin Elson
Craig
Craig Pedley (pedzdj)
Craig Rico
Cronelli
Damian Kenefick - Smiling since 92
Damo Pennells
Dan French
Darrell Wilde
Darren Collins
Darren Musk
Darren Thompson #real
Darryl Evans .UTST
Dave "Deev" Llewellyn
Dave Binney
Dave Kimberley
Dave Lee
Davey Bell
David Eve
David Guinan

David Lawson
David Lintott
Dawn Dale
Dawn Lee
Dean Halliday
Dean Sowden
Dean Weston
Declan Corr
Deelicious xXx
Dillon Gauld
Dipz
Disco Stu Glover
DJ Shock Leeds pirate radio operator legend
DJ WiKiD
Duan Yusef
Eammon Sturcock
Eddie Mulley
Em Thackeray
Emily Bowler
Emma 'Bradderz' Russell
Emma Lopez
Eric Beaurivage (Cyre)
Evie Clayton
Fadi Fakhouri (FadStar)
Fay Talula
Fiona (SmileySunshine) Scott xx
Francis Tabern
Fraser Brydson
Gary Simpson
Gav Smith
Gemma Smith
General Bounce
Glyn 'Dancefloor Legend' Hayler
Graham Pierce
Greavsie's
Griff
Helsinki
Ian "KIP-C" Kipps
Ian Mills
Indie Rose Benjamin
Ivan and Family
James
James Gould

James Nugent
Jamie Askew
Jane Angel
Jas
Jason 'JaceACE' Leggitt
Jay Palmer
Jay Viper
Jayne Elcomb Andrews
Jeff & Serena Booz
Jemma Leigh
Jennifer Batchelor
Jez Martin (Mr My House)
Jimmy
Jo DiscoBunny Bastow
Jo Fish
Jo Golds
Jo Mason
Joe
John Chilley
John Kay
John Reeder
Johnny Dangerous
Jon (Evil Genius) Edgecombe
Jon Kay
Jon Langford
Jonny & Claire Calder
Josh Foster
Juan Francisco Blanco
Julz (Julian Richards)
Karn
Kate Fairbrother
Kayleigh Blench
Kelly (OHF flag lady) & Dave 'the rave' Wood
Kelly Wright
Kennedy Moir
Kenny Deans
Kenny Stone
Kev
Kev Walsh
Kevin Marston
Kevin Roden
Kirsty Saville-Potter
Kizzy Lane

Kristi Blunt
Kyle Nathan Render
Lady Hani
Lady-Faith Jones
Lauren & Paul
Layla Harlow
Lee Hall
Lee Hulse
lee James
Lee 'Mert' Mattinson R.I.P
Lee Randall - Fresh
Lee Thompson
Leigh Strydom
Leyna Coates
Liam Foster
Liam Wright
Lianne Grew
Linds "Firthy" Firth
Lisa Bridge
Lisa Coop
Lisa Myers
Lizzie Curious
Lorna Devlin
Louise Strathie
Luke Matchett
Luke Randall
Luke Tandy
Lyds good vibes
Lynda Irvine
Lynne
Lynne Brimicombe (No1 fan)
Madeleine Lovejohn
Malcolm Tonto Ladkin
Mama P
Manda Ferguson
Mandy
Marc Lowley
Marcus Bennett
Mark Anderson
Mark Lewis
Mark Miley
Mark Stubley
Martin Jewell

Martin Walker

Martyn Beecroft Gallery crew

Mat Gonzalez

Matt Sears

Matthew Brignall

Melanie Ross

Merewyn Sayers

Michael James Wright

Michael Wood

Michelle Hold

Michelle 'Stewy' Stewart

Mick V

Mick Wright

Miguel Garrido-Letelier

Mike Devlin

Mike 'Hoopz' Hooper

Mike Palliser

Mike Stewart Sarasota

Millsy (Housewives Choice)

Mrs Squiggles

Muhammad Qasim

Nat 'Rob Tissera broke my Buffaloes!'
  Bowkett

Neil 'CLUBAHOLIC' Kemp

Neil Green

Neil Harding

Nhaill Morley

Nick The Kid

Nicky Hiller

NICOLA

Nigel  B Shine

Nigel Horne

Nikki Blacker

Nikki Bothwick-Adams

Nikki Whiles

Niknak

Olivia

Patricia Lowe (lady P)

Paul (Patty) Pattinson

Paul Browne

Paul Harrop

Paul Knaggs & Tammy

Paul Morgan

Paul Oakley

Paul 'T-bag' Teagle

Paulos Murray

Phil Horner

Phil Robinson

Phillip Robertson

Phillip Shortall

Pilly

Rachel McGuinness

RAGS & MANDY

Rich Elks

Rich Stevens

Richard (Raver) Freeth

Rick B.Viss Davey

Rob & Saskia Oakley

Rob Moore

Rob Powell

Robert Jan Bijleveld

Rocking Robin

Roger Keighley

Ross Canvin

Ross Currie

Russ Richardson

Ryan Galloway

Ryan Willmott

Sab's.

Sally Taylor

Sam Mitcham

Sam Piper

Sarah lane

Sarah WhittleAshcroft

Sasha & Pickle

Sasha Bryce

Scott McDonald

Scott Naylor

Sean Beare

Shazzzaa T

Si & Suzanne Frater (Rejuvenation)

Si Pi

SimmSound

Simon Cox

Simon Kenway

Simon Pratt

Simon Whitley

Slinky Angels

Speedy N Lyn

Ste Sandiforth/Vicky Lewis

Stella Timothy

STEPHEN DIXON

Stephen Fisher The original Gurner

Steve Kelly

Steve Killick

Stewart McAllister

Stuart Dee

Sue 'Suzie Q' Kinch

Suzanne Shield

Tara

Tasha Beaumont-Kaye (Tache)

The Vernon's

The Walker's

Tim Betterton

Tim Bulman

Tim Forrester

Tim Sim

Tina Hyslop

To DC..... Love TC x

Tom Frost

Toni Keen

Tory Le Sueur

Tracey

Vic and Nic

Vickie Medic

Vicky Craig

Wayne A

White disco slug

Will Morton

Winky

Yasuyuki Harada

Yvonne Salisbury

Zinky